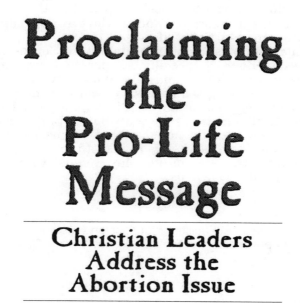

Proclaiming the Pro-Life Message

Christian Leaders Address the Abortion Issue

Larry L. Lewis, Compiler and Editor

APPRECIATION

My heartfelt thanks to all who contributed to this book to aid in the fight for life and to champion the cause of the unborn.

My special appreciation to Dr. Greg Martin, who suggested the idea for this book of sermons on abortion, helped me compile a list of possible contributors, assisted in editing the manuscript, contributed one of the sermons and provided an appendix of ideas for promoting the sanctity of life.

Also, many thanks to my office staff at the Southern Baptist Home Mission Board, especially my personal secretary, Mrs. Penny Grecni, for their hard and diligent labor, typing and editing the sermons, acquiring the necessary approvals and preparing the manuscript for publication. Thanks for a job well done.

My special thanks to all the contributors to this book. They tell a story, they speak a message that our nation and world desperately needs to hear. My thanks to you, too, for being concerned about the issue of life. May God use your concern to educate others and save lives.

Larry Lewis

National Facilitator for Mission America,
former President of the SBC Home Mission Board

DEDICATION

To my mother

Mrs. Mary Lue Lewis

Who in the most trying times

and the most difficult circumstances

chose life for me, her only child,

and the joy of motherhood for herself.

Table of Contents

ABORTION AND THE THREAT TO CIVIC ORDER

Charles Colson

It was a genial dinner party among friends—until the topic of abortion came up. Then strangely, people began to excuse themselves from the table. Finally, only one person was left facing me.

"Chuck," he said, leaning across the table. "This will surprise you but I can't buy your arguments against abortion."

It certainly did surprise me. My friend was in every other way a conservative evangelical Christian.

"Just look at our inner cities," he went on. "Kids having kids. Generations on welfare. AIDS babies, crack babies. My wife works with those kids. It's horrible to bring children into that kind of world. Birth control and abstinence don't really work. Abortion is the only way to stop the cycle."

"Wait a minute," I broke in. "Abortion is legal and available – and it *hasn't* stopped the cycle. It doesn't 'work' either."

"Well," he paused, "people need more education."

"Education? For the past twenty-one years, this country has had one of the most liberal abortion policies in the world – and you're suggesting that people still need to be educated on their legal right to choose abortion?"

His lips tightened but I went on: "What if after being 'educated' they still don't choose abortion? What's next? Forced abortions? Euthanasia? Don't you see what you're saying?"

At that moment, mercifully, our other dinner guests began reappearing, and the topic was dropped. But it left me with a troubling premonition of how easily even sincere and well-meaning people can gradually slide into accepting a culture of death.

That evening was three years ago; since then the gradual slide has given way to a free fall. The very thing that I warned my friend about has happened: The well-meaning people who want to "protect" children from the poverty and misery of ghetto life—along with those who want to ensure women's autonomous choice in abortion—have led us in a head-long rush into a culture of death. And in the process, they have threatened the very notion of a civil society, raising questions that go to the heart of maintaining public order in a free society.

"Liberty" Without Limits

The decisive moment occurred two years ago when the Supreme Court issued its decision in *Planned Parenthood v. Casey*. Initially, both sides heaved a sigh of relief. Prolifers were

7

glad that the Court had allowed states to impose some reasonable limits on abortion; prochoicers were glad that the Court had reaffirmed the basic holding of *Roe v. Wade*, namely that abortion is a fundamental right. The ruling seemed to be a middle-of-the-road decision by a middle-of-the-road Court.

But as the smoke of the political battles cleared, it became obvious that in fact the lines of battle had shifted decisively. *Casey,* it turns out, was a much more significant ruling than virtually anyone realized at first. It completely reframed the abortion debate; in fact, it redefined the very nature of the civic contract in a free society.

First, the Court made it virtually impossible to reverse *Roe.* In *Roe* the Court had based abortion on the right to privacy, a right found nowhere explicitly in the Constitution but only implied – making the decision vulnerable to reversal by subsequent Courts. But in *Casey* the Court transferred abortion from an implied to an explicit right – the right of liberty found in the Fourteenth Amendment. (The amendment says that no state may deprive a person of life, liberty, or property without due process of law.) In doing so, the Court enshrined abortion much more securely in the Constitution and made it as impossible to reverse as the *Dred Scott* decision once was.

Second, and perhaps even more important, the Court proceeded to define liberty in the most sweeping terms conceivable. The liberty protected by the Fourteenth Amendment, the majority said, includes "the most intimate and personal choices a person may make in a lifetime, choices central to personal dignity and autonomy." The majority then explained what kinds of personal choices it had in mind: "At the heart of liberty is the right to define one's own concept of existence, of meaning, of the universe, and of the mystery of human life." If the state were to set up a public standard regarding abortion, the Court implied, it would infringe on citizens' right to make up their own minds on the "intimate and personal choice." It would deny citizens a crucial, self-defining decision and rob them of those attributes of selfhood constituted by free choice.

At first sight, this passage may seem unremarkable. After all, beliefs about existence and the mystery of human life are religious, and religious freedom is guaranteed by the First Amendment.

What makes the court statement revolutionary is that it applies religious language specifically to *abortion.* It gives religious status to a completely individualistic act; an act that presumes the right of one person to take the life of another for purely private reasons, without any public accountability. As the editors of **First Things** put it, the Court was "asserting and endorsing a philosophy of at least quasi-religious status." And the philosophy it was endorsing was that of the autonomous individual defining his or her own reality in complete isolation—

even to the point of taking the life of another person.

In the words of Hadley Arkes, professor of jurisprudence at Amherst College, with *Casey* the Court "seemed to install solipsism for the first time as a rule in constitutional law." Solipsism is the philosophy that the self is completely isolated – that the individual self can know nothing outside its own direct experiences and states of mind. Whereas classical thought held that we can know an objective world outside our own minds, and whereas Christian teaching holds that we can know objective truth through divine revelation, the Court has now endorsed the philosophy that the self is an island, whose dignity is derived solely from individual "autonomy" in making purely "personal choices."

But if autonomous, personal choices may not be circumscribed in any way by the state, then the rule of law becomes impossible. After all, virtually *any* decision could arguably be related to the way a particular individual defines selfhood, existence and meaning in life. The Court has endorsed a definition of liberty so broad that it would eliminate not only any laws against abortion but any laws whatsoever.

For example, using the same line of argument, Lawrence Tribe, Harvard professor and constitutional authority, has argued that the state's attempt to control harmful drugs is an intrusion into the individual's right to autonomous selfhood. In his words, outlawing certain chemical substances represents "government invasion and usurpation of the choices that together constitute an individual's psyche."

Similarly, Stuart Taylor, Jr., in *The American Lawyer,* argues that liberty as defined in *Casey* gives constitutional support for gay rights. Surely, Taylor says, one's sexual relationships must count among "the most intimate and personal choices a person may make in a lifetime, choices central to personal dignity and autonomy." In fact, as Taylor sees it, "the rights to choose abortion and to intimate association (homosexual or otherwise) are likely to stand and fall together." He is likely to be right.

Most ominously, was the *Casey* definition of liberty which it applied to the early stages of life. In a stunning decision in May 1994, US District Judge Barbara Rothstein ruled that a Washington law prohibiting doctor-assisted suicide was unconstitutional. Rothstein specifically echoed the language of *Casey,* arguing that suicide, like abortion, "involves the most intimate and personal choices a person may make," that it "constitutes a choice central to personal dignity and autonomy," and that it deserves the same "protection from unwarranted governmental interference." Rothstein then appealed to *Casey's* sweeping definition of liberty: "There is no more profoundly personal decision, nor one which is closer to the heart of personal liberty, than the choice which a terminally ill person makes to end his or her suffering and hasten an inevitable death." The freedom to make this choice, Rothstein concluded, is protected by the Fourteenth Amendment's clause against state infringement of individual liberty.

The brief history of the *Casey* decision clearly proves the truth of Justice Scalia's dark prediction. In a dissenting opinion, Scalia pointed out that under the Court's expansive definition, liberty could encompass "homosexual sodomy, polygamy, adult incest, and suicide." Of course, that list is altogether too short. The truth is that liberty could now encompass virtually any decision by which an individual expresses his sense of "selfhood," "meaning" and "existence."

Public Justice

As Christians, our response ought to be that all this talk about personal choices and personal philosophy is completely beside the point. Our courts and legal system are not concerned with private religious and metaphysical beliefs; they are concerned with public justice. People of very different beliefs – from Christians to atheists to New Agers – may disagree vehemently over questions of existence and the meaning of life; yet we can all agree on standards of public justice and order, just as we can all agree to stop when the traffic signal is red.

We may each have different religious and philosophical reasons *behind* our willingness to stop at the signal – different convictions regarding the source of moral authority. Yet we can all still agree that such behavior promotes the public good. Christians have a distinctive ethic, revealed in Scripture, and empowered by the indwelling Holy Spirit. Yet as citizens we also contend for a public philosophy, justified on the basis of prudential arguments. This is a crucial distinction if we are to maintain freedom of conscience while also maintaining public order.

Passing on the Power of the Sword

The destructive implications of the *Casey* decision become even clearer if we consider biblical teaching on the function of the state. The distinctive characteristic of the state is its responsibility to use coercion – even lethal force – for the sake of justice in the commonwealth. In the language of Romans 13, the state bears the power of the sword to punish evildoers and protect the innocent. But this solemn responsibility is exercised legitimately (as Hittinger puts it) "only in the light of a public end, and even then only according to public procedures and the most exacting standards of accountability." Private citizens do not have the right to use lethal force, except in the rare case of self-defense.

In *Casey,* however, the Court stripped the state of much of its authority and responsibility, transferring decisions about life and death to private choice. And it did so without any requirement that citizens use that power only to public ends or that they adhere to careful standards of public accountability or justification. In abortion, a woman is permitted to ground her decision solely on her own estimation of her private good. In Hittinger's chilling words, "the abortion right is nothing less than a purported right of individual citizens to use lethal force without even the charade of being deputized to do so, and without any of the constraints that the government ordinarily imposes upon itself when it kills persons."

But a government that has given up the defining characteristic of the state – the power of the sword – is a government that has lost its legitimacy. Even secular political theorists recognize this. John Locke's political theory begins with a hypothetical "state of nature," in which each individual does what is right in his own eyes and is his own judge and executor. Civil society is created when citizens realize that it is in their interest to band together and invest the *state* with the power to judge between citizens and to execute sentences. In the civil contract, citizens give up private vengeance in favor of public justice.

But *Casey* threatens – and has perhaps even abolished – the civil contract. It has returned much of the state's essential power to individuals; it has privatized the use of lethal force. In effect, the Court has begun to unravel the civil contract that gives legitimacy to the regime. It has created a pre-civil condition, where each individual is judge and executor according to his own estimation of who deserves to live and die.

America has been cast back into a state of nature. And it is only a short step from here to barbarism.

The Watershed of Our Times

Christians who thought *Roe v. Wade* was disastrous must understand that *Casey* will be much worse. *Roe* legalized abortion; *Casey* will be used to legalize virtually any "lifestyle" choice, rooting it in the Constitution through an expansive definition of liberty.

It is crucial for Christians to take the lead in educating our fellow believers and our fellow citizens on what is at stake in the abortion controversy today. Critics have often derided concerns about abortion as a "single issue" mentality. But it is becoming increasingly clear that abortion is in fact the watershed issue of our times. By confronting us with matters of life and death, abortion forces us to face central moral questions – and even to weigh the legitimacy of the state itself.

The Marvelous Mystery of Mankind

W.A. Criswell

TEXT: Genesis 1:26-27, 2:7, KJV

SUPPLEMENTAL VERSES: Psalm 139:13-16

SUMMARY OF MESSAGE: W.A. Criswell's "The Marvelous Mystery of Mankind" is a unique look at the inherent value of mankind simply because of God's complex construction of our bodies. Criswell leads the congregation through the fascinating human body, from conception through adulthood, from the cell and chromosomes through the muscles.
Criswell concludes his message urging listeners to respect the life God has ordained and created and to pray that the "abortion holocaust will come to an end."

PREACHING TRACKS:

➤TRACK ONE: Preach the entire sermon.

➤TRACK TWO: Preach the points on the outline that best apply to your congregation. I, II and V introduce and describe the intricate development and construction of the body. III and IV give additional information about the workings of the body. Add your own illustrations, comments and Scriptures.

➤TRACK THREE: Preach a combination of points in this and in other sermons in this book.

THE MARVELOUS MYSTERY
OF MANKIND

And God said, Let us make man in our image, after our likeness...

W.A. Criswell

The wonder of that creative workmanship is not alone in the Garden of Eden. Nor is it a miracle of the beginning of the human family. A person's body is the most marvelous physical creation in the universe. The making of a star, of a continent, of an ocean, is not to be compared with the wonder of the skill that entered into the making of a human body.

But this miracle that was wrought by the skillful, infinitely wise and adroit hands of God in the Garden of Eden, is repeated every day, everywhere. We do not have to look back to that faraway age to wonder at the creative masterpiece of God. The Lord brings to pass the same miracle every day, in place after place.

In Psalm 139:13-16, David mentions this fearful and wonderful miracle of God. This is the marvelous mystery of the human body.

A person's body may be likened to a vast city, and on the inside of that city are ten times thirty trillions of inhabitants. Ten hundred thousand is a million; ten hundred million is a billion; ten hundred billion is a trillion. Ten times thirty trillion little citizens on the inside of that city are ten times thirty trillions of inhabitants. Ten times thirty trillion little citizens in the inside of that vast city, all of them with a task assigned. So tiny are those citizens that in one speck of blood no bigger than the head of a pin, there will be five million of them. The three hundred trillion are busy all the time doing their part to operate this infinitely intricate machinery.

THE CELL

Those living units that form this marvelous creative workmanship we call the human body are cells. And each cell is filled with the most amazing, remarkable and marvelous substance in this universe — protoplasm.

The cell is made like this: First, there is a cell wall. The containing cube has a membrane which is pervious. Some things can go through the cell wall, some things can come out of it and other things are prohibited. The tiny cell wall is a marvel in itself.

Then on the inside of that cell wall is a substance called cytoplasm. In the cytoplasm are infinitely small spaces filled with molecules of fluid, of proteins, of sugar and of salt.

But the most miraculous of all the miraculous things in that little cell is the tiny sphere called the nucleus that floats in the cytoplasm. That is the center of life. On the inside of the nucleus are small chromatin granules, and in the process of mitosis or cell division, those chromatin granules gather together into rods called chromosomes.

Every distinct family, every one of the unbreakable species God has made has its distinguishing number of chromosomes, and on those chromosomes a distinguishing number of genes. Drosophila, the common fruit fly, with which geneticists have been experimenting for half a century, has four chromosomes and on each of those four chromosomes are from twelve to fifteen thousand genes. Those genes have to do with heredity and the building of the body.

The distinguishing number of chromosomes in the cells of man is 46. All of those billions and billions of cells in the human body have 46 chromosomes in the nucleus of each one. Some have estimated that on those 46 chromosomes in the nucleus of a human body there may be as many as eight hundred million genes that have to do with the building of the body.

In the nucleus of each cell in the woman, there are two chromosomes called "XX" chromosomes.

In the man the two are different – "XY."

In the female reproductive cell, when those chromosomes are halved for the egg cell, there will be one X chromosome in each female egg (23 chromosomes, one of them an X).

In the male sperm, however, when the reproductive cell is created, and the chromosomes are divided in half, there will be 23 in one cell, one of them an X, and 23 in the other cell, but one of them a Y. When they are mated, there will be 23 from the female, 23 from the male, and again there will be the complete number of 46 chromosomes. If the 23 from the male are with the X chromosome, the new life will be female. But if the 23 from the female are fertilized with the 23 from the male with the Y chromosome, the new life will be male.

BUILDING A BODY

So without teaching and without training, those marvelous, infinitesimally small genes and chromosomes and cells begin their long and eventful journey building the marvelous body of the marvelous human body.

Some of the units seem to be leaders and directors and some of them seem to obey orders, which they do faithfully, immediately and meticulously. Some of those tiny citizens seem to be masons, some carpenters, some plasterers, some generals, some workmen, some doctors, some lawyers, some merchants, some sailors, some policemen, some soldiers. Without direction and without previous experience, without training, they begin to build this marvelous structure we call man.

Within the first few weeks, in one corner, there are some

pumping engineers who begin to construct a simple, one-chambered heart that begins to beat and to pump fluid.

About the same time, the plumbers are laying down all kinds of pipelines from that one-chambered heart the engineers have constructed, and the pump begins to pump fluid through those pipelines. When looked at closely, the system is like a moving cafeteria or a conveyer belt on which are all kinds of things to eat so all of those carpenters and plumbers and electricians can have their food laid right at their door.

Then, within about two months, out of nowhere, appear the bone-builders, beginning to lay down their structures, the way a man builds a great skyscraper.

Then, the teeth carpenters appear and begin to gather materials for the enamel, the dentine, the cement and all the things that go into the laying down of teeth buds. They say, "When the teeth are needed they will be right on time." Everything is done according to schedule, with nothing missing, nothing delayed.

They work and work and by three months, everyone is on the job. Everything is teeming and everything is busy. There are the bone builders gathering calcium and phosphorus in the right proportions and laying it down for the building of the skeleton. There are the plumbers laying all of those thousands and thousands of miles of pipeline. Then there are the electricians and they are laying down their cables all through the body so that it may have a fine communication system. There are those most marvelous of all tissues, the endocrine glands that are beginning to manufacture their hormones, messenger boys to be sent into any part of this marvelous body. Then there are the power machines — the muscles — that are being rigged up and made ready to work to generate power. They are being tied to all of the bones. Then from the photographic department and from the auditory department the technicians of photography and the technicians of the auditory system are called in and they begin to construct the most marvelous camera in this world, the cornea, the lens and the tiny muscle around that lens, the retina, and then the optic nerve. For protection an eyelid is built and on the inside a smooth membrane. Then on the outer side a little water fountain is constructed by which the delicate eye, that photographic piece, can be constantly washed and bathed and kept meticulously clean.

After everyone has done his part and all the little workmen, without teaching and without training, have all done their work, a day comes when the physician and the parents and the family and the neighbors and the friends hear the cry of a new-born baby. God has done it again!

Can you imagine the wonder, the miracle? You don't have to go back to Eden. You don't have to go back to the beginning, for before your eyes is the most marvelous, inexplainable mystery in this created universe.

But we haven't started!

THE MYSTERY OF GROWTH

We enter the mystery of growth. What makes that child turn into a man? What makes him grow? No one knows. But the days pass and there he is, growing and growing and growing. What tells him when to stop? His head will grow to the right size, then it will stop. His heart will grow to the right size and then stop. His arms will grow just to the right size and then stop. His feet and his legs will grow to their right size and then stop. Who tells them how long and how big and when to stop? No one knows. It is one of the mysteries of the marvelous human body.

"How can anyone ever believe such a marvel of creation is anything other than a miracle of God? Did man just happen? No! A thousand times, no! Every newborn child and every unborn child is a fantastic miracle of God!

How can anyone believe an unborn child is merely a glob of protoplasm to be disposed of at will? Every day the abortionists throughout America are destroying these little miracles and disposing of them as if they were garbage! God help us all!

THE PROBLEMS OF ANATOMY

As the child grows and turns into a man, think of the marvelous mystery of change and supply and rebuilding and reconstruction. It goes on fabulously, enormously, miraculously. Every minute and moment of every week of every month of every year of the whole life, the entire body, all of it, is being marvelously rebuilt. Solid bone, piece by piece (the way workers take timbers out of a railroad bridge), is being torn down and reconstructed. Every unit of the eye is being taken apart and rebuilt, yet it never loses a moment of life. The steam is never cut off, the electricity is never shut down. It never stops. Each little workman comes in, picks up where his predecessor has been working, and carries right on without a moment's hesitation.

This is an amazing thing! We have to have new lungs, but we never lose breath. We have to have new stomachs, but we never lose a meal. We have to have new hearts, but they never cease to beat. All of this marvelous work is being changed piece by piece every moment of every day and every night, and we never realize it, nor are we conscious of it at all.

Can you think of a factory where even the operator is not conscious of the changes in his factory, and yet his factory is being rebuilt from top to bottom?

The most amazing thing about these cells that inhabit by the millions and billions this house we call the body of man, is their know-how. Their knowledge is astounding. It is the knowledge of God Himself. Such unbelievable things these cells know how to do!

Let us take some of them, for example. What a marvelous chemical know-how enters into the manufacture of blood. In an ordinary, healthy man, there is about a gallon and one-half of blood. On the inside of that blood, there are at least thirty trillion cells called corpuscles. They die, they are injured, they are destroyed at the rate of about seventy-two million a minute, so they have to be replaced. They have to be remade at the rate of seventy-two million a minute!

THE CHEMICAL FACTORIES

How is a corpuscle made? On the inside of that tiny corpuscle is a red substance called hemoglobin. It is a protein and has a vast capacity for oxygen. When it comes to the lungs it grabs all the oxygen that it can possibly care for, four times as much as itself, and then takes it down to all those living cells that have to have it to breathe and live. Did you ever try to make a piece of hemoglobin? I want you to look at the miraculous chemical know-how of these factories that create hemoglobin. A molecule of water is made of two atoms of hydrogen and one atom of oxygen —H_2O— that's water. Carbon dioxide would be made of one atom of carbon and two atoms of oxygen. One molecule of glucose, which is body sugar, would be made out of six atoms of carbon, 12 atoms of hydrogen and six atoms of oxygen ($C_6H_{12}O_6$). One molecule of some fats would be 18 atoms of carbon, 36 atoms of hydrogen, three atoms of oxygen ($C_{18}H_{36}O_2$). Now, one molecule of hemoglobin, that scarlet red protein on the inside of that little cell (and there are three hundred million molecules of this chemical on the inside of the cell) is $C_{758}H_{1203}N_{195}S_3Fe_1O_{218}$, which means one molecule of this red hemoglobin has in it 758 atoms of carbon, 1203 atoms of hydrogen, 195 atoms of nitrogen, 3 atoms of sulphur, 1 atom of iron and 218 atoms of oxygen, making a total of 2378 atoms in each molecule of hemoglobin. Now molecules of hemoglobin have to be made exactly like that. If they are not, they are something else.

Those red cells are made at the rate of seventy-two million a minute. Can you imagine the job of the chemist who had to take our 758 atoms of carbon, 1203 atoms of hydrogen, 195 atoms of nitrogen, 3 atoms of sulphur, 1 atom of iron, 218 atoms of oxygen, and count them up — 300 million to the cell, 72 million cells to the minute? And yet the bone marrow cells do it like the snap of a finger all the time!

Where is the chemist who can do that? Yet those little factories do that day and night, silently, unobtrusively, skillfully, and we never realize it.

Where are the little factories? Just as a bank vault is put down in the foundations of a building, so the all-wise architectural Designer and Engineer put those factories in the most protected parts of the human frame, deep down on the inside of the marrow of the bone. There we find those little factories coining out cells, counting out atomic numbers in the right proportion and manufacturing them by the millions and the billions every minute. What an amazing process God has done!

A chemist can figure out what is in hemoglobin. But there are other little chemical factories in the body that have knowledge to construct things that no human mind in this earth can enter into. So delicate, so intricate, so deep, so unfathomable are they, that no one knows what they are or how they are made.

For example, does anyone know what an enzyme is, how it is made, how it is constructed? An enzyme is an organic piece of matter that can change other things but is not changed itself. It can take starch, for example, and change it into sugar. What are those enzymes, how are they constructed and how are they manufactured? What is their component part and what is on the inside of them? The answer is known but to God Himself.

Again, I do not know of anything that is more amazing than the creation of the ductless glands, called the endocrine glands.

You have two kinds of glands in your body — you have a duct gland that will pour out its secretions through a pipe in a designated place in your body. An example of a duct gland is the gall bladder. But there are in your body marvelous little pieces of tissue that are the most amazing pieces of tissue on earth. You have in your body pieces of tissue that secrete chemicals which are poured directly into the blood stream, which in turn carries them wherever they are needed. These chemicals carry messages to tell the different parts of the body what to do.

The activity of your body is regulated by two means. One is the nervous system. Little cables and wires of communication run all over your body from the spinal column, providing one way for body activity to be coordinated. The other way your body activity is coordinated is through these messengers that are secreted by the endocrine glands.

Until recently, evolutionists looked at the endocrine glands and said: "Why they are just vestigial remnants. They were useful in the day when man was a beast. But now since the ape has evolved upward, they are useless and these are just the remnants of those useless organs that he once had to have."

They did not know why the beast had to have them. They did not know what function they served. The evolutionist did not see any reason for these glands, so he said they were vestigial remnants. They were doubtlessly useful to the beast, but to the man they are not useful at all. That is typical of the evolutionist's reasoning and it is also typical of what happens to his argument when we finally know the facts. These glands are not mere remnants. The most important tissues in our bodies are the endocrine glands, and we are just beginning to find that out. Far from being remnants, they were put there by the marvelous creative hand of God Himself.

The adrenal glands above the kidneys are sometimes called

the glands of flight and fight. They are there for preserving life.

If something scares you and you have to jump, the adrenal gland will send a hormone messenger to the liver and the liver will immediately turn loose glycogen that is immediately turned into glucose, into blood sugar, and the muscles are ready to work. Then the adrenal gland will send a hormone messenger to all of the little blood vessels of the body. They constrict and more blood pressure results. Then the adrenal gland will send a hormone messenger to the heart and the heart muscle is toned up and is ready to do twice as much work. The adrenal gland will manufacture a hormone messenger and send it through the blood stream to the pupil of the eye which is dilated. You are then ready for fight or for flight. The manufacture of the chemical of that gland is a marvel!

No one on this earth understands how a muscle is made, or how it moves. Man has already discovered 15 chemical reactions in the functioning of a muscle. One enzyme will take what the other has done and work on that, then another enzyme will come and take that product and change it until finally energy is liberated. How? No one knows. And yet an athlete can jump his height and a skilled violinist and a fine pianist can use their fingers and arms almost automatically. But the reaction, the chemical reaction of just moving a muscle, is beyond man's reasoning.

We have not even begun. Oh, that I could speak of the mystery of the mind, the mystery of memory and the mystery of the human soul. The greatest spiritual creation in this earth is a man's soul, his mind, his memory, his personality, the spirit that resides within him, "And man became a living soul."

When the silver cord is loosed
When the golden bowl is broken
When the pitcher is broken at the fountain
And the wheel is broken at the cistern
When the dust returns to the earth as it was
And the spirit unto God who gave it.

Oh, the marvelous mystery of man. We can but bow our heads and humble our hearts in the presence of the great Designer and Creator and Architect Who made us and fashioned us in His own likeness and in His own image.

I close this message urging your respect for life, born and unborn. All human life is a marvelous, miraculous act of God. The formation of a child in the mother's womb is the crown of God's creation!

Selfish, non-therapeutic abortion is an abomination! It must be stopped! More than 60,000,000 abortions are performed annually throughout the world, more than 1,000,000 here in the United States.

I appeal to you to elect congressmen and senators who will stand for the unborn and for a president who will lead in the fight for life.

Above all, let's pray that this abortion holocaust will come to an end and for those who have been affected by this tragedy. Let's pray sanctity of life will be restored and people everywhere will realize we are truly "fearfully and wonderfully made."

19

The Death of America

James T. Draper

TEXT: Psalm 139:1-17, KJV

SUPPLEMENTAL VERSES: Genesis 29:31, Job 31:15, Isaiah 44:2,24; 49:1, Exodus 21:22-25, 1 John 1:7-9, Romans 8:1-2 Hebrews 10:16-17, Psalm 103:10-13, Luke 1:41;2:12,16;18:15, Colossians 2:14

SUMMARY OF MESSAGE: James Draper's "The Death of America" asks the question, "Why have we Christians of America been silent about abortion?" Draper exposes the contradictory laws in our nation and offers some reasons for Christians being so quiet and complacent in standing up for life.

Draper's message is also for those who need healing. He uses Psalm 139 to paint a clear picture of God's live for us and presence with us, of His involvement in our lives, and of His creation of each individual. Using Scripture from the Old and New Testaments, he shows that complete cleansing is available for all who come to Jesus Christ.

PREACHING TRACKS:

➤ TRACK ONE: Preach the entire sermon.

➤ TRACK TWO: Preach the points on the outline that best apply to your congregation. I and V strongly challenge church members to speak out for life. II, III and IV show God's wonderful plan in creating each person. VI brings a message of pardon and change for those who have experienced abortion or been silent when they should have spoken.

➤ TRACK THREE: Preach a combination of points in this and other sermons in this book.

THE DEATH OF AMERICA

Psalm 139:7-16

James T. Draper

We Americans like to pretend that if we do not recognize something, it does not exist. If we hide our eyes where we cannot see it, it is not real. We insulate ourselves. Our whole society and our whole culture is built to insulate us, to keep us from really seeing reality. We insulate ourselves religiously. We insulate ourselves socially, politically, internationally, and the feeling is as long as we are not aware, then it is somebody else's problem. I speak to you about what may be the greatest tragedy in American society.

One and one half million babies are killed every year; four thousand everyday; one every twenty seconds in this country. One out of every four pregnancies – 25 percent – in the United States ends in an abortion. We cannot escape the dreadful consequences of this tragic killing of four thousand unborn babies every day.

We can say it is the Supreme Court's fault. They legalized abortion. We can blame the philosophy of the secular humanist. Or we can blame the radical feminists—the organizations that are pushing for what they call women's rights; the right of a woman to make a choice.

Hear me very carefully! The truth is that we must lay the blame at our own feet. If we were few in number, maybe we could blame somebody else. But evangelical Christians in the United States number more than 40 million. Couple that with more than 51 million Roman Catholics, who are very much against abortion, and the total is almost 100 million, approximately 45 percent of the population of this country who could make a difference. We cannot blame others.

The tragedy is that we think the church is suffering for the sins of the world, but the truth is that the world may be suffering for the sins of the church. We could make a difference.

We have demonstrated a tragic cowardice of silence in the midst of this tragedy. We have accepted compromise and pretended it does not exist. Thus the salt has lost its savor and the light has gone out. We do not want anybody to think we are prejudiced or bigoted, so we do not speak out. But by our cowardice and by our silence we have consented to the death of millions of babies.

In the state of Maryland, a wounded eagle was found. They were so distraught over the wounding of an American eagle that a $5,000 reward was offered to find the individual who injured that American eagle. Yet, in that state and other states a teenage girl can get an abortion without her parent's consent, but she has to have her parent's consent to get her ears pierced. Unbelievable paradox!

It is illegal to ship a pregnant lobster. If you ship a pregnant lobster, the punishment is $1,000 fine and one year in jail. Why? Because the unborn lobster may be injured!

The Massachusetts State Supreme Court ruled that goldfish cannot be given away in games of chance. In a lottery, or some form of bingo or gambling goldfish cannot be given away. They said it might contribute to the moral decay of society, and yet the same Supreme Court in Massachusetts decreed mandatory payment for abortion. What a tragedy!

When abortions first began to be performed with frequency in New York City, do you know who protested it? Not the political philosophers who have been fighting for homosexual rights and for the rights of prostitutes. No church voices were raised against the abortions that went on. It was the garbage collectors who said, "We will not dispose of the carcasses." A great moral stand was taken, not by ecclesiastical leaders, but by the garbage collectors!

We have had a hoax perpetrated upon American society. In the 1960s, when there was the great push to legalize abortions, the pro-abortionists lied to the American public. Dr. Bernard Nathanson once was very much pro-abortion and has since become an anti-abortionist. He once was known as the abortion king. He had performed over 1,500 abortions and had supervised over 60,000 others. He admits now, "Back in the 60s we misled the public in order to get what we wanted."

For instance, they said five to ten thousand women died every year through illegal abortions. Do you know what the truth is? In 1967 there were 160 deaths from illegal abortions. In 1972 there were 39 deaths. That was the year just before the abortion ruling by the Supreme Court, and in 1977 there were 33 maternal deaths from abortions that were legalized and we swapped that for 1.5 million babies killed.

In every abortion, whether it is legal or illegal, one person dies. The argument for legalizing abortion so that no one gets injured is like legalizing bank robbery so no one will get injured in the robbery. It does not make any sense at all.

Why have we remained silent?

One, we've remained silent because we honestly reject anything that requires sacrificial involvement on our part. We do not want to be involved in anything that may threaten our comfort. As long as we can live well and expect a comfortable retirement, we're indifferent to the things about us. Our own personal comfort and our own affluence is number one to us.

Another reason is that we have accepted the world's values. We have accepted the values of a world system. We have compromised and thus we have lost our ability to challenge our culture. We have become so much like the world that the world has no example of godliness to follow.

It is ironic. The unborn child has legal protection in his right to die but not in his right to live.

If an abortion is attempted and fails after the child is born, the mother, on behalf of the child, can sue the doctor for malpractice. Now what is the crime in the malpractice suit? The crime is the failure to kill the baby. The baby has a right to die, but it doesn't have a right to live.

It is ironic how twisted we have become in our society. We have done the same thing with the matter of a woman's right to do whatever she wishes with her body.

If a baby can be destroyed within a mother's body, there is no consistent argument against allowing the same mother to destroy the same baby after birth in her home. Both the home and her body are hers. Life must be precious in both places if it is precious at all. And anyone who supports abortion has no legal, moral or practical defense against deliberately killing newborn children.

Some may ask, "What about rape and incest?" If that was the real aim of the abortion decision, why did not the Supreme Court allow an exception that we would legalize abortion in cases of rape but not in other cases. The truth is pregnancy following a rape is very rare. In one ten-year period in one hospital they processed 3,500 rapes and reported not one pregnancy. And even today the very liberal, generous estimates are that less than 5 percent of the abortions performed in the United States are performed from those who have been raped. The truth is abortion has become the American way of birth control.

In 1973 the Supreme Court gave some medical reasons. Let me just give you one of the medical reasons for legalizing abortion. I'm going to quote. "Mental and physical health may be taxed by child care." Now did you hear that? Mental and physical health can be taxed by child care. What a reason! I suppose that if a child is injured in an accident, becomes a quadriplegic, it would be taxing upon the parents, so by that reasoning we could kill the quadriplegic. In other words, if it is inconvenient, kill it.

We have to recapture the truth of God's word regarding the sanctity of human life.

In July of 1983 in *Pediatrics Magazine*, the official journal of the American Academy of Pediatrics, the lead editorial contained this statement, "We can no longer base our ethics on the idea that human beings are a special form of creation, made in the image of God, and singled out from all other animals and alone possessing an immortal soul."

Clearly, we have come to a time where the sanctity of life is under attack. The word of God teaches us and history confirms that the only thing that stands between a society and brutal tyranny is that society's commitment to the sanctity of life.

I recognize I am speaking to some who have had abortions. I

am speaking to many others who will contemplate it. God's grace is sufficient and cleansing is complete and total. If you have been through an abortion, you do not have to live under guilt. God's grace forgives and cleanses us completely. But, I want you to see what a beautiful picture the word of God paints about life and about God's intention for us.

I. God's Purpose For Us

In Psalm 139, the first six verses speak about God's knowledge of us and God's purpose for us.

He knows all about us. He knows our thoughts and our actions. He hears every word. He surrounds us with His care. His plan is so marvelous it is beyond comprehension. God has a wonderful purpose and wonderful plan for every person in the world.

Ps. 139:1-6; "O Lord thou has searched me and known me. Thou knowest my downsitting and mine uprising, thou understandest my thought afar off. Thou compasses my path and my lying down, and art acquainted with all my ways. For there is not a word in my tongue, but, lo, O Lord, thou knowest it all together. Thou has beset me behind and before, and laid thine hand upon me. Such knowledge is too wonderful for me; it is high, I cannot attain unto it."

Can you imagine anything more beautiful? God knows everything about you and about me. He knows our thoughts. He knows the intent in all that we do. He knows everything about us. He surrounds us everywhere we go. We cannot be out of his compassionate concern. "He lays His hand upon me." Would you like to live knowing that God's hand was on you? God's hand resting upon you, knowing that everywhere you went, the hand of God is there. That is what God says He wants to do in your life. God wants you to live with such a consciousness of Him that it is as though someone laid their hand on your shoulder. His Spirit is there always watching, always guiding, always guarding, always protecting. That is God's desire for you.

No wonder the Psalmist says, "Such knowledge is too wonderful for me; it is high, I cannot attain unto it."

II. God's Presence With Us

Ps. 139:7-10; "Whither shall I go from thy spirit? or whither shall I flee from thy presence? If I ascend up into heaven, thou art there: if I make my bed in hell, behold, thou art there. If I take the wings of the morning, and dwell in the uttermost parts of the sea; even there shall thy hand lead me, and thy right hand shalt hold me."

These verses tell us that everywhere we go God is already there. This is not really saying God is everywhere. It is saying wherever I go God is. It is a lot more personal, is it not? Wherever I go, God is there. Wherever you go, God is there. His presence, His interest is so intense, His concern is so great for us, that wherever we go God is there. In every circumstance God is there.

Ps. 139:11-12; "If I say, Surely the darkness will cover me (I'm going to do some things and God won't be able to see); even the night shall be light about me. Yea, the darkness hideth not from thee; but the night shineth as the day: the darkness and the light are both alike to thee."

God is saying in every circumstance of life I see you. In every circumstance I am there. Do you see the beautiful teaching of the presence of God? Everywhere I go, God goes. Every experience I have God is there. God observes. God is in the midst of it. What a difference it makes if we can comprehend that. What a difference it makes in our lives if we understand God is there.

III. God's Providence Guiding Us

Ps. 139:13; "For thou hast possessed my reins: thou hast covered me in my mother's womb."

Notice that God is the initiator. Covering me, possessing my reins means He formed our bodies.

Ps. 139:14; "I will praise thee; for I am fearfully and wonderfully made: marvelous are thy works; and that my soul knoweth right well."

God formed us. God's love for us began before we were born.

Genesis 29:31; "And the Lord saw that Leah was hated, he opened her womb."

He enabled her to have children. God initiated, moved, in order to let that come to pass.

Job 31:15; "Did not He that made me in the womb make him? And did not one fashion us in the womb?"

God made me in the womb. He fashioned us in the womb.

Isaiah 44:2. "Thus sayeth the Lord that made thee, and formed thee from the womb, who will help thee..." Look in verse 24, "Thus sayeth the Lord, thy redeemer, and he that formed thee from the womb..." We know God is our Redeemer. He is also the one who formed us in the womb.

Isaiah 49:1; "...The Lord hath called me from the womb; from the bowels (from the inner being) of my mother hath he made mention of my name."

Before the child was born, God called him and even knew him by name.

Look at verse 5, *"And now, saith the Lord that formed me from the womb..."* From a scriptural standpoint, when the child is conceived in the mother's womb, he or she is a person. That child is an individual.

Exodus 21:22-25 speaks about the punishment of someone who injures a woman so severely that she has a miscarriage. And it is very clear from that passage that in God's eyes someone is killed when that happens.

In 1967, the first international conference on abortion met in Washington, D.C. Twenty scientists from various backgrounds concluded, "The change occurring between implantation, a six-week embryo, a six-month fetus, a one-week child or a mature adult are merely stages of development and maturation."

We recognize the only difference is that one is inside the mother's womb and the other is outside. The argument that as long as the life is dependent upon the mother it cannot be considered killing is ludicrous. When is a child more dependent than after it is born? How many children do you know that came out with teeth and were ready to cut up their steak and eat it. They are as dependent and more so after birth than they are before.

The word for baby in the Greek language is *brephos*. In Luke 1:41 it is used after Mary came to her cousin Elizabeth, "the babe leaped in her womb." In Luke 2:12 and Luke 2:16 the word baby, speaking of a newborn baby, is *brephos*. In Luke 18:15, concerning the children that they brought to Jesus, it says that they brought infants to Jesus that He might touch them, and the disciples said leave him alone, and Jesus says, "Suffer little children to come unto me, and forbid them not:..." The word infant there in Luke 18:15 is *brephos*. II Timothy 3:15, "...from a child thou hast known the holy scriptures...", the word child is *brephos*. It is used to denote children from the unborn to a teenager. No distinction is made between the born and unborn children.

He formed you in secret. Psalm 139:15 and 16 are really beautiful verses as he tells what God saw that nobody else saw. "My substance was not hid from thee,..." It was hid from everybody else "...when I was made in secret, and curiously wrought in the lowest part of the earth." No one else saw what God saw. He saw your substance when it was not yet complete. It was not hid from Him. He watched as you grew. Isn't that beautiful? That means that for whatever reason God grew us like He wanted us. Who are we to say that one form of life is higher than another? Who are we to say that certain handicapped children do not deserve a right to live? God formed you. He knew something nobody else knew. It was not hid from God.

The next verse tells us that nobody else did what God did. "Thine eyes did see my substance, yet being unperfect;..." God saw you before all the warts and the freckles and everything was formed.

"...And in thy book all my members were written, which in continuance were fashioned, when as yet there was none of them."

God wrote down everything about you physically before you were ever formed. In His book, while you were still in the process of being formed physically, when your members were in development, when as yet there was none of them, God wrote it down in His book. Life is precious to God. Clearly, the unborn child is a person and abortion is murder.

That was the position of the church until the last 25 years. You can go back to the earliest Christian writings, and there are many writings in the second century dealing with the subject of abortion, and every one of them treats the unborn as a child and the one who takes the unborn is guilty of murder. Yet in our sophisticated, liberal, human-centered theology today, we have concluded that it does not matter.

The tragedy is that those who are not even Christians have led the way in this matter. Doris Gordon is an atheist. She is the head of a group called Libertarians for Life. She declares: "The right to choose does not include the choice to harm innocent people. As a Libertarian I am strongly pro-choice, but never where there is a victim. We affect children without their consent when we choose to have sex. And they are conceived in a state of dependency. Being in the womb and needing parental care is a situation parents impose upon their children. Children do not impose it upon their parents. If we are responsible for causing those needs, and if we negligently or intentionally fail to provide care and then harm results, we are accountable. The right of children to parental care is fundamental. Caring for someone else's children should be voluntary for we have no choice about causing their existence and thus their dependency."

This does not mean that we may choose to kill them. Pro-abortionists grant that someone else's children have at least one right against us. Yet according to their thinking our own children have none. This means that a child next door or halfway around the world has more rights against us than our own child. Does this make sense to you? Abortion is a wrong not a right. Legalizing abortion is not neutral as some say, but incredibly dangerous, for it creates a class of victims; innocent persons whose killing is permitted and protected by law. Both sides of the abortion debate should see such an idea as absolutely incompatible with liberty." Now listen to this. "If mothers may kill their own children, then whom can we trust? If the womb is unsafe, then where can we be safe? Abortion not only violates children's rights, it endangers us all."

It is a tragedy that we who know the Word of God and who hold it precious and cherish it have been silent in the midst of this tragic slaughter of the children of our country. We have begun to market the carcasses of these babies. Ladies, the cosmetics you wear may contain the fetuses of aborted babies. This is so prevalent that Mary Kay cosmetics has stated all of the gelatin used in their cosmetics is animal gelatin. But if you use cosmetics that do not specifically state animal gelatin, the chances are that part of it is the marketing of the carcasses of aborted babies. It has become big business. Doctors and abortion clinics have made millions and millions of dollars. In American society, while we concern ourselves with the extinction of the whooping crane or with some little minnow, we are killing 4,000 babies every day.

IV. God's Pardon For Those Who Have Sinned

I know that I am speaking to some of you who have been through the experience of abortion. Please hear me.

I John 1:7, "But if we walk in the light, as he is in the light, we have fellowship one with another, and the blood of Jesus Christ His Son cleanseth us from all sin."

All sin. Does *all* mean every sin? Does *all* mean murder, does it mean lying, stealing? *All* sin. The blood of Jesus Christ cleanses us from *all* sin.

I John 1:8-9 "If we say that we have no sin we deceive ourselves, and the truth is not in us. If we confess our sins, He is faithful and just to forgive us our sins, and to cleanse us from all unrighteousness."

Forgiveness is what happens between us and God. It is justification, redemption, where God applies the saving work of Jesus Christ. And then it says *"...cleanse us from all unrighteousness."*

Cleansing is what happens in my own sight. I am cleansed because I know I am forgiven. I am cleansed and clean and pure because God has forgiven me. And so He forgives me in His sight, and He cleanses me in my sight. That is what God wants to say to us.

Romans 8:1-2; "There is therefore now no condemnation (no judgment) to them who are in Christ Jesus, who walk not after the flesh, but after the Spirit. For the law of the Spirit of life in Christ Jesus hath made me free from the law of sin and death."

Law says that murder is punishable by death. Jesus died and set us free from the judgment of the law. When we come to Him, his forgiveness is total and complete. There is now no condemnation to those in Christ Jesus.

Hebrews 10:16-17; "This is the covenant that I will make with them after those days, saith the Lord,..." He is talking about the days after the coming of Christ. "...I will put my laws into their hearts, and in their minds will I write them; and their sins and iniquities will I remember no more."

He will remember them no more. And what God has forgotten we best forget! What God has forgotten is gone.

Psalm 103:10 "He hath not dealt with us after our sins; nor rewarded us according to our iniquities."

God does not treat us according to what we deserve. He has not dealt with us according to the way we lived; according to the way we acted. When we come to Him he does not treat us that way.

Ps. 103:11; "For as the heaven is high above the earth, so great is his mercy toward them that fear Him."

For those who fear Him, who come to Him for forgiveness, His mercy is as high as the heaven above the earth.

Psalms 103:12-13; "...as far as the east is from the west, so far hath he removed our transgressions from us. Like as a father pitieth his children, so the Lord pitieth them that fear Him. For he knoweth our frame; he remembereth that we are dust."

Whatever your past has been, if you will come to Jesus Christ, He will remove your sin as far as east is from west. Whatever your sin may have been, if you will come to Jesus Christ it will be forgiven. If it is forgiven it is covered, if it is covered it is forgotten, it is cast away and you are as pure as the purest virgin. You are as pure as the most sinless child. You are pure in the grace of Jesus Christ. That guilt which you carry, that burden which you have fostered need not be yours anymore. When He nailed His Son to the cross, He nailed that which was against us to the cross. He nailed that list of the sins, the list of all of my sins, to the cross. (Col. 2:14) He erased it out of the record when He nailed that record to the cross. It meant it is covered. It is forgiven!

You do not have to live with guilt and despair and defeat. You can know forgiveness and liberty from the sins of the past whatever they may be. That is the message that God has for us. That is the message that we claim today. We stand and raise our voice against the injustice and the crime that is being perpetrated in our society. We must bow before a holy God claiming His perfect provision for every need in our life.

Some of us need to repent of the sin of silence. Some of us need to repent of the sin of cowardice. We have been unwilling to speak. We have been afraid and fearful.

Some of us need to forever remove from our hearts the reality of an abortion. Let God take it away. He will do it. He will remove it. Some of us need to be obedient to God's call for our life. Only in obeying Him will we find the freedom that is ours in Jesus Christ.

A Testimony on Behalf of Life

Mrs. Carol Everett

TEXT: 1 John 1:9, KJV

SUPPLEMENTAL VERSES: Isaiah 41:9

SUMMARY OF MESSAGE: Carol Everett's "A Testimony on Behalf of Life' is not a sermon to be preached. Rather, it is a story to be told, a testimony of God's forgiveness and power to answer prayers.

Mrs. Everett tells of her experiences of owning and managing abortion clinics, assisting in abortions, and having an abortion. She tells how God changed her from being calloused toward unborn babies and money-centered to being clearly pro-life and trusting in God to lead her. Everett's testimony is touching and convincing.

PREACHING TRACKS:

➤TRACK ONE: Share the entire testimony with no supplemental information.

➤TRACK TWO: Select parts or all of the testimony to share, adding your own Scripture and commentary. I and II tell the story of Mrs. Everett's involvement in the abortion industry and her life-changing counseling experience. III tells about her continuing growth. V offers ideas for solving the abortion problem from the core.

➤TRACK THREE: Preach a combination of points from the testimony and from other sermons in this book.

A TESTIMONY ON BEHALF OF LIFE

The Scarlet Lady – Confessions Of A Successful Abortionist.

Mrs. Carol Everett

Nineteen years ago today is the anniversary date of my abortion. I was married and I had two children. I should have been thrilled for a third pregnancy. But we had a premarital agreement: There would be no more children. And when I found myself pregnant my choice was my husband or my child, and I chose my husband.

The moment I woke up, I knew I had killed my baby. But who can you share that with? You can't say, "I'm depressed. I killed my child." My husband didn't share my remorse so I acted out my anger at him. I continued by abusing one child physically and mentally, and overprotecting the other, actually expecting him to be killed and for the police to come to my door and say, "Mrs. Everett, your son has been killed. You had an abortion, didn't you? Well, you're even now." Nothing would satisfy the feelings of inadequacy, of killing my child.

Strange as it may seem, I became the manager of an abortion clinic. I became involved to the point eventually of owning part interest in two abortion clinics in Dallas.

I had to hold those babies still in the second and third trimester. You say, "The head's here. The buttocks are here." And you push that baby down into the instruments and watch those baby parts coming out. I knew it was a baby. But I trained myself to say, "I'm helping the woman. I'm helping the woman. I'm helping the woman." As I trained my employees, their eyes would roll back in their head when they saw body parts. I told them, "We're helping the woman. Remember the woman." I trained them not to think about the baby.

Of course, you know a baby dies in every abortion. But we were also maiming and killing women. We would carefully get them out of the clinic before they died so that we could always tell the girls on the phone that we had never had a death. There were hysterectomies and colostomies, because the woman's uterus was perforated or her bowel injured. The last 18 months, 20 women either died or had major surgery. Those people were my children's age. And I was questioning it all.

I worked on a straight commission. My commission was $25 for each abortion. That doesn't sound like a lot of money, but the last month we did 545 abortions. And 545 times $25 means my

31

last month's income was $13,625. Most people today don't recognize that not only the owners and the managers, but the abortionists work on a straight commission also. They are only compensated for the number of abortions they actually perform.

I had a plan. I was going to make $250,000 to $260,000 in 1983, but I wanted to be a millionaire. And the only way I could be a millionaire was to have five clinics open.

There is so much infighting in the abortion industry. I had to solve those problems. The problem was the doctor and with him came his wife. I couldn't get along with her. We needed to solve those problems and with that in mind, I found a counselor.

I will admit to you that this was a very strange counselor. First of all, he wouldn't talk about money, and, to me, everything in my world revolved around the dollar sign. He made us agree we would meet with him for an hour each week. I can talk to anybody for four hours, and if he would solve my problems, I didn't care how much he charged. So we sat down with him. The second time I noticed something very different about him — I couldn't control him! I started interviewing him, and I don't know why to this day, but I finally said, "Are you a preacher?" He said, "Yes," and I said, "What in the world are you doing here?" He said, "God sent me."

I knew this man was crazy and I told him so. "I'll have you know I am a Christian. I have a Bible in the top right hand drawer of my desk. I want you to know that I pray every day" (of course, I didn't tell him I prayed none of those women would die, and I prayed there would be a lot of abortions). But when I told him I tithed all that money and he wasn't impressed I knew I was in trouble.

He had a very different story to tell. He said that not only he, but he and his deacons, had been praying for some time. They felt that there was someone inside that abortion clinic that God wanted out. He said, "Someone will be leaving in 30 days." Of course, I assumed the one who would be leaving was the doctor and I was so glad he was going to go and take that wife with him.

But then he went on. He told me about his God, this God who loved all of us but was a just God who was going to punish us for our sins. And this God knew that we couldn't be good enough, we couldn't work hard enough. He said, "Carol, you can't buy your way into heaven. But it's simpler than that. You can by this simple act of faith in Jesus Christ accept Him as your Lord and Savior and have eternal life. Would you pray with me, accepting Jesus as your Savior?"

I honestly prayed that prayer to shut him up. And it did. It was this kind of prayer, "Dear God, I am a sinner. Please forgive me of my sins. Thank you for sending your son, Jesus Christ, to die for sinners. Reign on the throne of my heart as Lord and Savior. Make me a worker in your vineyard. Amen."

That was the strangest prayer I had ever heard in my life. But

I ran back to the clinic. I only had to work two more weeks, and I would be a millionaire, but I couldn't wait.

When I got back to the abortion clinic something had happened. When I left, they were running in the front door saying, "Isn't this great. I'm pregnant." They were excited about being there. Now, when I came back, they were coming in the same door but they were crying. I had never seen that before. So I started taking them in my office and saying, "Why are you crying?"

Don't misunderstand. I knew how to sell abortions. You take that fear, amplify it, tell them abortion will fix it, get their money, push them through.

But I started saying, "No, you don't have to have an abortion. Your parents will not kill you. Would you like for me to go home with you and help you tell your parents?"

Now I was confused. I was not saying, "Isn't this great. I saved three babies today." I was saying, "I lost $75." And again, money, money, money. I've got two children in college, they need a thousand dollars a month allowance. As I fell to my knees on the floor of that abortion clinic, my prayer was, "Lord, if there is a Lord, if this is not where you want me, hit me over the head with a two-by-four." He did. Channel 4, the CBS affiliate in Dallas, did an expose on abortion clinics doing abortions on women who were not pregnant. They sent their reporters to a doctor to be certain they were not pregnant then wired them for sound and sent them in our abortion clinic to see if we would attempt to abort them, even though they clearly were not pregnant. They caught us red-handed and aired a five-day special with those reporters walking in the clinic and sketches of how we sold abortions to non-pregnant women.

And it was 27 days after that pastor said, "Someone will be leaving in 30 days." I knew it was me!

The man who introduced me to Jesus was Jack Shaw. The Shaws discipled me for 18 months feeding me the Word of God, changing my life with the Word of God. And I started to understand that I had been involved in the murder of 35,000 babies! That was very heavy. I found 1 John 1:9, "If we confess our sins He is faithful and just to forgive us our sins and cleanse us from all unrighteousness." And I started moving through that.

I didn't want to be a pro-lifer. I watched television and I thought the only thing pro-lifers did was get arrested and I didn't want that. I am a different kind of pro-lifer. I am the kind you won't see on television. The Lord continues to work in my life, and through Isaiah 41:9 He said, "You whom I have taken from the ends of earth and called from its farthest reaches, do not fear." He's with me and He's continuing to work in my life. The writing of a book was the most healing experience because through it I was able to reconcile all of those experiences I never planned to tell anyone about.

Some asked me if I think there is ever a reason for abortion?

No. God tells us clearly in Psalm 139 that He ordains life. And even if it's rape (and let's be honest… yes, we hear about rape and incest all of the time, but abortions for rape and incest in this nation are less than one percent. The abortionists will admit that 93 percent of abortions today are for birth control.) God tells us in Psalm 139 that life begins at conception, and if it is in a rape or incest, that's Him taking an evil and using it for good. We have to stand on that.

Many of us might lie or cheat, but none of us thinks we will ever kill. But when I had my abortion, I killed! I killed a baby that my body was supposed to protect, that God designed me to nurture. I assume if I tell you that, you're going to hate me. You can't love me. So we who have had abortions have a very difficult time sharing that. I was never going to tell anyone I was bad enough to kill my baby.

But again God had a plan, and one night I did my testimony in front of my church. I wasn't going to talk about this. You know, I do my testimony all the time. I thought I would have no problem. But I made a mistake. I said, "Lord, speak through me." When I stood up, out of my mouth came, "I had an abortion." In my mind I was thinking "Where did that come from? Why did you say that?" Then, I was looking around at that audience at these people who loved me and saying, "Okay, when I finish I will grab my purse and run down that aisle and they will never see me again." And, yes, I was crying. Yes, I was hurting.

But when I walked down from that platform there was a big fight, but it was my church trying to see who could hug me the tightest and the longest. I realized that the Bible really means it when it says we're supposed to confess our sins one to another. 1 John 1:9 says if we confess and repent, He is faithful and just to forgive. The part of that Scripture we forget is, "Cleanse us from all unrighteousness."

In my life it is an ongoing process. He continues to work. Many times I am reminded, "You killed your child." Every day someone gets in my face out there on that pro-life trail and says, "How in the world can you be forgiven?" If I didn't understand those Scriptures, I would be lost.

The people in the pro-life movement are busy behind the scenes ministering. They are there with the 2000 Crisis Pregnancy Centers across this nation that are ministering to the needs of women, and you never see them. We're there for them. We never charge the women. And last year, the combined Crisis Pregnancy Centers of this nation, saved at least 300,000 babies. So, if you just multiply 300,000 times $200 (which is a cheap abortion), we cost the abortion industry $60 million last year. They're mad and they are attacking us. That's where the pro-life women are. And there are men in this movement. There are men in this movement who are out in front of the abortion clinics, who are protesting, who are doing all of those things.

We are letting our youth talk about safe sex when we know there's no such thing. We are cheapening life. We've got to get back to God's plan for life, God's plan for sex. You see, abortion is not the problem. There's a bigger problem. We've got to take our Christian principles out of our pews and into the streets, and especially into the schools. The kids are dying to hear the truth. Everywhere they hear the abstinence message, they stop having sexual intercourse. Our message is critical to those young people. They are really hurting!

Life is truly a precious commodity, and we know from reading God's Word that He has created each and every one of us for a specific purpose. We must have that life, and we must make Him Lord and Master of that life in order to fulfill that purpose. We all do make mistakes but I am so glad that God does not freeze us in our past mistakes, but rather He warmly, lovingly forgives and changes us.

Your Body, God's Temple

Gerald Harris

TEXT: 1 Corinthians 6:19-20, KJV

SUPPLEMENTAL TEXT: 1 Peter 1:18-19, Philippians 3:20-21, 1 Thessalonians 5:23, Revelation 20:11-15, Isaiah 44:2, Acts 17:28, Luke 1:15, 41, Romans 5:20, 1 John 1:9, 1 Corinthians 3:17; 15:42-43, Psalm 46:1; 100:3; 139:13-16

SUMMARY OF MESSAGE: Gerald Harris' "Your Body, God's Temple" uses I Corinthians 6:19-20 to explain the value and sacredness of all human life. Dr. Harris states that a mother does not have the right to abort her child, first because the child is his own life and not part of her body, but also because each person's body is the potential temple of God. What God would indwell, Harris says, we should not kill.

PREACHING TRACKS:

➤ TRACK ONE: Preach the entire sermon.

➤ TRACK TWO: Preach the points on the outline that best apply to your congregation. I and V include the story of a woman who was advised not to have an abortion then came to realize that was the best advice. III teaches that each body God creates is a sacred treasure, a sacred trust and a sacred temple.

➤ TRACK THREE: Preach a combination of points in this and in other sermons in this book.

YOUR BODY, GOD'S TEMPLE

*"Know ye not that your body is the temple of the Holy Ghost
which is in you, which ye have of God, and ye are not your own?
For ye are bought with a price: therefore glorify God in your
body, and in your spirit, which are God's."*
1 Corinthians 6:19-20

Gerald Harris

Several years ago the director of our weekday preschool ministry entered my study with some information that shattered my day. Someone had told her that one of the part-time employees in our daycare program was going to have an abortion. A mutual friend persuaded this church employee to seek my counsel about this critical matter. When the young woman entered my study it was apparent that she was there more out of an obligation to her friend than to seek any kind of advice.

When I inquired about her intention to have an abortion she admitted that she had an appointment the next day to see a physician at the "New Woman's Clinic" several miles from the church. When I made my appeal for her to go to the Crisis Pregnancy Center instead of the "Clinic" she had chosen, she vehemently protested.

"Don't interfere with my life," she defiantly retorted.

I said to her, "I know you love children. You have spent hundreds of hours caring for the dear children in our weekday preschool ministry. You'd be devastated if anything ever happened to one of the children under your care. Is that not correct?"

Her eyes filled with tears as she replied, "Of course, I would be devastated if anything bad ever happened to any of those children."

"Why, then," I asked, "would you destroy your own child through an abortion?"

"Because this is my body," she answered, "and I can do whatever I want to do to my body."

For more than an hour I tried to use all of the logic, all of the reason, all of the theology, and all of the persuasiveness at my disposal to convince her not to proceed with her intended plans. However, what rights does a woman have over her own body?

First of all, we realize that the unborn child is not a part of the mother's body. The body of the child in the mother's womb is distinctly different from that of the mother. When 23 chromosomes in the male sperm and the 23 chromosomes of the female ovum unite into 46 chromosomes at the time of conception, the result is a human being. These 46 chromosomes carry the genes that determine the hereditary characteristics and the lifelong identity of this human being in embryo. Therefore, there is no qualitative difference between a fetus after the moment of conception and a human being. The only difference is quantitative.

The child growing within the body of the mother develops a heart that beats, tiny hands and feet, ears and eyes—all within the first five weeks in the mother's uterus. Quite often the child's blood type is distinctly different from that of the mother. The child has its own sexual identity, personal heredity, and eternal destiny. So, the unborn child is neither a part nor an appendage of the mother's body.

Therefore, the woman who says, "I can have an abortion because it's my body and I have a right over my body," is simply ignorant of the facts . If you look at the evidence produced by embryology you can come to no other conclusion but that an unborn child is a living human being.

However, for the sake of argument, let's move from the sublime truth as stated above to a ridiculous hypothesis. Let's suppose, just for the moment, that the unborn baby were part of the mother's body. The mother still does not have the right to do whatever she wants to her own body. No woman has the right to mutilate or disfigure her body. She does not have the right to take her life by committing suicide.

In fact, our text informs us that we were created with a God-shaped vacuum that we might be inhabited by the Holy Spirit. The apostle Paul declares, *"If any man defile the temple of God, him shall God destroy; for the temple of God is holy, which temple ye are" (1 Cor. 3:17).* Any woman who has an abortion is simply giving evidence of ignorance, not information; selfishness, not stewardship; and the gratification of self rather than the glorification of God. Such a woman is also giving evidence that she is more interested in rights than responsibility.

So, whether you ascribe to the truth that the unborn child is not a part of the mother's body and a distinctly different human being, or to the fallacy that the fetus is a part of the mother's body, the principle remains. The woman has no right to abort an unborn child. Indeed, the woman who has an abortion is an agent of death instead of the agent of life.

Therefore, let us consider what the text has to say about the human body.

I. THE BODY IS A SACRED TREASURE

In writing to the church in Corinth, the apostle Paul informs us that these bodies which we have are "of God" (verse 19). Mankind is the product of God's own hands.

At the dawn of creation, before the tempter had touched the world, and the forbidden tree had yielded its fateful fruit, God scooped up a handful of dirt and fashioned the first man, Adam, and breathed into his nostrils the breath of life. When God viewed His creative handiwork, He saw that "it was very good" (Gen. 1:31). God's designing and shaping of that first human being was a mighty miracle. But, the miracle of conception and the fashioning of each and every child is also a miracle of mighty proportions. Every human body is a sacred treasure because it is a miracle product from the hands of an omnipotent God.

A. A Sacred Treasure Because of Its Magnificent Design

The body is a sacred treasure because of its design. The Psalmist declared, *"I will praise thee; for I am fearfully and wonderfully made..." (Ps. 139:14a).* Consider a larger portion of this same passage from *The Living Bible: "You made all the delicate, inner parts of my body, and knit them together in my mother's womb. Thank you for making me so wonderfully complex! It is amazing to think about. Your workmanship is marvelous – and how well I know it. You were there while I was being formed in utter seclusion! You saw me before I was born and scheduled each day of my life before I began to breathe. Every day was recorded in your Book!" (Ps. 139:13-16, TLB).*

Our body is a mosaic of miracles, from the crown of the head to the sole of the foot. The body is an intricate machine of symmetry, utility, and mystery. The configuration and the construction, the composition and connections, the compressions, the coordinations, and the compensations all attest to the truth that the body is "fearfully made."

Think about the intricacies of the human body. An adult body has 650 muscles, about 206 bones, over 100 joints, 60,000 miles of arteries, veins, and capillaries, and 13 million nerve cells – all encased in 20 square feet of flexible, waterproof covering called skin. Amazingly this skin wears away and is replaced every few weeks. Set in the skin are up to five million hairs which last about three years.

The heart is the engine that keeps the human machine going moment by moment. The heart is a hollow, muscular organ about the size of a man's fist. This organ pumps the blood throughout the body by an alternate contraction and dilation action. The heart pumps ten pints of blood through veins, arteries, and capillaries every minute. This means that the heart pumps 1,800 gallons of blood through the body each day. The capillaries, the smallest vessels of the blood-vascular system, have a total surface area of about 60,000 square feet, or about one and one-half acres. These tiny vessels, many of which are microscopic in size, open and close in perfect rhythm so that the blood is distributed through the body according to God's precise design.

Indeed, every part of the body is an amazing miracle of construction. The eye, with its optic nerve, sensitive retina, cornea, lens, and iris lodged in a bony orbit in the skull for protection, is a miracle of design. The brain, with its billions of components controlling and coordinating our thoughts into actions, is a creation of such complexities that only an omnipotent God could fashion it.

Even God's design and creation of the hand has captured the wonder of brilliant men. Dr. Chris Ethridge, a fine Christian physician in Jackson, Mississippi, has narrowed his interests to hand surgery. Often I have heard him speak of the amazing flexibility, proficiency, and capability God has provided in His creation of this grasping organ of the body. And, just think—the tiny hand of a child, complete with distinctive personalized fingerprints, is formed in the mother's body within five weeks of conception.

B. A Sacred Treasure Because of Its Miraculous Destiny

The body is a sacred treasure, not only because of its design, but also because of its destiny. It is difficult to believe that God would create such a complex, yet delicate, instrument as the human body, only to permit it to occupy a brief span of time and then disintegrate into the dust of oblivion.

Would a master craftsman fashion an exquisite violin of rare beauty and precision, play a song upon its strings, and then smash it across his work bench? No! A thousand times no! Likewise, God would not allow man, His masterpiece of creation, to walk upon this earth for a few brief years and then allow the darkness of death to be the culmination and consummation of His existence.

God has created us body, mind, and spirit for eternity. At conception when those 46 chromosomes unite, a trinity of body, mind, and spirit comes into being that will outlast the stars and planets. The apostle Paul underscored this truth when he wrote, *"...and I pray God your whole spirit and soul and body be preserved blameless unto the coming of our Lord Jesus Christ"* (1 Thess. 5:23).

Those who have trusted Christ for salvation will one day experience a bodily transformation. Those believers who are dead when Christ returns will experience a physical resurrection. Concerning the body of the redeemed, the apostle Paul writes, *"It is sown in corruption; it is raised in incorruption; it is sown in dishonor; it is raised in glory; it is sown in weakness; it is raised in power"* (1 Cor. 15:42-43). Those believers who are alive when Christ returns will go through a metamorphosis. To the Philippian church Paul describes it thusly: *"For our conversation is in heaven; from whence also we look for the Savior, the Lord Jesus Christ: who shall change our vile body, that it may be fashioned like unto his glorious body, according to the working whereby he is able even to subdue all things unto himself"* (Phil. 3:20-21).

All of us, and especially a woman with child, need to remember that our bodies – including the body of the precious child in the womb – are sacred treasures because of their design and because of their destiny. Women have a unique role in God's divine plan for the creation of life. How gloriously good it is when women decide to facilitate rather than impede God's marvelous creative process.

II. THE BODY IS A SACRED TRUST

Consider the text once again: *"What? know ye not that your body is the temple of the Holy Ghost which is in you, which ye have of God, and ye are not your own? For ye are bought with a price: therefore glorify God in your body, and in your spirit, which are God's" (1 Cor. 6:19-20).*

This Scripture clearly states that we cannot claim ownership over our bodies. We are not our own. We belong to God. Our body is an entrustment from God. He is the owner. We are trustees or stewards of our own bodies.

A. A Sacred Trust By Creation

Our bodies belong to God because we are created by Him. He made us. The Psalmist wrote: *"Know ye that the Lord he is God: it is he that hath made us, and not we ourselves; we are his people, and the sheep of his pasture" (Ps. 100:3).* The body of the woman may be the instrument God uses for the creation and development of a child, but the Father in heaven forms, fashions, and finishes the child in the womb. Isaiah declared, *"The Lord that made thee, and formed thee from the womb,...will help thee" (Is. 44:2).*

B. A Sacred Trust By Preservation

Furthermore, our bodies belong to God because He preserves us and sustains us. God did not create us, then abandon us. He wants our lives to be meaningful and fulfilled. *"God is our refuge and strength, a very present help in trouble" (Ps. 46:1). "In him we live, and move, and have our being" (Acts 17:28).*

Therefore, what God would sustain and preserve we are not to destroy. He alone has the keys of life and death and those who would try to wrest those keys from His hands are seeking to usurp the place and the authority of the Almighty.

C. A Sacred Trust By Redemption

However, He not only has the right of ownership by virtue of His creation and His preservation, but also by reason of redemption. The saints are His purchased possession. Paul avows, *"For ye are bought with a price..."* (1 Cor. 6:20). Peter affirms, *"...Ye were not redeemed* (purchased from the slave market of sin) *with corruptible things, as silver and gold...but with the precious blood of Christ, as the lamb without blemish and without spot" (1 Pet. 1:18-19).*

We are not our own. Our lives, our bodies, our minds, our

spirits are entrustments from God. The redeemed are God's because of creation and preservation and redemption.

Notice the word "therefore" in our text. It is a big word. *"For ye are bought with a price: therefore glorify God in your body, and in your spirit, which are God's" (1 Cor. 6:20).* Paul is speaking under the inspiration of the Holy Spirit and he says, "You are not your own." Your body is not your own to abuse or pollute or defile. Neither does anyone have the right to abuse or to destroy the body of another. Our bodies are the vehicles God must use to do His work on this earth. He has no hands but ours, no feet but ours, no voice but ours to tell the world of His redeeming love.

When God says, "therefore," you had better listen. The "therefore" in this verse puts each of us under a divine imperative to live for Christ, to surrender to Him, and to serve Him. In view of all that transpired at Calvary, we cannot be arbitrary. It is not an incidental matter. Christ is our substitute, our sacrifice, and our sovereign in redemptive love; thus, we belong to Him. Our bodies are entrustments from God and must be surrendered to His will and His control.

This truth also means that children, even from the womb, are entrustments from God. The Old Testament story of Hannah, who gave her son Samuel back to God in temple service, is an example of a mother who recognized her trusteeship.

III. THE BODY IS A SACRED TEMPLE

In our text the apostle Paul referred to the body as "the temple of the Holy Ghost" (1 Cor. 6:19). It is incredible to think that the human body can become the royal residence of the Spirit of the living God. The body of every unborn child is a potential dwelling place of deity. In fact, when the angel of the Lord foretold the birth of John the Baptist, he said, *"And he shall be filled with the Holy Ghost, even from his mother's womb"* (Luke 1:15). So totally dedicated to God was the baby John that God had the unborn child leap in his mother's womb when Mary hailed Elizabeth and informed her of her holy conception (Luke 1:41).

Those who allow the Holy Spirit to be resident and president in their lives go on to do mighty exploits for God. Who can measure the souls saved, the advancement of the kingdom, and the good accomplished by those indwelt and filled by the Holy Spirit? Peter, filled with the Spirit, preached a mighty sermon on the day of Pentecost and 3,000 souls were saved. Paul filled with the Holy Spirit, established churches throughout the Roman empire in the first century. D. L. Moody, filled with the Spirit, shook two continents closer to God.

Ethel Waters, whose Christian testimony and songs of faith have thrilled millions, was nearly aborted. Years ago in a Billy Graham crusade she affirmed, "Jesus is my rock, my sword, my shield. He's my wheel in the middle of the wheel. He's the fairest of 10,000 to my soul." Then she sang, "His Eye Is On The Sparrow,

And I Know He Watches Me."

Though many years have passed since I saw that television crusade, the glory of God was so manifestly evident upon her countenance, I remember it as if it were this morning. Ethel Waters brought joy and faith to many souls. This world would have been deprived of a great saint of God had she been aborted. Every aborted child is a potential singer or soul-winner, a preacher or president in embryo. In the wombs of expectant mothers we have new hopes and dreams, new friends and companions for eternity. These bodies of ours are extensions of Christ into the present day. He dwells in every believer and God desires that the temple (body) of every child of God become a palace of praise and honor to Him.

CONCLUSION

Oh yes, do you remember the young woman who came to me saying, "Why can't I have an abortion? I can do whatever I want. It is my body." Sadly, tragically, she followed through with her plans. She exercised her "right" to have an abortion. However, she soon discovered that her "right" was filled with suffering and regret that she never could have imagined.

Two days later she was heard to say, "Oh how I wish I had listened to those who tried to counsel me to have my baby. I've made a tragic, irreversible mistake." I wonder if her little girl would have been a nurse, a school teacher, or perhaps even a missionary.

For those who have had an abortion, however, there is good news. The glorious news of the Gospel is that God's grace is greater than all of our sins. Our God is the God of a second chance. He has graciously given all of us far more chances than we deserve. The Bible teaches that where sin abounds, grace does much more abound (Rom. 5:20). God has graciously promised that "if we confess our sins, he is faithful and just to forgive us our sins, and to cleanse us from all unrighteousness" (1 John 1:9).

Honor the sanctity of life. Nourish and care for the body for it is a sacred treasure, a sacred trust, and a sacred temple. Remember that even the tiny body of the unborn child has the capacity for eternity and can become a palace of praise to the eternal God.

Choose Life So You May Live

O.S. Hawkins

TEXT: Deuteronomy 30:19, NIV

SUPPLEMENTAL VERSES: Matthew 1:20, Acts 7:19, 2 Timothy 3:15, 1 Peter 2:2, Luke 1:31, 41, 44; 2:12, 16; 18:15, Jeremiah 1:5; 20:17, Ephesians 1:4, Proverbs 6:17; 24:11-12, Joel 2:17; 3:19, Deuteronomy 27:25, 2 Chronicles 7:14, Psalms 139:13-16, 51:5, Genesis 25:23, 1 Corinthians 6:19-20, Romans 8:1, 1 John 1:9

SUMMARY OF MESSAGE: O.S. Hawkins' "Choose Life So You May Live" confronts the abortion issue and pro-choice arguments with personal testimonies from women who have experienced abortion—and still feel the pain of it.
Hawkins explains that life begins at conception from irrefutable scientific and biblical points of view, then exhorts Christians to do something about the murder of innocent babies that is taking place in our land. Hawkins closes his message by encouraging those who have had abortions to receive the loving acceptance and freeing forgiveness of Jesus Christ.

PREACHING TRACKS:

➤ TRACK ONE: Preach the entire sermon.

➤ TRACK TWO: Preach the points on the outline that best apply to your congregation. II shows that life starts at conception. IV directs and instructs Christians in how to respond to pro-abortion arguments and slogans. V offers those who have experienced abortion hope and healing.

➤ TRACK THREE: Preach a combination of points in this sermon and in other sermons in this book.

CHOOSE LIFE SO YOU MAY LIVE

"I have set before you life and death, blessings and curses, now
CHOOSE LIFE so that you and your children might live."
Deuteronomy 30:19

O.S. Hawkins

Legal personhood does not exist prenatally..." So declared the United States Supreme Court in the now infamous Roe vs. Wade Decision handed down on January 22, 1973. Since that day, over twenty-five million babies have been legally aborted in our nation. In its aftermath has not only come the elimination of millions of lives, but tragic trauma to millions of mothers. "Legal personhood does not exist prenatally." Tell that to the lady who wrote me these words: "Nearing 40 years of age and after four children, I found myself pregnant. My husband suggested abortion. I knew in my heart it was wrong. I have suffered supreme remorse ever since. Our home has one empty bedroom — a constant reminder! The doctors could control my problem, but nobody can control my hurt and loss of a very precious life that God Himself created. I carry this around now and for the rest of my life, this awful memory, the hurt is all mine. You can tell young women who may be considering abortion that a woman **never** forgets her baby. The memory lives on and on."

On July 1, 1976, the week of our National Bicentennial Celebration, the Supreme Court expanded its 1973 Decision by declaring that abortions may be performed on minor daughters without the knowledge of their parents. It is a strange nation in which we are living where an adolescent cannot get an aspirin in a school infirmary without parental permission, but can have an abortion without such! The 1976 Decision also expanded the 1973 Decision to allow women to obtain an abortion without the knowledge or consent of the baby's father. While a father must pay child support in other cases (and rightly so), he is often left with no say as to whether his own child comes into the world or not.

It is ironic that often when a man suggests an abortion he is thought of as insensitive, uncaring and selfish, while at the same time, a woman is often thought of as exercising her rights! Sometimes fathers are the forgotten victims of the abortion agenda.

I. When Does Life Begin?

Perhaps no other moral or social issue is as many faceted as is the abortion debate. Any serious discussion of the matter will eventually come down to one central issue — when does life begin? This is "the big question." Some say life begins at birth. They contend that until the baby is out of the womb it is not to be considered a human being, but simply a "fetus." Others say life begins when the fetus has grown and developed enough to live outside the womb or life begins at five to six months. Others say life begins when the baby has a measured brain wave or approximately six weeks after conception. Still others claim that life begins when the baby develops a measured heart beat at approximately three to four weeks after conception. And others say that life begins at conception when the male cell and the female cell unite, thus beginning the life process.

When does life begin? Consider for a moment the argument from science. The nucleus of a human cell is composed of 46 chromosomes. Twenty-three are furnished by the father, and 23 are furnished by the mother. The abortionists argue that during the embryonic stage of development and in the early stages of fetal development, the baby could not survive apart from the mother's body. Thus, it is moral to eliminate the fetus. But the truth is, the same baby could not survive apart from the mother's care after it is born at nine months either. To follow this erroneous concept to its conclusion would be to go ahead and eliminate the baby even after birth.

It is a fact of biological science that the only cell that the mother contributes to the baby is the first one (23 chromosomes) when it meets the father's cell and they combine. At this point conception takes place, and a new person is formed. In the cell structure, the baby is as much a part of the father as the mother. Obviously, during gestation the baby is nourished through the umbilical cord by the mother. But it should be noted, that only the baby is nourished. The same baby, after birth, is also dependent upon being nourished outside the womb. After conception, the child receives no new or additional life from the mother. It is not a part of her body that can be removed like a wart or a tumor. It is an individual person.

It is amazing how abortion activists refrain from using the term "baby" for the unborn and instead cling to the less intimate word, "fetus." It is as though this gives more of an appearance that the baby is simply a part of the mother's anatomy like a gall bladder or an appendix. It sounds so much better to say the fetus was extracted than to say the baby was killed. The pro-abortion activist might be interested to know that the word "fetus" is a Latin word. What does it mean in Latin? It is the word for "child." Life is a continual process, and each of us is a part of it. Some of us are newly conceived. Others are developing in the womb. Some are just born. Others are toddlers in the nursery. Some have completed the first day of school. Others are adolescents. Some are adults. Others are elderly. But we are all in a stage of gradual development. Man is no more or less a person at any stage of this development!

When does life begin? Consider for a moment the argument of Scripture. Just because many influenced by New Age persuasions have placed the Bible on the shelf as a worn out book of antiquity, does not mean it is. Millions of people still hold its truths near and dear to their hearts. Its words and laws have been the foundation blocks for every decent democracy and republic in world history. We believe it is revealed truth and our ultimate standard. Jesus stepped into manhood, not at his birth at Bethlehem, but at his conception at Nazareth. The Scripture records, *"An angel of the Lord appeared to Joseph in a dream and said, 'Do not be afraid to take Mary home as your wife, because what is* **conceived** *in her is from the Holy Spirit' " (Matthew 1:20).* To Mary, the angel announced, *"You will be with child and give birth to a son and you will give him the name of Jesus" (Luke 1:31).*

As many are aware, the New Testament was written in the Greek language. It was the universal written language of the first-century world. The Greeks have more than one word for our English word, "child." The most common word, found over 98 times in the Greek New Testament is the word *teknon.* The word speaks of a child as viewed in relation to a parent. However, there is an interesting word that is found only eight times in the Greek New Testament which throws much light upon what the Bible teaches regarding the unborn. It is the Greek word, *brephos.* Note its usage in the following verses:

Acts 7:19: "He dealt treacherously with our people and opposed our forefathers by forcing them to throw our their **newborn babies** *(brephos) so that they would die."*

Luke 18:15: "People were also bringing **babies** *(brephos) to Jesus to have him touch them. When the disciples saw this, they rebuked them."*

II Timothy 3:15: "And how from **infancy** *(brephos) you have known the Holy Scriptures which are able to make you wise for salvation through faith in Christ Jesus"*

I Peter 2:2: "Like **newborn babies,** *(brephos) crave pure spiritual milk, so that by it you may grow up in your salvation."*

Luke 2:12: "This shall be a sign to you: you will find a **baby** *(brephos) wrapped in strips of cloth and lying in a manger."*

Luke 2:16: "So they hurried off and found Mary and Joseph and the **baby** *(brephos) who was lying in the manger."*

In all the above verses the word, *brephos* describes a baby who has already been born. One who is outside the womb! That is, a real live human being. But there are two other verses in Scripture in which the same Greek word *(brephos)* is used. One is in Luke 1:41 where Scripture records, "When Elizabeth heard Mary's greeting the baby *(brephos)* leaped **in her womb** and Elizabeth was filled with the Holy Spirit." The other is found in Luke 1:44, "As soon as the sound of your greeting reached my ears, the **baby** *(brephos)* in my womb, leaped for joy." Note in each of these cases, the *brephos* (baby) is still in the womb. It is blatantly clear that God considers an unborn baby more than simply a wad of tissue. He considers him *brephos,* as much a human being as the child who is already born and playing, running up and down the street. In God's vocabulary, the little package of love in the uterus is *brephos* just as much as the toddler in the playpen! He uses the same word to identify them both.

The argument of Scripture is absolute. Those who do not believe that life begins at conception should be consistent and throw away the story of the virgin birth of our Lord Jesus Christ. You cannot have it both ways! One cannot believe the Bible and believe in abortion at the same time. The Bible is explicit – life begins at conception. There is even a sense in which the issue of life goes back beyond science and Scripture. Yes, back even before conception into the Eternal Councils of Creator God. God deals with us not only **after** our birth for all eternity, but **before** our birth and conception and all eternity past. To Jeremiah, God said, *"Before I formed you in the womb, I knew you, before you were born I set you apart: I appointed you as a prophet to the nations" (Jeremiah 1:4-5). "My mother could have been my grave" (Jeremiah 20:17).* If an abortion had been performed upon the fetus in Jeremiah's mother's womb, he still would have been Jeremiah. Although his mother may not have known his name, God did! Yes, life begins even before conception in the eternal councils of God. The great apostle Paul put it like this, *"For he chose us in him **before** the creation of the world to be holy and blameless in his sight"(Ephesians 1:4).*

II. What Should The Christian Do?

Thus, if life is present at conception, as both science and Scripture certainly reveal, then as a Christian there is no such thing as neutrality. Solomon, the wisest man who ever lived, said, *"Rescue those being led away to death: hold back those staggering toward slaughter **if you say, but we knew nothing about this,** does not he who weighs the heart perceive it? Does not he who guards your life know it? Will he not repay each person according to what he has done?" (Proverbs 24:11-12).* Here is a definite call to action. Life begins at conception, therefore, to take a life is murder. We call abortion murder, but many of us do not act like it is. Therefore, the law **must** be changed. And Christians, and moralists alike from other faiths, must become involved.

The main reason convenience abortions on demand are the law of the land is not because of the militant minority of the women liberationists and the liberal politicians, but primarily because moral people do nothing and say little as we walk by on the other side of the street ignoring this national blight. Perhaps the thing that is most amazing is the silence of the grand old flagship churches in the hearts of cities across America. Where are all the voices from all the First Baptist Churches of our land? Where are the voices from the First Presbyterian Churches and The First Methodist Churches? Some denominations in recent conventions have even taken pro-abortion platforms and stands. Perhaps Joel asked the question best 2,500 years ago when he cried out, "Where are all the prophets and preachers weeping between the porch and altar over the sins of the people?"

The church is virtually silent today when a child who by state law is too young to drink alcohol, too young to vote, and too young to drive a car, is at the same time legally permitted to destroy an unborn life and never even notify her parents. What kind of a nation have we become? By and large, the church and synagogue remain silent on the sanctity of life and surrender the truth of the Torah and the good news of the Gospel to the lies of the abortionists. Moses' call comes thundering down through the centuries, *"This day I call heaven and earth as witnesses against you that I have set before you life and death, blessings and curses. Now **choose life** so that you and your children may live"* (Deuteronomy 30:19). What is the bottom line for you? What do you believe? Is that a human life in the womb? So, then to abort is murder. You would not pass by on the other side of the street or keep silent while men and women were taking two and three-year-old children and scalding them to death in hot water. As Solomon said, how we need to "rescue those being led away to death." Dr. James Dobson has astutely observed that "all the abortion arguments descend to whether one believes an unborn baby is a live human being. If you believe the unborn is a person, then all the peripheral exclusions like rape and incest become folly." Would you kill a one-month-old baby in a crib because he was a victim of rape? Of course not! Then the same baby shouldn't be killed just because he is a few weeks behind in his development still in the womb! Yes, God has "set before us life and death, blessings and curses. Now **choose life** so that you and your children may live."

III. How To Respond To Pro-Abortion Arguments?

A few abortion rights activists rallied at the Federal Court House Building across the street from the First Baptist Church in downtown Fort Lauderdale. I walked across the street to watch their demonstration and listen to their arguments. What amazed me most was the signs they carried. They bore on them the most paradoxical and hypocritical statements imaginable. In fact, our very arguments for choosing life are found in the placards and themes which they promote. They carried such signs as: "Don't impose your morality on me," "Keep abortion legal," "Keep your laws off my body," and "Keep abortions safe." As I watched them and thought about these signs, several thoughts rushed through my mind. Let's think about their slogans for a moment. At the abortion rally, one lady, attractive and in horn-rimmed glasses, with the obvious appearance of a lawyer or professional woman, was carrying around a sign on a wooden stick which said, **"Don't impose your morality on me!"** Now, think about that sign for just a moment. If indeed life begins at conception, the fact is plain — abortion is murder and murder is a moral issue!

For centuries when medical doctors have obtained their medical degrees they have taken an oath called the Oath of Hippocrates. Many doctors have it displayed on their office wall, framed beautifully and written in flowing script letters. A portion of this Hippocratic Oath states: "I will give no deadly medicine to anyone if asked, nor suggest such council, and in like manner, I will not give to a woman a pessary (instrument) to produce abortion." In listing the things which God hates, Solomon says one of the things is, *"hands that shed innocent blood" (Proverbs 6:16-17).* As I looked at that sign, I pictured the bloody hands of a physician who took the Hippocratic Oath promising to never knowingly administer any drug that would injure life. For many medical doctors today it is no longer the Hippocratic Oath, but the Hypocritic Oath! It would do well for all women to find out if their gynecologist performs abortions in his office. Some of you might be surprised and might need to change doctors. A physician who is financially profiting from the abortion business is under severe judgement. From God's Torah thunder these words so applicable today: *"Cursed is the man who accepts a bribe to kill an innocent person" (Deuteronomy 27:25).*

At the rally as I looked at the lady's sign, I also pictured the blood of the innocent victim who never had a chance to "pursue life, liberty and justice" as guaranteed by our Constitution. How long will God continue to bless a nation which is so blatantly oblivious to His Word? Joel, the ancient Jewish prophet, said, *"But Egypt will be desolate, Edom a desert waste, because of violence done to the people of Judah, in whose land they shed innocent blood" (Joel 3:19).* Why did they become desolate? Because they "shed innocent blood in their land." And the woman continues to carry her sign – "Don't impose your morality on me!"

CHOICE! That is the password for the pro-choice advocates. Their cry is loud and long: "You people who are pro-life are trying to take away my power of choice. Don't impose your morality on me!" Now think about that. We are taking her power of choice? Think about the many choices that are made which lead up to so many convenience abortions on demand. Consider the choices a particular lady has already made. Should I go out with him or not? And she makes a choice – yes! Should I have sex with him or not? And she makes a choice – yes! Should I have sex without any preparation or birth control? And she makes another choice – yes! And then she becomes pregnant! And then she begins to scream that we are trying to take away her freedom to choose. She chose all right, and what is now in her is a live human being. She chose. It is not a question of us imposing our morality on her, but she imposing her immorality on us... and the unborn, and often asking us to pay for a federally funded abortion at the same time.

"Don't impose your morality on me." Do pro-abortionists really mean this? Are they then saying, "I am personally opposed to sex discrimination; however, if others want to discriminate on the basis of sex, that is their right. Don't impose your morality on me. I am personally opposed to racial discrimination. However, if others want to discriminate on the basis of race, that is their right. I don't want to impose my morals on them." How hypocritical can these men and women be who carry around signs saying – "Don't impose your morality on me!"

Morality is the strength of any nation. If America falls, it will not be the result of a weakened military, but the result of a weakened morality. America's hope is in a genuine repentance. God said, *"If my people who are called by my name will humble themselves and pray and seek my face and turn from their wicked ways, then will I hear from heaven and will forgive their sin and will heal their land" (II Chronicles 7:14).*

Another lady carried a sign which said, **"Keep abortion legal!"** Now let's think about that sign for a moment. There are many who say, "abortion is all right because it is legal." But just because something is legal does not mean it is moral or right. It is interesting what the pro-abortion people are saying about the unborn. They say that the fetus is a non-person. They say the fetus possesses no soul. They say the fetus possesses no legal rights. The fetus, in their opinion, is simply a piece of property belonging to the mother and can be disposed of at will. And, it is all legal!

Now, that sounds very familiar doesn't it? It should certainly sound familiar to every black American. Our American history books are replete with the smudge and shame of slavery upon our nation's character in the last century. What did slave owners insist about their black slaves? They called them non-persons. They possessed no legal rights. Some even went so far in their stupidity and blindness to say they had no souls. They were simply a piece of property belonging to the master and could be disposed of at will. And, it was all legal!

Does that sound familiar?

Abortion advocates are no different from slave owners in the sense that they are fighting for **their** rights and are ignoring what should be the legal rights of others. Thank God that good and moral people took a stand against slavery! It brought about a civil war, but they stood for what was right. Thank God today that good and moral people are once again making a stand against abortion. Not since the days of the abolitionists and of Abraham Lincoln has the conscience of America raised its voice so loud and long over such a disgraceful national practice.

At the abortion rally I attended, one particular vocal and vindictive protester wore a sandwich board type of sign which read, **"Keep your laws off my body!"** Now, that sign sounds right. And, it is. I agree with it! I don't want the government making laws regarding my rights or health care. There are many medical decisions that ought to be personal. Some readers of this book have had plastic surgery. That is your personal decision. Some have desired to donate organs. That is a personal decision. Some have undergone different types of cancer treatment. That is a personal decision. There is nothing wrong with the desire to be free of government intervention upon our bodies. I agree with the sign that says, "Keep your laws off my body." However, for the one who is pregnant, there is no longer one body to think about — there are two!

It is God himself at work through the creative processes in a woman's body when she is pregnant. What other explanation can one give for two tiny specks of protoplasm coming together and developing into all the intricacies of a nervous system, a circulatory system, a respiratory system, a digestive system, etc. Yes, *"You created my inmost being, you knit me together in my mother's womb." (Psalm 139:13).*

The abortionists tell us that removing the fetus is no different from removing a blood clot. In the womb God sees life, individual life. A nurse in our church tells of a turning point in her own experience. When she was working the late night shift at one of our local hospitals, a young girl was admitted with lower abdominal pain. Two days previously she had a saline abortion. She requested to be placed on a bed pan. The nurse when removing the pan, among the clots of blood and tissue, saw a fetus of about two months. In her words, "the little heart was beating and the cord was attached as the baby was still alive. I cannot tell you how terrible I felt. I began to cry. That was not just a blob of tissue, but a human life. If only women who are pro-choice could witness an abortion, things might be so different."

Another lady wrote me telling of her experience. She was engaged and living with her fiance when she became pregnant. His business was expanding and he unequivocally threatened to terminate the relationship if she did not have an abortion. By her own testimony she rationalized that since the baby was just a blob of tissue, only a mass at this stage, everything would be fine. She tells of going to the abortion clinic. In her own words, "They placed me on the table and I felt fine. They explained the vacuum machine method as if it were an every day household kind. No problem. I was ready. They began the machine and there was some tugging and some pain. I felt something lift out of my chest as though a dark cloud was hovering over me. And in that same instant I heard a child's voice within me loud and clear call, 'Mommiee.' A taste of hell followed. Right then I wanted to save the child. I cried out to stop them, but it was too late. The nurse said in a sing-song way, 'Well, it's all over.' I wretched in agony as I knew I had done a very real and horrible thing. I cried. I wanted the baby. Can I still have it? No, it is too late. In the recovery room I pulled a blanket over my head and cried and cried. I harbored hatred for the man who had me do it. If only I knew before that the 'mass or blob of tissue' was already a soul, already a being, a little girl, my little girl! Had I really known it, I would have left the man to protect my baby. Later, I discovered that the age of my baby was that which would match the pro-lifer's pin with the little feet with ten toes. Please tell men and women not to be fooled. It is not a blob of tissue, I killed my own child in ignorance!"

Until a child is born, a baby is obviously unseen by the human eye. I am convinced that if the womb were transparent, there would be far fewer abortions. If the young pregnant girls who are having abortions could see inside and see the baby being formed, they would seldom abort. One lady wrote of an abortion she had ten years earlier at the age of 18. Afraid her parents would be disgraced and disown her, she sought out a doctor to perform the procedure for three hundred dollars. She said, "As I entered the clinic doors, the nurse at the desk took my name and age. She said I was eight weeks pregnant and that it was just a mass of tissue not yet formed. As I lay on the table where the procedure was about to take place. I saw a covered jar on the table close to my feet. Terror ran through me and I asked why this jar was covered up if this thing they say is inside me is just a blob of white tissue? After seeing the jar I knew deep down inside something was not told to me. I felt betrayed and sick. It wasn't until years later when I saw the fetal growth chart, that I realized why they covered the jar. The one thing I lacked was the visual knowledge of what was really happening after conception in my body. The biggest thing I had to get over was to forgive myself for what I had done. The memory will always be there." No wonder the abortionists' clinics do not want to show fetal charts as to what this "blob of tissue" looks like a few weeks after conception.

Children were visible on the steps of the Courthouse at the pro-abortion rally that day. One little girl holding her mother by one hand held a sign in the other hand which said, **"Keep abortions safe."** Now, think about that one. Safe for whom? Certainly not for the baby! Just how is the baby extracted from the womb? There are several methods that are used, and if one carrying the picket sign reading "Keep abortions safe" ever witnessed the trauma and tragedy of the unborn, they would never carry that sign again. Abortion is certainly not safe for the baby.

One method of abortion is commonly referred to as "D & C" (dilation and curettage). The procedure is performed by the physician inserting a spoon-shaped instrument with sharp edges into the uterus. The baby is then cut into pieces and scraped from the uterine wall. And all the while the pro-choice advocates carry the popular sign which reads, "Keep abortions safe." For whom?

Another method is the suction type of abortion. A tube is inserted in the uterus and attached to a strong suction apparatus. This creates a powerful vacuum which tears the fetus from the womb in a mass of blood and tissue. The baby is torn to pieces and sucked into a jar. And all the while the pro-choice advocates carry their sign reading, "Keep abortions safe." For whom?

The third method is used for those farther along in their pregnancy. It is commonly referred to as the saline injection. A long needle is inserted into the mother's abdomen and into the baby's sac. Most of the fluids are removed and a strong salt solution is injected therein. The helpless baby is poisoned by the solution and kicks and jerks violently. He is literally being burned alive. Generally within 24 hours, labor sets in and the mother gives birth to a dead baby. However, the abortionist's greatest horror comes true, when this aborted, burned baby sometimes comes forth, still alive and then must be left to die of starvation and neglect rather quietly. Kathleen Malloy, a registered nurse in Jacksonville, Florida, describes one such live birth. "There was a baby in this bassinet, a crying perfectly formed baby, but there was a difference in this child. She had been scalded. She was the child of saline abortion. This little girl looked as if she had been in a pot of boiling water. No doctor, no nurse, no parent to comfort the burned child. She was left alone to die in pain." And all the while the pro-choice abortion advocates carry their signs, "Keep abortion safe." For whom?

Another method is the Cesarean Section which is generally performed the final three months of pregnancy. Here the physician enters the womb by surgery through the wall of the mother's abdomen and then removes the baby. The baby whose lungs are often not yet adequately developed is left alone to die of neglect. And all the while the pro-choice advocate carries her sign reading, "Keep abortions safe." For whom?

Not only is it not safe for the baby, but what about the mother? Remember, we have more than one facet of our being. We are not simply talking about the physical, but also the emotional and spiritual. The truth is, abortion is never one-hundred percent safe, whether it is legal or illegal. The constant cry of the pro-choice advocate is "Don't send us back to the back alley abortions." I have watched them at their rallys carrying coat hangers wrapped in women's bras and undergarments as protest symbols. How degrading to a woman! These women must not think very much of a lady's ability to make a wise choice so as to insinuate that she is to retreat to some back alley, take some rusty coat hanger and insert it in her body to abort her baby. If I were a woman, this would be an insult to my intelligence. How degrading!

Abortion is certainly not safe for a mother psychologically. The pro-choice organization which councils so many ladies to have abortions seldom, if ever, talks to them about the tremendous weight of guilt and emotional scarring that awaits them in the aftermath of abortion. One young lady in our church tells of such counsel from the Planned Parenthood Organization. She tells of going away to college and having the representatives from Planned Parenthood coming to her dorm to make a presentation on birth control. She says, "Their presentation convinced most of us that, yes, we need to have sex and it was expected of 'mature' 18-year-old women. And yet, our background had us believing otherwise. The first semester my roommate got pregnant and the first thing we did was call the 'nice friendly young women' at Planned Parenthood. They calmly explained that there was no problem. They could take care of it. My roommate did not have enough money so I, thinking I was helping her, loaned her the extra one hundred dollars she needed. After her abortion, she was deeply affected and dropped out of school. During the course of the following year, my five best friends each had an abortion. Why? Was it because they were too poor, too young? No! They were 19 and afraid to tell their parents. But the main reason was they had been told, and really believed, that it was a little operation that **did not hurt anyone!** Had I become pregnant, I too would have probably believed the 'great lie' told by those at the abortion clinics. I grieve for each of these babies and feel ashamed of my part in their deaths. The abortionists of Planned Parenthood were kind, gentle, attractive young women. I believe they were being deceived themselves in this spiritual battle."

The sign reads, **"Keep Abortion Safe."** For whom? As a pastor I have dealt with the aftermath of abortion in many lives. One lady in our congregation had an abortion at the age of 20 as a result of premarital sex with her boyfriend who is now her husband. She says, "It has been over ten years and I still feel the pain and loss of it as if it were yesterday. It was a decision we reached together, one based mostly on preventing embarrassment and shame to our parents and the local church. We simply wanted to get rid of an untimely problem. The college clinic and local planning council set up an appointment to have a suction vacuum procedure done. Not once did anyone tell me just how my ten-week-old baby looked, or how it was growing. If only there had been someone with the truth. 'If only' are words I have said a hundred times! When I had my first baby, there was both joy and sadness in my heart. Joy because of the tremendous miracle God had given, and sadness because I fully realized that there really was a baby which I destroyed earlier. It was especially difficult when I began to think how old my child would be and wondered what he or she might have looked like and been like. Time has a way of healing so many emotional scars, but abortion is a scar that is carved on my heart. And I don't think time will ever change it completely!"

Another lady wrote to say, "I became pregnant when I was 16. I did not want to have an abortion, but I felt I had no choice. The abortion clinic told me to lie about my age so I wouldn't have to get permission from my parents. As I was in the abortion clinic, I could hear my baby being sucked away during the procedure. I immediately felt the loss and cried. Terrible nightmares started – every night! I became obsessed with wondering what my baby would have looked like and whether it was a boy or girl. I had that abortion in 1975, and until I accepted the Lord Jesus as my Savior, my life and self worth continued to decline. After I came to know Christ, I had a hard time forgiving myself. For me, I realized abortion does kill, not only my baby, but in a very real sense a part of me too! I honestly could say, I don't think I would be alive today if not for the Lord's forgiveness and healing." As I read that letter I thought about the lady who carried her sign, "Keep abortions safe." For whom?

Long ago Moses brought his people to decision with these words: *"This day I called heaven and earth as witnesses against you. That I have set before you life and death, blessings and curses, now* **choose life** *that you and your children may live"* (Deuteronomy 30:19).

III. Can Abortion Be Forgiven?

To the many who have had abortions, please remember: abortion is not the unpardonable sin! Many live with the haunting longing that if only that moment could be lived again. The grief you feel is normal. You should thank God that your conscience is not seared. The good news is that Jesus Christ died on the cross to make a way for you to be free of your failure and saved from your sin. How beautiful are the words of Paul in Romans 8:1, *"Therefore, there is now no condemnation for those who are in Christ Jesus."* God is not mad or angry at you. He hates sin, but He loves you! He stands with open arms to forgive you. *"If we confess our sins, he is faithful and just to forgive us and cleanse us from all unrighteousness"* (I John 1:9). If you have aborted a child, God will forgive you right now if you ask Him. Through His forgiveness you can know the true freedom which comes in placing Him as Lord of your life. You can purpose to follow Him, accept His cleansing, and then not call unclean what He has cleansed. You can forgive yourself!

> *In a far away place and a different time*
> *I killed my first child, a most heinous crime.*
> *The state didn't come, and I didn't stand trial,*
> *Judge Blackmun was calm when he said with a smile,*
> *"Killing is legal," say we the High Court*
> *"But don't call it murder, Just call it 'abort.' "*
> *The judge in my heart would not let the case rest.*
> *I had no defense when once put to the test.*
> *Found guilty I was by my heart's Supreme Court.*
> *"You murdered your baby!" they screamed in retort.*
> *With tears on my cheeks it was too late, I knew*

to bring back the life of the child I once slew.
The gavel slammed down, and it rang in my head,
"You are guilty as charged, and deserve to be dead.
We now give you torment to pay for your sin," was the
sentence passed down from my own court within,
"You will never escape. You're branded. Don't hide.
Your just due is death. You should try suicide."
I was beaten in prison by daily attack
I was paying a debt, so I never fought back
No hope of escaping, and this I knew well.
I cried out to God from my own self-made hell.
That day I met Jesus; He smiled in my face.
He said, "I forgive you. Come walk in my grace."
"Lord, I believe you forgive me and yet.
Blameless you are. Can you pay for my debt?"
And Lord, please don't touch me for I am unclean.
I'm filthy with murder, a most wretched being."
I poured out my story. He showed no surprise.
I gazed up with awe at the love in His eyes.
He said, "I paid for your crime, yes, was nailed to a tree.
There's no condemnation if you'll trust in Me.
I took on your blame and your curse on My soul
So you may be free without judgment and whole."
I sputtered, "Dear Lord, where's the justice in this?
I killed my first son, and you offer me bliss?"
Tears blurred my vision, yet there in His face
Were eyes of compassion, blue oceans of grace.
I thought to myself, "Now the past has been buried?
I'm free of the guilt that for years I have carried?"
He said to accept. It's a gift that is free.
This is atonement, not justice for me!
My judge was dismissed, my accusers, and jury.
The truth of His love made them leave in a fury.
He smiled, "Walk with Me and come learn My way."
And grasping His hand I began a new day.

Surviving an Abortion

Jim Henry

TEXT: Luke 7:36-50

SUPPLEMENTAL VERSES: Ezekiel 36:25-27, 33-36, 1 John 1:8-9, Psalms 32:5; 127:3, 2 Samuel 12:15-23, Leviticus 5:17

SUMMARY OF MESSAGE: Jim Henry's "Surviving an Abortion" offers compassionate help to women who have had abortions and to others involved in the decision to abort. Henry uses testimonies from women who have experienced abortion to expose the deceit, negative effects and long road to recovery of abortion.

Henry outlines a plan for restoration, including such steps as admitting guilt and responsibility, forgiving others and receiving forgiveness from Jesus Christ.

PREACHING TRACKS:

➤TRACK ONE: Preach the entire sermon.

➤TRACK TWO: Preach the points on the outline that best apply to your congregation. The testimonies in I, IV.B.1, and IV.B.2 speak a strong, personal message about the wrongness of abortion. II.A, V and VII offer forgiveness and hope in a loving, accepting way.

➤TRACK THREE: Preach a combination of points in this and other sermons in this book.

SURVIVING AN ABORTION

Luke 7:36-50, I John 1:8-9

Jim Henry

(This story is told by Jenny Clark, guest speaker in the service)

Yesterday my family and I went to the beach, and I was watching my three little children playing in the water. It was the first time they had ever been to the ocean, and they were having a wonderful time.

But in my heart I remembered another child that was missing. One who would never be able to experience the wonders of God's creation. Every woman who's had an abortion has her own story, her own set of circumstances and her own reasons for having an abortion.

I was raised in a Christian home. I had Christian parents with godly values, but at 18 I found myself pregnant and unmarried. At that time my life was a series of failures. I was dishonoring and disobedient to my parents. I had violated all of the principles that I was taught from my childhood. I had compromised my own integrity and degraded my God-given femininity. So although I felt in my heart that abortion was really wrong and I knew that my little baby I was carrying was unique and unrepeatable, for me abortion was the next logical step in a pattern of rebellion and self-destruction.

The decision to abort was extremely painful. But at the time I really saw no alternative. So I went ahead with my plans to end the pregnancy.

I remember feeling my little child being ripped out of my body. I remember when the baby died. And I remember the grief that wrenched my heart.

It says in Hosea 8:7 that when you sow to the wind, you reap the whirlwind. I never wanted to kill my baby, but I had sowed immorality and I reaped abortion.

When I became a Christian a year later, my heart was still broken, and I was still carrying a heavy load of guilt. But I got married and by God's power I became a faithful wife. God filled my longing for another child, a beautiful little baby girl. But the hurt and the guilt in my heart just wouldn't go away. None of the things God gave me seemed to take care of that empty place in my heart.

I found myself mourning on the anniversary of the death of my first child. It was difficult to beg for forgiveness over and over. I didn't understand the way I was treating the abortion was unhealthy. I thought I was going to pay the penalty for the rest of my life in my grief.

Fortunately for me there was a counselor who knew what I was going through wasn't what God intended. She helped me understand that Jesus even pays for abortion. He paid for it on the cross. Accepting God's forgiveness was an act of my will. I asked and then accepted God's forgiveness. Forgiving myself was an act of my will, and God gave me the power. My healing began.

That was four years ago, and since then God has been seeing me through. I've forgiven my parents, the child's father, and the abortion clinic personnel (that was a hard one to forgive), and the process has continued.

My most recent difficulty has been a feeling of unworthiness with the children that I have now. God has forgiven me and I am worthy to command their respect and to discipline them because God has restored me.

I want everybody to know that what God has given me back is an undeserved gift. The Lord impressed that upon me after the birth of my fourth child.

I want to read in Ezekiel 36. God was prophesying to Israel His intention to restore them to their former glory during the Babylonian captivity. *"Then I will sprinkle clean water on you and you will be clean. I will cleanse you from all your filthiness and from all your idols. Moreover I will give you a new heart and put a new spirit within you, and I will remove the heart of stone from your flesh and give you a heart of flesh. And I will put my spirit within you and cause you to walk in my statutes, and you will be careful to observe my ordinances. Thus says the Lord God, on the day that I cleanse you from all your iniquities, I will cause the cities to be inhabited and the waste places will be rebuilt."*

I liken the desolation that Ezekiel describes to abortion. The husband that God has given me loves me and leads me, and my children are the inhabitants of those cities. It continues, *"And the desolate land will be cultivated instead of being a desolation in the sight of everyone who passed by, and they will say, 'This desolate land has become like the garden of Eden and the waste, desolate, and ruined cities are fortified and inhabited.' Then the nations that are left round about you will know that I the Lord have rebuilt the ruined places and planted that which was desolate, I the Lord have spoken and will do it."*

(End of Jenny Clark's Testimony)

Thank you so much, Jenny, for your courageous testimony. What a beautiful lady she is, and what a wonderful witness for God's mercy and grace.

Please open your Bibles with me to Luke 7:36: *"Now one of the Pharisees invited Jesus to have dinner with him, so He went on to the Pharisee's house and reclined at the table. When a woman who had lived a sinful life in that town learned that Jesus was eating at the Pharisee's house, she brought an alabaster jar of perfume.*

And as she stood behind Him at His feet weeping, she began to wet His feet with her tears. Then she wiped them with her hair, kissed them and poured perfume on them. When the Pharisee who had invited Him saw this, he said to himself, 'If this man were a prophet He would know who is touching Him and what kind of woman she is. She is a sinner.' Jesus answered him, 'Simon, I have something to tell you.' 'Tell me, teacher,' he said. 'Two men owed money to a certain money lender. One owed him five hundred denari, the other fifty. Neither of them had the money to pay him back, so he canceled the debts of both. Now which of them will love him more?' Simon replied, 'I suppose the one who had the bigger debt canceled.' 'You have judged correctly,' Jesus said. Then he turned toward the woman and said to Simon, 'Do you see this woman? I came into your house, you did not give me water for my feet. But she wet my feet with her tears and wiped them with her hair. You did not give me a kiss, but this woman from the time I entered has not stopped kissing my feet. You did not put oil on my head. But she has poured perfume on my feet. Therefore I tell you her many sins have been forgiven for she loved much, but he who has been forgiven little, loves little.' Then Jesus said to her, 'Your sins are forgiven.' The other guests began to say among themselves, 'Who is this who even forgives sins?' Jesus said to the woman, 'Your faith has saved you. Go in peace.' "

Now turn to I John 1:8: *"If we claim to be without sin we deceive ourselves and the truth is not in us. If we confess our sins He is faithful and just and will forgive us our sins and purify us from all unrighteousness."*

In the *Tempe Daily News,* Saturday, October 20, 1984, this letter to the editor appeared. "Dear Editor, I've read letters to the editor from persons who feel abortion is morally wrong and others who feel abortion is a matter of choice. I would like to present a side of the abortion debate that few people consider. That is a position of one who has had an abortion. This is what the right to choose has meant to me.

"In 1980, I aborted my first child. I was told at Planned Parenthood that this little blob of tissue would be as easily removed as a wart. Terminating a pregnancy, I was told, was no more significant than removing a tiny blood clot in my uterus. Sounds harmless, I reasoned. Exercising the right to choose I opted for abortion. At that time no other option such as adoption or single parenting was explained. At the abortion clinic I was not administered pain killers. When the suction aspirator was turned on, I felt like my entire insides were being torn from me. Three quarters of the way through the procedure I looked down and to my right I saw the bits and pieces of my baby floating in a pool of blood. After I screamed, 'I killed my baby!' the counselor in attendance told me to shut up. Suddenly I felt very sad and alone.

"But the worst was yet to come. I was not forewarned about the deep psychological problems I would encounter in the months and years to follow. I was never told that I would have nightmares about babies crying in the night. Neither was it explained previous to the abortion that I would experience severe depressions in which I would contemplate suicide. I didn't mourn the loss of my appendix, so why would I grieve the passing of an enigmatic uterine blob? The answer was that it wasn't a mere blob of tissue. It was a living baby. I realized this the moment I saw his dismembered limbs. I realized too late.

"By now the reader may be asking him or herself 'isn't this an extreme example of an abortion experience?' Actually, no. Mine was a routine suction abortion. Millions have been done. Why do women who have had an abortion have a higher incident of suicide than other women? And why do the chances of losing a subsequent wanted baby double or even quadruple following a safe, legal abortion? Since when has death become good for us?"

This letter is signed by Karen Sullivan, Arizona state president of "Women Exploited By Abortion," Taylor, Arizona.

This last year 1.5 million children were legally killed. That means that more than 4,000 such killings took place each day in America alone. That does not count tremendous numbers around the world.

Somewhere along the way someone has forgotten to help those who have had an abortion, including men who may have encouraged their wives or girlfriends to have an abortion, how to deal with the aftermath of an abortion. Many of us have preached on abortion, as well we should. Thank God the sensitivity of the American people is being raised to a higher level. With courageous legislators and judges, we hope to get this issue turned around. Once again, human life is considered sacred. Yet for those millions who have had abortions, there have to be some good words and some help. There's got to be some honesty and integrity. It has to be dealt with and faced. And so, I would like to deal with surviving an abortion.

I. Who Is At Risk?

I want to ask three questions and then seek to answer them. First, who is at risk when an abortion is performed? Actually, anyone connected with an abortion is at risk has to come to grips with it. A husband, a boyfriend, a girlfriend, a wife, a daughter, a grandchild, anyone who is connected with the abortion has to have some help in surviving it.

A Canadian survey recently found, and this is fairly new information, that those who have had an abortion have deep psychological problems afterwards, and they need help. A British study showed the same thing. A psychiatrist in Vancouver said, "Until recently we have overlooked the fact of the guilt and the remorse and the grief that's tied in with having an abortion." Only in recent years have we begun to deal with those who have had an abortion, who are seeking to be reached and helped.

So when we say, "Who is at risk?" no one who's had an abortion can say, "It won't affect me." Everyone who has had anything to do with an abortion is at risk.

II. What Are the Effects?

Second, what are the effects of an abortion? First of all, let's realize that there are physical effects. A pamphlet from "Women Exploited by Abortion," lists just a few: sterility, miscarriages, stillbirths, menstrual disturbances, bleeding, infection, shock, coma, perforated uterus, peritonitis, passing blood clots, fever, cold sweats, intense pain, loss of other organs, crying, insomnia, loss of appetite, weight loss, exhaustion, constant swallowing, nervousness, decreased work capacity, vomiting, gastrointestinal disturbances, and frigidity. This is just a partial list of some of the difficult physical effects of an abortion.

There are other effects, maybe more powerful and as deeply painful, and those are the psychological effects of an abortion. Depression becomes a real problem with one who's had an abortion. Many people in trying to help a person have an abortion, tell them there's nothing wrong with it, and if they will deal with it properly, then they shouldn't feel bad about it. Consequently, the feelings become internalized. The woman begins to feel all the pressure of the blame and guilt. Then depression sets in. There's no one to lash out at, no one to talk to, no one who will say, "Hey, there is a problem here. You *do* have a sense of guilt. It's normal to feel guilty and you do need some help."

Another psychological effect is denial. There may be a denial that it really happened. In one sense, this can be worse than depression. Denial of feelings show up sooner or later.

Another effect is disappointment. Sometimes a baby is aborted so that a career or family plans, or college will not be prevented. The abortion takes place, and then disappointment comes because those things that the baby was aborted for are empty. Deep disappointment comes because a baby has been sacrificed for a career, for money, for parental relief, or to keep a boyfriend from embarrassment. What was substituted does not satisfy.

Another thing that happens psychologically is a sense of "drivenness." If a baby has been aborted, I must make up for it. I must succeed to cover for this loss of life. So there comes a tremendous push to succeed in a career, or whatever, only to find emptiness in success.

Another effect psychologically is grief, deep long-lasting grief.

In a 1976 *New York Times* article, in which the person wrote under a pseudonym: "We were sitting in a bar on Lexington Avenue when I told my husband I was pregnant. It is not a memory I like to dwell on. Instead of champagne and hope which has heralded the impending births of our first, second, and third child, the news of this one was greeted with shocked silence and scotch. We tried to rationalize that night as a starting time for the careers that we wanted to have. My husband talked about his plans for a career change. To stem the staleness of fourteen years with the same investment banking firm, he wanted a change. A new baby would preclude that option. The timing wasn't right for me either. Having juggled pregnancies and childcare with freelance jobs, (jobs I could fit in between feedings), I had just taken on a fulltime job. A new baby would put me right back in the nursery just when our youngest child was finally school age. It was time for *us*, we tried to rationalize. There just wasn't room in our lives now for another baby. We both agreed and agreed and agreed.

"How very considerate they are at the women's services, known formerly as the center for reproductive and sexual health. Yes, indeed I could have an abortion that very Saturday morning, be out in time to drive to the country that afternoon. I must bring my first morning urine specimen, a sanitary belt and napkins, money order or $125.00 in cash, and a friend. My friend turned out to be my husband, standing awkwardly and ill at ease as men always do in places that are exclusively for women, as I checked in at 9:00 a.m. Other men hovered around just as anxiously, knowing that they had to be there, and wishing they weren't. No one spoke to each other. When I would be cycled four hours later, the same men would be slumped in their same seats looking downcast in their embarrassment."

She goes on then to relate the abortion and I won't deal with that, but let me close with this. She says, "What good sports we women are and how obedient. Physically the pain passed even before the hum of the machine signaled that the vacuuming of my uterus was complete. My baby was sucked up like ashes after a cocktail party. Ten minutes, start to finish, and I was back on the arm of the nurse. There were twelve beds in the recovery room, each one had a gaily-flowered draw sheet in soft green or blue and a thermal blanket. It was all very feminine. It was very quiet in that room. The only voice was that of the nurse locating the new women who had just come so she could monitor their blood pressure and checking out the recovered women who were free to leave. Finally, it was time for me to leave. I checked out. My husband was slumped in the waiting room clutching a single yellow rose which was wrapped in a wet paper towel and stuffed into a baggie. We didn't talk the whole way home, but just held hands very tightly.

"At home there were more yellow roses and a tray in bed for me and the children's curiosity to divert. It had certainly been a successful operation. I didn't bleed at all for two days just as they predicted. Then only moderately for a few more days. After a while my body felt mine again instead of the eggshell it becomes when it's protecting someone else. My husband and I are back to planning our summer vacation and his career switch. And it certainly does make more sense not to be having a baby right now. We say that to each other all the time. But I have this ghost now, a very little ghost that only appears when I'm seeing something beautiful, like the full moon on the ocean last weekend. The baby waves at me and I wave at the baby. 'Of course we have room,' I cry to the ghost. 'Of course, we do.' "

Bill Stout was for many years a nationally known CBS network correspondent. He does commentary work for station KNXT in Los Angeles. He wrote an article in the Los Angeles Times that appeared in February of 1976. In the article he talks about 1952 when he took his wife to have an abortion. Over 20 years later, close to the time that he wrote this article, he got stopped in a traffic jam. As he was stopped he looked up to a second floor window and saw the initials of the name of the doctor that aborted their baby. He said, "Suddenly, like a kick in the groin, everything that happened that day came back to me as clear as a bell. All the way home every detail of that event 23 years before was clear and fresh to my mind. I kept saying, 'he or she would have been 23 today.' "

When Jenny said that she kept mourning the birthdate, that's part of the psychological effect. The due date is a part of the process of dealing with the guilt of an aborted child. Preoccupation and other effects, suicidal impulses, sense of loss, unfulfillment, regret and remorse, withdrawal, lower self esteem, preoccupation with death, hostility, self-destructive behavior, anger, rage, despair, helplessness, loss of interest in sex, inability to forgive yourself, feelings of dehumanization, nightmares, seizures, frustration, feelings of being exploited, child abuse, intense interest in babies, thwarted maternal instinct; all of these are part of the psychological price that an abortive mother faces, and often the father has to deal with some of these same feelings.

III. How Does One Deal With An Abortion?

Who is at risk? Anyone close to an abortion. What are the effects? They are physical and psychological and spiritual. How do you handle it?

First of all, you must face the reality that abortion is real, it's wrong, and your grief is normal and natural. In fact, it is abnormal *not* to have grief. Family, friends, clergy, or others may seek to help a person over it by saying, "Don't feel bad." But the reality of the matter is real. Face the reality of the grief.

Second, face your sin and your guilt. The Christian Scriptures teach that a person owes three things to God in the face of sin. Number one, responsibility. We are responsible even if at the time we didn't know. We are responsible even if family and clergy say it's okay. We are responsible even if the doctor says, "You may be running a risk to have this child. Go ahead." For example, suppose you go through a speed limit in a strange town and the policeman stops you. You say, "I was only doing 45." And he says, "Yes, but the speed limit here is 25." And you say, "But I'm new to this area." And he says, "I'm sorry but that's the law, and ignorance of the law does not excuse you. You're guilty and responsible." *"If a person sins and does what is forbidden in any of the Lord's commands, even though he does not know it, he is guilty and will be held responsible." (Leviticus 5:17)*

The Bible says children, the fruit of the womb, are a heritage of the Lord. That innocent blood that is spilt must be atoned for. Therefore, the person who is seeking to survive an abortion must recognize and face the reality, deal with it as sin, recognize responsibility, recognize the blame, and submit to punishment and the consequences of that sin.

The third thing you must do is face the lack of support. Maybe you didn't have much support. Maybe the baby's father, encouraged you to get the abortion to help his career or not to get in the way of his future. Maybe your family was facing the feelings of embarrassment, and they were trying to help you, and downplayed the seriousness of abortion. Maybe the counselors at the abortion center said, "It's all right. This is normal. Go ahead." Maybe those at the clinic, as kind as they sought to be to you, were not honest with you and did not support you in what you were facing. Maybe you equated legal rights according to the Supreme Court for what is right before God. Maybe you were too young and didn't know the consequences. Maybe you were mature and knew the consequences, but you faced a lack of support and tried to deal with your abortion by yourself. Face that lack of support and recognize that it did contribute to some of your difficulty.

There's a fourth thing and that is forgiveness. You've got to forgive. You've got to forgive the father of the child. You've got to forgive the doctor. You've got to forgive the nurses. You've got to forgive the clergy who may have given you help but in the wrong way. You've got to forgive those at the clinic. You've got to forgive anyone that you feel hard toward about the abortion. You have got to forgive them, or bitterness will continue to be a cancer in your soul. Forgive every one who had anything to do with the abortion.

Fifth, turn to Jesus for healing and acceptance. Jesus will heal your depression. Jenny shared that in her testimony. She went back to Jesus and Jesus brought inner healing.

I John 1:9 says, "If we confess... He is faithful and just to forgive us of *all* our sins." God can use your past to build humility and character and love for Him.

Have you thought about that woman who washed the feet of Jesus with her hair and the perfume? Jesus said to her, "Your sins are forgiven." I imagine until the day she died she loved Jesus in a very special way because He forgave her.

My friend, Jesus loves you, and if you confess your sins, Jesus forgives the sin of abortion just as He forgives any other sin. He'll build out of the past, gratitude for Him, humility in your life, and a stronger character. Some of you have never applied God's plan of salvation. You've never asked Him to forgive you, never asked Jesus Christ into your life. That's very simple to do. It's a matter of repentance. Repentance is going in another direction.

The Bible says we must confess our sins and then place our faith in Jesus Christ. Ask Him to come into your heart and He will forgive all the sin of your life, including abortion. Maybe it was your immorality that led to the baby and the abortion. He will forgive that, too. There is no sin that Jesus Christ will not forgive, if you'll repent and confess and ask Him to come into your life and into your heart.

In Psalm 32:5, the psalmist says, "Then I acknowledge (that's the confession) my sin to you (that's God) and did not cover up my iniquity (I didn't hide it, I faced up to the reality that I was guilty)." And look what happens, "I will confess (got it out, told somebody) my transgressions to the Lord." And I told Him (and look what happens), "and you forgave the guilt of my sin." Did you get that? I simply say, "Lord, I had an abortion." And God says, "Daughter I forgive your sin." I say, "But God it was terrible." And He says, "Daughter I forgive your sin." I say, "Father, I told her to get that abortion, I'm sorry, can you forgive me?" And He says, "Son, I forgive your sin." He forgave the guilt. But when did it happen? When I acknowledged it, faced it and confessed it to the Lord. Maybe some of you just need to get on your knees in a quiet place, acknowledge your sin and your guilt before Holy God who loves you, ask His forgiveness and He'll forgive.

IV. What Happens To The Aborted Baby?

Someone may ask, "What about the baby that was aborted?" There's been discussion for hundreds of years about when life begins. So let me read II Samuel 12. There was a little baby born, and that little baby belonged to King David. Beginning with verse 15, *"The Lord struck the child that Uriah's wife had born to David and he became ill. David pleaded with God for the child. He fasted and went into his house and spent the nights lying on the ground. The elders of his household stood beside him to get him up from the ground, but he refused and he would not eat any food with them. On the seventh day the child died. David's servants were afraid to tell him that the child was dead for they thought, 'while the child was still living we spoke to David but he would not listen to us. How can we tell him the child is dead? He may do something desperate.' David noticed that his servants were whispering among themselves and he realized the child was dead. 'Is the child dead?' he asked. 'Yes,' they replied, 'he is dead.' Then David got up from the ground. After he had washed, put on lotions and changed his clothes he went into the house of the Lord and worshipped. Then he went to his own house and at his request they served him food and he ate. His servants asked him, 'why are you acting this way? While the child was alive you fasted and wept, but now the child is dead and you get up and eat.' He answered, 'While the child was still alive I fasted and wept. I thought, who knows, the Lord may be gracious to me and let the child live. But now that he's dead why should I fast? Can I bring him back again?'* (Here's the answer.) *'I will go to him but he will not return to me.'* " David said, "I'm going to see that boy again someday, that tiny little baby. I'll go to him."

You see in the hospital today at one end of the hall they may be aborting a four or five month old baby. Down at the other end of the hall they may be saving the life of a premie who is four, five, or six months old. They're now able to push back further and further the ability to make life viable down to infants just a little over one pound. Some of you ask me about this little lapel pin I'm wearing. There are ten toes on two little feet, representing a ten week old baby in its mother's womb—a fetus. This is the size, perfectly formed, of a little baby's feet ten weeks after conception.

We believe, as Christians, that the little fetus at whatever age, aborted or dying of natural causes, goes to be with God in heaven. So if you aborted a child, that baby is in heaven, as best we understand from the Scripture and from what we know of the grace of God. One mother wrote it this way and I think it's beautiful (it may be the prayer of some of you today).

*"If I knew then what I know now, you never would have died.
I'd have held you close and nurtured you and kept you by my side.
I'd have sung you songs and treasured you more than silver, more than gold,
But this song is all I'll give to the babe I'll never hold.
I've never written poetry that hasn't been a praise
to the Lord who wept with me and held me through those days.
Jesus, now I'm asking, I know you hear my plea,
Won't you take this child in your hands and hold my babe for me?*

And we believe Jesus does that. Mothers can survive abortion. I want you to know that the church of the living God holds out arms of love and acceptance and forgiveness in the name of Jesus Christ and offers to you the good news. Somebody will listen and somebody will care and God will forgive and Jesus will make you new.

It is my prayer that our church will adopt a child agency. I pray we will provide the finances to give an option to the increasing numbers of mothers who want to keep and not abort their babies. Get ready, for in the future we will have such a place. We will open our homes. Many of you will open your home to expectant mothers who have no place to go. You will take in that mother until she has her child and places the baby for adoption or raises that baby for Jesus.

You can survive an abortion through Jesus Christ. Deal with your guilt, receive forgiveness and help in the struggle for life. That's the good news that we offer. Praise God!

RAPED AND PREGNANT!

A TESTIMONY OF TRAGEDY AND TRIUMPH

Dr. Ron Herrod

Honey, Twila has just told me that she is pregnant... that she was raped here in our home and is pregnant."

Those were the shocking, stunning words that my wife, Emily, struggled to share with me through her sobs about our beautiful youngest daughter who had just turned sixteen.

As I sat in my home study late that Wednesday evening, I could barely speak and my mind raced with a thousand thoughts.

"Could it really be true that our daughter, who I thought to be pure and a virgin, could be with child at such an early age?

"If she was, indeed, pregnant, was she telling a story of rape to cover up her own impurity and immorality?

"Was this some cruel joke of the Devil knowing that we already had more pressure than we could hardly deal with in our lives?

"If our daughter had truly been raped, who was the rapist and how soon can I get my hands on him?

"What will this do to our family and our ministry in this small town?

"When did it happen and why didn't I know about it long before now?

"If she was truly raped, why has she hid it from us for so long?

"If this is true, she must be devastated. What can we do to help her?"

And then came that fleeting momentary horrible thought: "Is this the exception when *abortion* is the *quick fix* and the easy answer to a tragic unwanted pregnancy?"

As the three of us struggled through the night these thoughts and hundreds of others flooded our minds and hearts. Who could we turn to and what was the answer.

Thus began months of experiencing every negative emotion that one family can experience. They were all there. Anger, guilt, bitterness, failure, defeat, fear, desire for revenge and so many others.

I wanted to blame myself. Had I come to this place out of God's Will? Was there some failure in my life that left my daughter morally unprotected? Was this God's chastisement and correction upon us? Why hadn't I provided an alarm system that would have prevented the assailant from entering our home? Why were we away when she needed us?

As the story unfolded, the actual events began to fall into

place. The rapist entered our home one evening while we had been at the church for a function. Twila had returned downstairs from studying and was violently attacked. As in most cases of rape, she did not want to tell anyone, especially those closest to her. She felt guilt, shame, and embarrassment. She felt that if she kept it to herself, it would go away.

She also considered abortion when she discovered that she was pregnant. However, her pilgrimage led her to share with her Sunday School teacher and our son-in-law who was our Minister to Students. Then she reluctantly shared with her parents and her greatest concern was "what will this do to my dad's ministry?" What an enormous burden for a 15-year-old child to face.

Our society has made it very easy to view abortion as the quick fix to an unwanted pregnancy. Especially are we conveying that in the case of rape or incest it is the appropriate thing to do. Because this is true, it was natural that the momentary, fleeting thought of abortion would pass through our minds.

However, upon reflection on the truth of God's Word and our settled convictions, there was really no choice – this was a child. Whatever else we felt or chose to do, this was a living human being and deserved the opportunity to be born and to live.

Psalm 139:13-16; For You have formed my inward parts; You have covered me in my mother's womb. [14] *I will praise You, for I am fearfully and wonderfully made; marvelous are Your works, and that my soul knows very well.* [15] *My frame was not hidden from You, when I was made in secret, and skillfully wrought in the lowest parts of the earth.* [16] *Your eyes saw my substance, being yet unformed. And in Your book they all were written, the days fashioned for me, when as yet there were none of them.*

Until now, since 1973 when the Supreme Court rendered its deathknell decision, we have had almost 30,000,000 babies legally killed in America. One in every three pregnancies in the U.S. now ends in abortion. A baby is aborted every 20 seconds in the U.S.; three per minute, 180 per hour, 4,320 per day – over one and a half million per year. The most dangerous place in America is in the womb of your mother.

Now the possibility of abortion was more than just a statistic to me and our family. Now we were faced with the reality of the decision. I had been told so many times that a woman should have the right to abort in cases of rape and incest.

I want to say that rape is an unspeakable terrible crime against women. I am angry at the rapist but I am also angry at the pro-abortionists using rape victims as their big gun for keeping abortion legal in this country.

Only a small percentage of rapes result in pregnancy. Our family is one of the victims of that small percentage. Even if the mother is the victim of rape, the child in her womb is created in the image of God and deserves to live and become all that God intended that child to be.

Perhaps the next time you are in a crowd you will want to look around and observe all the people. Can you point out the ones who are products of rape?

Following that tragic night when we learned of our situation, I felt as if our lives were in shambles. It was already the most stressful and pressure-filled time in 30 years of ministry. Now it seemed our world had fallen apart. I could not sleep and I would spend my fretful hours walking and weeping and praying. I continued to be swept by every emotion one can feel.

Over those next several weeks, God showed us that we had to do three things in order to put the pieces back together.

First, we had to give him *praise* and *thanksgiving.* God's Word exhorts us to give thanks in all things. It was a difficult day as Emily and I knelt in the Prayer Room of our church to praise God for our situation. That is when we began to learn of the power of praise. This was the test. God had promised that *all things* work together for good to them that love Him and are called according to His purpose. *Can even this work together for good?* We praised Him in faith believing that it would.

Secondly, we knew we had to *forgive.* Another difficult day was when I took the trip to the jail. As I sat across the table from the alleged rapist, I sought the strength of the Holy Spirit to give forgiveness in my heart. I can honestly say that when I sought it, God gave me the power to forgive and even gave me a tenderness and love for this young an who was a victim himself.

We discovered it even more difficult to have forgiveness toward some in the Christian community:

The policeman who handled Twila with such insensitivity, unkindness, and suspicion.

Those church members who whispered that we lied about the rape to cover up immorality.

Those prominent lay-leaders who spread slander about us throughout the country.

Those "pastor friends" who had "needed us" in the past but now were nowhere to be found.

Those people we needed to come and hug us and say, "We understand," but they were few and far between.

But again, God in His graciousness, gave us a true spirit of forgiveness and then gave us others who did understand and met that great need in our lives.

Thirdly, God convicted my heart that we had to go on in ministry and not turn back. My commission was to be the pastor of the First Baptist Church of Fort Smith, Arkansas, and I must give myself to that task with enthusiasm and fervor. It was difficult but we gave ourselves to that task with a fresh new enthusiasm.

The six-month period of time between learning of our

daughter's rape and pregnancy and the birth of her child were the most difficult days of our lives. Emily had major surgery and serious complications from that. Our house flooded three times. There were, of course, the financial challenges of this situation. I sensed an intense rejection from my peers and that was one of the greatest difficulties.

Then there were those wonderful people who offered such gracious support.

Twila's Sunday School teacher, Carolyn Plummer, who was a great strength to her.

Dr. Larry Hyde, an OB/GYN doctor who was one of God's great gifts to us at this time.

The Bradfords, the Geans, the Morrises and other sweet Christian friends who walked with us through our valley and experienced our darkness as true friends.

Miles and Jeanne Seaborn, who immediately offered their home in Fort Worth and the ministries of their church that were committed to this kind of need.

Family became more precious and real than ever before. The bonding that took place with an already close family was wonderful.

So the decision was made that *abortion* was *not* an *option* because this was a *child* and *not* a *choice*. Now there were other decisions to make.

Where would Twila stay during this time? How would she continue her education?

Would she keep the child or would the child be adopted?

If adoption were our option, would it be an open adoption or closed?

If this were to be adoption, what agency would we use and how would we go about it?

As God gave us leadership, the decisions were made. Twila would stay in Fort Worth, Texas, with the Seaborns and attend school there. She would receive home schooling when she was too far along to continue to go to class. She would receive ministry from the Birchman Baptist Church and their crisis pregnancy ministry. We would use an adoption agency there and it would be a closed adoption.

But still the questions lingered. What good could come from such a tragic situation? It was a pilgrimage of prayer, of pain, of pressure, but also of praise! We believed God's promises and discovered that all the truths we had preached were, indeed, real.

God continued to confirm, in my prayer time, that He had a special purpose for this child. I sensed that these sorrows would not be wasted. I knew the decision for the child to be born was the right one. I even had an impression that this child would be a great man of God and I still feel that very strongly.

It is impossible to describe the emotions of the birthing day. We all gathered at the hospital where Twila was to give birth to our first grandchild. Because of her age and other complications, it soon became apparent it would be impossible for her to have natural childbirth. A C-Section was required and our grandson was born late that afternoon. We experienced mixed emotions of joyfully holding our first grandchild and yet knowing that we would probably never see him again. Our emotions were impossible to describe. We were both happy and hurting at the same time.

The next day we told the little baby goodby, thinking that we would never see him again. However, we knew that some couple who had been praying for a child would soon hold him and love him. We thought that we would never know them. We knew, however, they would be wonderful Christian folks because of our agreement with the adoption agency. We could only obey and trust our wonderful Lord.

But our story had another turn of events far beyond our expectation. It is recorded in the book by Lila Shelbourne, *When Evil Strikes.*

That next year the emotions continued. We would correspond in a limited way with the adoptive parents through the agency. We sensed that he was in a wonderful home and would receive the kind of spiritual training that we desired for him.

Then came the unexpected. On my final Sunday as pastor of the First Baptist Church of Fort Smith, Arkansas, in January, 1991, we held our grandson in our arms and rejoiced together with his adoptive parents. They had felt that God had led them to locate us and with our permission, would make this an open adoption. The feelings of joy, confirmation and delight brought ecstatic celebration to our hearts.

Now what good has God brought from this rape? What triumph has come from this tragedy?

A fetus that could have been aborted is now a beautiful, healthy, energetic and enthusiastic child.

A godly couple who had prayed for years for a child now are investing their lives in this special little boy.

Our daughter is a healthy, happy college student with plans for a career and marriage. She does not have to live with the mental and emotional scars of knowing she took a life in her womb. The doctors tell us that giving birth to a child in this manner is less damaging to her than to have carried the inward scars of the rape without ever sharing it with anyone (this is what most rape victims do for life).

Thousands of others have been encouraged by our story to live through their tragedy and believe God to bring the triumph.

Because we have decided not to waste our sorrows, the book is now available in Christian bookstores (or from the publisher, Hannibal Books – 1-800-747-0738) to encourage and strengthen others when evil strikes in their lives.

Two Crisis Centers have been opened to meet the needs of

young women faced with unwanted pregnancies.

My wife, Emily, has received special training in rape and pregnancy crisis and now is a source of information and inspiration to many others faced with needs in their lives.

God has given us more than just sermons to preach. Now we have a life message that can affect the lives of others.

Our family has a closer bonding and love-relationship than we could have ever known without this tragedy in our lives.

We now have an extended family. Our grandson's adoptive parents have become like our own children. We visit with them and they with us and we will be able to see God do His wonderful work in our grandson's life and will be able to contribute to his spiritual development.

I am preaching with greater anointing and with deeper sensitivity to the needs of people than ever before in my ministry.

We have learned that God is "at work" not only in the good times of our lives but also in the bad. We learned the most during those times of greatest hurt.

We have learned that unless there is a very definite threat to the mother's life, which is very rare, there is no other reason to take the life of a child before he has the opportunity to be born.

From a Biblical perspective, there is no qualitative difference between a fetus and a living, walking human being. It is only quantitative. The only difference in a newly conceived fetus and a newborn child is time.

Frances Schaffer said, "If the Christian church will not stand on the abortion issue, where will it stand?" I recently listened to one of Dr. Schaffer's tapes that was almost 15 years old—he was truly a prophet. We are already seeing his prophesy fulfilled. The longer we tell people it is okay to kill before birth, the more they will believe they can kill after birth.

It is true that our wonderful Lord offers full forgiveness for those who have been involved in abortion. His grace is sufficient and the Blood of Jesus cleanses from *all* sin.

However, it is also true that our hearts in America should be breaking like the heart of Jeremiah, the prophet.

Jeremiah 9:1,21; ¹*Oh, that my head were waters, And my eyes a fountain of tears, That I might weep day and night For the slain of the daughter of my people!* ²¹*For death has come through our windows and has entered our palaces; to kill off the children, no longer to be outside And the young men, no longer on the streets.*

Jeremiah understood the need because he understood his origin.

Jeremiah 1:15; "Before I formed you in the womb I knew you; Before you were born I sanctified you; And I ordained you a prophet to the nations."

You may be saying, "What can I do, I am only one?" Please take another approach and say, "I am one and I can do something."

What can you do?

➤ 1. Make a firm and total commitment that you will live by the principle of the sanctity of human life and do whatever is required of you to protect the life of the unborn.

➤ 2. Help to begin Crisis Pregnancy Centers and perhaps open your own home to help young girls who are faced with unwanted pregnancies.

➤ 3. Be sensitive to the needs and hurts of families and young women faced with the option of abortion. Do all you can to reach out to them in love and let them know of your understanding.

➤ 4. Realize that God's forgiveness and His redemption is available to those who have participated in abortion. God is always ready to completely forgive and restore.

➤ 5. Pray for our national leaders in the Administrative, Legislative, and Judicial branches of government. Pray that God would open their eyes and turn the tide against the awful scourge of abortion in this nation.

➤ 6. Pray that preachers will have the courage to speak on this issue with boldness in our pulpits. Encourage your own pastor to do so in your church.

➤ 7. Be actively involved in electing officials who take a strong pro-life stance.

The tragedy of our hour is that the Church of Jesus Christ has the answers to the problems of our nation but very few want to listen to our answers because we have lost our credibility. Because we have ceased to walk in the community as a servant as Jesus walked when He was on the face of the earth, people no longer want to hear us. They don't care what we know until they know that we care.

We must take a stand and let our prophetic voice be heard simultaneously with that. We must walk as a servant in the community of need standing in the gap on behalf of the innocent that are being slaughtered.

Let me ask you, if not us, who? If not now, when?

Children in The Fire

Junior Hill

TEXT: 2 Kings 17:7-17, KJV

SUPPLEMENTAL VERSES: Job 42:2, Jeremiah 32:35, Acts 7:51, Ephesians 6:4

SUMMARY OF MESSAGE: Junior Hill's "Children in the Fire" explains that our society is following the steps the children of Israel, God's chosen people, took to spiritual destruction. These steps are becoming defiled because of callousness, denying God's commandments, delighting in conformity and destroying children.

Hill says that our society destroys children on the altars of abortion, abuse and abandonment, and he encourages Christian parents to follow biblical guidelines for parenthood: exhorting, nurturing and molding them in Christlike love.

PREACHING TRACKS:

➤ TRACK ONE: Preach the entire sermon.

➤ TRACK TWO: Preach the points on the outline that best apply to your congregation. II gives the steps God's people took to destruction, III outlines the ways our society harms and kills children and IV encourages parents to evaluate their perspective on parenthood and their attitude and actions toward their children.

➤ TRACK THREE: Preach a combination of points in this sermon and in other sermons in this book.

CHILDREN IN THE FIRE

II Kings 17:7-17

Junior Hill

I have just read one of the most unbelievable and astounding statements in all of the Word of God. Here was a generation of people who had departed so far from the Lord that they actually made their children walk through fire. They offered them as sacrifices unto the pagan god Baal!

The other day, while reading the Bible, I saw a passage of Scripture that I have never seen before. Quite often we talk about God being omniscient, that He knows all things, and that nothing ever takes Him by surprise. Obviously that is true. Job summarized that fact so succinctly when he said, "...No thought can be withholden from thee" (Job 42:2). As someone has so wisely said, "Has it ever occurred to you that nothing ever occurred to God!"

And yet, there is a passage of Scripture which indicates that sometimes God is so astounded by man's sin that it seems even to surprise Him.

Jeremiah said, *"They have built the high places of Baal, which are in the valley of the son of Hinnom, to cause their sons and their daughters to pass through the fire of Molech; which I commanded them not, NEITHER CAME IT INTO MY MIND, that they should do this abomination, to cause Judah to sin."* (Jeremiah 32:35)

These people had departed so far from God that it never entered into His mind that they would do such horrible and abominable things. Their unthinkable wickedness surprised even God!

Now, how did that happen? How did a nation divinely chosen as God's special possession come to that loathsome and sordid place? And once there, what was the tragic outcome?

The Scripture passage we are considering answers those questions by pointing out four steps the house of Israel took — all of them progressively downward.

I. They Were Defiled by Their Callousness

In the first place, they were defiled by their callousness. The Bible describes them as a "hardened" people. That hardness and callousness expressed itself in three significant manifestations.

First, they had EARS THAT WOULD NOT LISTEN. II Kings 17:14 says "Notwithstanding they would not hear..." And that is precisely where we are in our society today. We have more being said, more being presented, and more being preached than ever before, but we don't have many ears that are willing to receive it.

Second, verse 14 goes on to say that they had WILLS THAT WOULD NOT BOW. The Scriptures say that they "...hardened their necks, like to the neck of their fathers, that did not believe in the Lord their God."

These who "hardened their necks" are similar to those whom Paul described as "...stiffnecked and uncircumcised in heart and ears" (Acts 7:51). Both terms are references to stubbornness and obstinacy. It is a picture of a hard-hearted and cold-spirited person who is resolutely determined to do something regardless of the outcome. That is exactly what happened to the house of Israel. Not only would they not listen with their ears, but they had hardened their hearts and stiffened their necks so that they would not respond to the clear proclamation of God's will.

And the tragedy is, our day follows in their steps!

I was in a revival several months ago and a woman came to me at the close of the service for counsel. She was 25 years old and very attractive. "Brother Hill," she said, "The Lord spoke to my heart tonight and I really believe that He convicted me that I need to make a decision."

"But before I do," she continued, "I want to ask you one question. I am 25 years old, I am not married, and I am living with another woman's husband. What I want to ask you is this: If I get right with God will I have to give up that man?"

"Ma'am," I replied, "not only will you have to give him up when you get right, but you're probably not going to be able to get right until you are willing to give him up."

She stood up, folded her Bible, and as she walked out the door she replied, "Then I don't want to be right!" Now what is that? That is a stiff-necked person. That is someone who has become so hardened in heart that their will supersedes the will of God. That calloused spirit is reflected in one of the popular Country/Western songs which declares, "If loving you is wrong, then I don't want to be right." Those may be only the clever words of a song, but they reflect the callousness of a stiff-necked and hard-hearted society.

Third, they had HEARTS THAT WOULD NOT BELIEVE. Again in II Kings 17:14, "...they did not believe in the Lord their God." In spite of all His manifold miracles, the unbelievable outpouring of His grace, and the tender appeals of His anointed prophets, the house of Israel continued to provoke the Lord to anger. Their callousness defiled their spirits.

II. They Denied God's Commandments

In the second place, they denied God's commandments. II Kings 17:15 says, "And they rejected his statues, and his covenant that he made with their fathers, and his testimonies which he testified against them; and they followed vanity..."

That is an inevitable fact. It never fails. When a person rejects

God he will reject the Bible which God wrote. These hard-hearted people began by closing their ears to the voice of God and ended up denying the laws of God.

That's why you and I need to be very careful not to give one quarter to those who would deny the integrity of the Word of God. Many critics would say, "I don't understand all this argument about the Bible. What does it matter?"

I will tell you why it matters. God's character is inseparably bound up with the Word which He has given. If you deny the Word which God has spoken, then you must deny the God who spoke the Word.

We are not babbling about words and paper and semantics, we are talking about the character and integrity of God. Either the Bible is the Word of God or it is not the Word of God. J.M. Frost summarized it well when he said, "We accept the Scriptures as an all-sufficient and infallible rule of faith and practice, and insist upon absolute inerrancy and sole authority of the Word of God. We recognize at this point no room for division, either of practice or belief, or even sentiment. More and more we must come to feel as the deepest and mightiest power of our conviction that a 'thus saith the Lord' is the end of all controversy."

That is where every Christian needs to stand! Those who cannot anchor their faith on that kind of sure foundation are destined, like jaded Israel, to reject "...his statues, and covenant that he made with their fathers..."

III. They Delighted in Conformity

In the third place, they delighted in conformity. Verse 15 says, "...and they became vain, and went after the heathen that were round about them, concerning whom the Lord had charged them, that they should not do like them."

Having rejected the commandments of God which were designed to make them distinctive, they conformed to the standards of their day. What should have been their greatest shame, turned out to be their greatest pride. They were just like everybody around them!

Sadly, that is where the modern church finds herself today. Rather than be salt that preserves, we content ourselves to be sugar that pleases. Intimidated by trends and infatuated with acceptance, we become pawns, rudely shapened and molded by the movers and shakers of our day. Rather than falling upon our faces and looking to Christ, we sit in our chairs and study charts.

We are told what to eat, what to wear, how to talk, and what to believe. Church convictions must always answer to social correctness. Pagans must be appeased and the world applauded. Rather than being broken and remade in the likeness of Christ until we have become like bread to hungry men, we find ourselves compromised by convenience and stripped of New Testament authenticity.

The only hope for the modern church is that we can get back to being salt that is salty and light that is bright. All else is religious fodder. Somehow we need to be reminded that sickness always affects wellness but wellness never affects sickness. For instance, suppose you, a well person, says, "I believe I will go over and spend a week with some sick folks." Chances are that sickness will affect your wellness. But suppose you were sick and you went to be with some folks who were well. Their wellness is not going to affect you, is it?

No, wellness does not affect illness but illness does affect wellness. When we conform to the world we are not going to make the world more like God, but the world is going to make us more like the world.

That is exactly what the nation of Israel did. Having refused to hear His word and obey His commandments, they eventually found themselves enslaved to a way of life they would never have thought possible.

IV. They Destroyed Their Children

In the fourth place, they destroyed their children. Verse 17 says, "...They caused their sons and their daughters to pass through the fire..." They actually offered them up as living sacrifices to the pagan god Baal. Can you imagine a person doing such a thing? Can you conceive of anyone taking an innocent little child and allowing them to be burned to death in order to appease his own perverted conscience?

I think one of the greatest delights of any Christian family is to take their little children to the house of God where they can be taught about Jesus and how He loved them and died for them. What a privilege that is!

Sunday after Sunday as I stand to preach, my heart is deeply blessed to see scores and scores of precious little boys and girls sitting in church with their mamas and daddies. For many of them, it is all still a mystery. They are not there because they understand all the elements of faith and of worship. They are there because their mamma and daddy brought them. Thank God for parents who care—for parents who believe it is important for children to learn at an early age that God is real and that we have a responsibility to worship Him.

Although for a vastly different reason I suppose it was like that back in the days of II Kings. I can almost see some daddy coming home from work one night and saying to his little eight-year-old daughter, "Honey, you need to go to bed early tonight and get some rest for tomorrow we are going to a special place."

"Where are we going, Daddy?"

"We are going up to the temple to worship our god Baal."

I can see that little girl getting up in the morning all excited about the day. Perhaps, just like you parents do for your children, mother helps her get ready with that special dress and those shiny new shoes.

As they are walking down the road to the temple that little girl sees the belching smoke coming out of the building. "Daddy, what is that smoke from? Why do they have a fire?" "Oh, that's the place of worship, Honey. Don't worry about it. Everything is going to be just fine."

In front of the temple that man probably turns his little girl over to the high priest who takes her, binds her hands and feet, and lays her on the altar of fire.

Can't you hear that little child screaming, "Daddy! Mamma! Daddy! Mamma! I'm in the fire! I'm in the fire! Save me, Daddy! Help me, Mama!"

"Oh, its all right, Honey, you're worshipping god. You are our sacrifice to Baal!"

A living child burned on the altar! And why? Because they would not listen to what the true God said. Obsessed with the lure of the world's popularity, these chosen people of God sank into the absolutely unthinkable position of burning to death their own little children. When you conform to the world, the inevitable result will be the destruction of your very own offspring.

No doubt some of you are saying, "Why listen, preacher, I would never take one of my children and put them in the fire. I would never let my little child be offered up as a sacrifice." And yet, despite all of the pious protests, it is happening every day. All over this country, every hour of every day, precious little children are being placed into the furnace.

Millions of them are being thrust into the furnace of ABORTION. There are thousands of little boys and girls who never see the light of birth because a mother or a daddy thinks they know more than God knows. Their little innocent bodies will be brutally dismembered, sucked out in tubes, or burned to death in saline solutions. And all in the name of personal choice!

Since the infamous Roe/Wade ruling more than 30 million babies have been butchered and murdered. Oh, my God! Oh, my God! What must the sovereign God of the universe think! How long? How long, will His wrath be held back?

I had a man say to me the other day, "Well you ought not be so radical about it. There are good people on both sides of the issue." I could not help but reply, "Sir, I beg to differ with you on that! There may be sincere folks on both sides of the issue, but you will never get me to say that anyone who kills little babies is a good person in the sight of God!"

I think it is high time that the Church of the Living God stood up and cried out against this blasphemous slaughter of the innocents. We may not be able to stop the killing or to shut down the abortion clinics which flow with little children's blood. They may go on covering their bloody hands with the court laws of this land, but as long as we have a breath in our bodies, and a voice in our mouth, Oh, God, help us to cry out!

Others of them are being placed into the furnace of ABUSE. I read the other day that one out of every eight little children born into our country can expect to be sexually molested before they reach adulthood. One out of eight!

I am by nature a very mild person. I don't get angry very often or very easily. I certainly have no desire to sound harsh toward anyone. But there is one kind of person whom I have no patience with—child abusers! I believe child abusers have the judgment of God upon them. The Bible says it would be better for a man that a millstone were hanged about his neck and that he was cast into the sea than to offend a little child. I would not want to stand before the just God of Heaven as a child abuser. Oh, may God have mercy upon their souls!

Then there are other little children who are being placed into the furnace of ABANDONMENT. Every day thousands of little trusting children are forsaken by parents who no longer want them. I was in a home just the other day where a daddy had walked out on his wife and children leaving behind two little girls, broken and disillusioned. That wife said to me, "Brother Hill, he just told me he no longer wanted to be tied down. He no longer wanted the responsibility of children." And so he just left. With calloused disregard for his position as a father he laid those precious young lives on the altar of abandonment and offered them as sacrifices to his god—SELF!

Why the crocodiles aren't even that mean! The lowest animal forms of the field have an innate will to love and to protect their offspring. The Bible says, "...If any provide not for his own, and specially for those of his own house, he hath denied the faith, and is worse than an infidel" (I Timothy 5:8). I am not sure what being "worse than an infidel" means, but I certainly wouldn't want to stand before God in the judgment day with that designation!

Dear parent, what are you doing with the children God has given you? What is your attitude toward them? Are you aborting them, abusing them, or abandoning them? Or are you doing what Paul said in Ephesians chapter 6, *"Fathers, provoke not your children to wrath, but bring them up in the nurture and admonition of the Lord"* (Ephesians 6:4). Are you admonishing them? Are you teaching them? Are you setting a proper standard of conduct by the way you live before them? Are you praying for them?

Like pliable clay in a potter's hand, God places those previous ones in our care. Oh, may God help us to love them to Jesus.

Several years ago, a pastor and I went to a home to witness to a woman who was not a Christian. As we talked with that mother about being saved, her son, probably no more than ten years old, literally laughed and made fun.

The way he acted was simply unbelievable!

Realizing our visit was accomplishing very little, the pastor called upon me to pray before we left. As I bowed my head to pray, that young boy, with a loud and boisterous voice, began to say,

"Jabber, jabber, jabber!"

I could hardly believe my ears. As I opened my eyes, I saw that young boy standing right in front of me with his eyes gleaming in resentment. Not wanting to hurt his feelings but deeply impressed that I should make him aware of the seriousness of his actions, I put my hand on his shoulder and said, "Son, I don't want to offend you, but I want to tell you that unless you change your attitude, you may one day grow up and go to hell."

Without so much as blinking an eye, that young boy looked me squarely in the face and said, "Preacher, I want to go to hell. That's where my daddy is going, and I want to go with him." And the chances are that he will!

As we left that home I thought in my heart, "Oh, God! Here is a daddy that is leading his son to hell, and the tragedy is, he probably doesn't even know it. Preoccupied with self and engrossed in his own pursuits, he blindly leads his little son into the fire!

Oh, dear parent, don't put your children in the fire!

Moral Crisis #1

Anthony Jordan

TEXT: Psalm 139:13-16, KJV

SUPPLEMENTAL VERSES: Luke 1:41, 44

SUMMARY OF MESSAGE: Anthony Jordan's "Moral Crisis Number One" shows how the immorality of killing babies is the most crucial moral issue facing the United States. Jordan says that respect for life is the benchmark for other moral decisions.

Jordan uses biblical principles to explain why abortion is wrong, then encourages his audience to get involved. He closes the message with a powerful personal testimony, saying his adopted baby girl could have been aborted just a few months earlier.

PREACHING TRACKS:

➤ TRACK ONE: Preach the entire sermon.

➤ TRACK TWO: Preach the points on the outline that best apply to your congregation. I explains the detrimental standard abortion sets for other moral decisions. II gives a look at where our society is today in regard to abortion and valuing life. IV gives basic information about ways to combat abortion.

➤ TRACK THREE: Preach a combination of points in this sermon and in other sermons in this book.

MORAL CRISIS #1

Psalm 139:13-16

Anthony Jordan

Today America stands in the midst of a deep moral morass. The number of pressing moral issues are legion. Homosexuality and AIDs, pornography, child abuse, incest, alcohol, gambling, all call for the voices of God-fearing people to be raised.

In the midst of this moral decadence I find myself positioned as Edmund Burke when he said, "An event is happening about which it is difficult to speak, but about which it is impossible to remain silent."

It is the event which Margaret Heckler has called "the greatest moral crisis facing our country today." The moral crisis which I have come to speak to you about is abortion. It is that event about which I can no longer remain silent.

But why? Why is abortion such a critical issue?

Let me answer by asking another question. If a society does not hold a high view of the sanctity of life, then where is the benchmark? If life is not viewed as sacred and God-given, then why should there be such grave concern about other moral issues. I believe what we decide about the unborn child is the key moral question of today.

This moral question demands that the voice of Christians be raised. We as Christians have a responsibility to be the moral conscience of our society. We are under marching orders from our Lord to be the applied "salt" and revealing "light" in a decaying and darkened world. We are to be the moral watchmen on the walls of the city crying out against evil.

For this reason we can no longer remain silent while innocent unborn children are slaughtered in the abortion clinics across this land. It is to our discredit that we have not spoken before now. We can no longer remain silent.

I. Where Are We Today?

For many the subject of abortion is best left in the closet. Often abortion is given short shrift because we have been doped into believing it is none of our business, only the woman and her doctor should discuss such things. For others, the fact that the Supreme Court has made abortion-on-demand the law of the land, causes them to view abortion as a closed subject. After all, if it is the law, it must be right.

Therefore, since 1973 when the Supreme Court handed down its landmark decision, abortions have been performed in astronomical numbers while the Christian community at large has remained strangely silent. But can we remain silent any longer? The facts suggest we are a society bent on the destruction of the unborn. In 1970 there were less than 200,000 legal and illegal abortions in America. In 1973, the first year of abortion-on-demand, 750,000 unborn children were killed by abortionists. After 1973 we destroyed 1.5 million unborn children per year. Can you believe that? Yes, and it is still happening. One and a half million a year are still being killed!

These numbers are hard to comprehend. Consider that 30 million is the equivalent of the combined populations of the states of Washington, Oregon, Nevada, Idaho, Montana, Wyoming, South Dakota, Nebraska, Kansas, and half of Oklahoma. That's fifteen states.

In our 213 year history we have fought six major wars with combined casualties of 1.3 million. In 20 years after Roe vs. Wade, over 20 times that number of unborn children were killed through abortion.

We, the nation which fights for human rights and defends respect and sanctity of life around the world, are categorically denying this basic right to our voiceless, defenseless, and innocent unborn.

What an incredible disregard for life! Albert Schweitzer said, "If man loses reverence for any part of life, he will lose reverence for all of life."

Tragically, America has lost the reverence for life. We are on a slippery slope which will lead us to disregard for life.

Let me illustrate. *Newsweek* magazine did a special edition called, "The 21st Century Family." Included is an article entitled, "Made to Order Babies." A survey done by the New England Genetics Group indicates one percent would abort on basis of sex, six percent if a child was likely to get Alzheimers in old age, and eleven percent would abort a child predisposed to obesity.

The Supreme Court decision overturned nearly 200 years of protection for the unborn in this land. It also ignored 2,000 years of Judeo-Christian history. Will Durant, the great historian, points out that Rome, before Christian control, practiced abortion freely. In fact, 99 percent of families killed their girl babies after the first one. Judaism, on the other hand, outlawed abortion and punished those who practiced it by death.

In Christianity the history of opposition to abortion is long. Almost without exception the early church fathers stood against abortion. When Christianity took control over the Greco-Roman culture abortion was stamped out and didn't return until the demise of the Christian consensus in the 20th century — first Russia, then in Nazi Germany, then in Western Europe, and now in the United States.

While we were the last to fall, we have overtaken the others. Today, America aborts more babies than any nation in the world. In America, the mother has absolute right over the life or death of her unborn child. Parents of pregnant minor children have no legal right to stop their children from getting an abortion. The father of an unborn child cannot stop the mother from having an abortion and can be sued to pay for it.

In over 14 cities in the U.S. there are more abortions than live births.

All of these statistics became painfully personal when in 1982 the lifeless bodies of 16,500 unborn children were discovered in a cargo container behind an abortion clinic.

Again I ask can we remain silent any longer?

Consider the schizophrenia displayed by our society concerning the sanctity of life.

A wounded American eagle was found in Maryland and was rushed for emergency treatment but to no avail. It died. A $5,000 reward was offered for its killer. Yet in America abortionists are paid to destroy unborn children to the tune of $500-600 million per year. Abortion clinics are so lucrative they are being franchised.

Under California law a newborn cat or dog is given protection from undue suffering. It may be killed only by use of drugs, chloroform, or a decompression chamber.

Unborn children are not so fortunate. A saline abortion, for example, causes the unborn child to "feel the same agony as an adult who has suffered burns on 80-90 percent of his body." The child squirms, throws himself around, and shows a total grimacing pattern of withdrawal.

We gasp at the news reports of the grotesque scene left after Patrick Henry Sherril entered the Post Office in Edmond, Oklahoma and murdered 13 fellow employees and then killed himself. The carnage left us stunned and shocked. But where is the outcry when an unborn child is torn systematically piece by piece, limb by limb, from the mother's womb. When the limbs have been suctioned into the abortionist's jar, he carefully takes forceps and grasps the baby's head and crushes it because the head will not pass through the suction tip in one piece.

In most states minors, who cannot legally purchase liquor or cigarettes, can have abortions without parental consent or knowledge.

In America there are 1.5 million abortions a year while 1.6 million requests for adoption go unfilled.

If we have such little regard for the life of the unborn child, will it be long until we have no regard for the life of the handicapped, elderly, or anyone else who gets in our way?

This thought was underscored in my mind a few summers ago during a trip to Europe. We visited a small but infamous town in Germany called Dachau. There we visited the Nazi extermination camp where thousands of Jews were systematically exterminated because someone decided they did not measure up. I saw the bath houses which were really gas chambers. Next door were the ovens where the bodies were burned. A short distance away was the blood ditch which ran full with blood from prisoners shot to death.

But perhaps the most striking of all was the sign prominently displayed in five languages. It read, "Never again."

Sadly, today in America, it is happening again. Not to Jews, but to an even more defenseless group—the unborn children.

This brings us to another question. What does God say about the unborn child and the sanctity of life?

II. What Does God Say?

The Psalmist describes God's view of life in beautiful terms. Turn to Psalm 139. We want to look at verses 13-16.

A. God is the author of life. David says it was God who formed him and weaved him in his mother's womb. God made him and skillfully wrought his body. David saw his conception and development as in God's hands.

B. The unborn child is a human being. David declares that God saw his unformed substance and ordained his life even before birth.

The use of the word *"brephos"* in the New Testament substantiates the humanness of the unborn child. *"Brephos"* is defined by scholars as a breathing, nursing infant. But this word is used by Luke to describe John the Baptist leaping in his mother's womb in the presence of Mary and the unborn Jesus (Luke 1:41,44). It also was used to speak of the children who were coming to Jesus.

C. Science has confirmed that a child is growing and developing from the moment of conception. In fact, due to the discipline of medicine called fetology physicians now see the unborn child as a second patient.

Listen to this. At the moment of conception all the necessary elements that create a new human being are present. When the chromosomes of the father and mother unite, they form an absolutely unique, never-to-be duplicated human person. At that moment, life begins. From that moment on, any further formation of the person is purely a matter of development, growth, and maturation. From the moment of conception, the child grows, and keeps growing until life ends.

At three weeks, the tiny human being, only one-tenth of an inch long, already has the beginnings of eyes, spinal cord, nervous system, lungs, stomach, and intestines. The primitive heart, which began beating on the 18th day now pumps more confidently. All this before the mother is aware of new life within her.

The child is making body movements a full 12 weeks before the mother may notice such stirrings.

At eight weeks, the developing child can make a tiny fist, hiccup, suck a thumb, wake and sleep.

While growing inside the mother, the child develops separately from her with a separate individual blood supply. The child's life is not the mother's life, but a separate individual life. And the child has as much right to life as the mother has or any other human being of any age.

This right to life is the most fundamental right of every human being. To violate this right, to destroy life, to kill a human being, at any age or state of development – whether in the womb or out of the womb – is a crime against society, against man, and against God.

Yet, in spite of the clear teaching of God's Word and science, the unborn continue to die at the rate of 4,400 per day. While almost inconceivable, the mother's womb is the most unsafe place in America to live.

But what can we as Christians do? How can we be salt and light in our society?

III. What Can We Do?

Edmund Burke said, "All that is necessary for the triumph of evil is for good men to do nothing." But we can and must do something! Let me suggest some ways we can help stop the slaughter of the unborn.

A. Be informed. We can no longer remain ignorant of the facts. Go to your Christian bookstore and get books about abortion. I will gladly recommend some to you. Seek out literature and films which deal with the subject.

B. Be involved. Preach the Word! The most powerful place in a Baptist church is the pulpit in which a pastor stands with an open Bible, preaching the unchangeable truths of God's Word.

Support the effort of your denomination to minister to pregnant women. We have Crisis Pregnancy Centers lines for counseling. Start one in your town. Counselors and financial resources are needed. Lead your church to be a part.

Work for legislative change of the abortion laws.

C. Be compassionate. There are in every church, women who have been traumatized by abortion. They need our love and need help in finding God's forgiveness.

I want to close my message with a living picture. I hope it will be etched in your mind and will become unforgettable as you consider the issue of abortion. You see, my stand on abortion begins with the clear teaching of God's Word on the sanctity of life. It is formed and confirmed from the field of medicine called fetology. But my stand against abortion is based on a much more personal and precious reason.

I hold in my arms Alisha Suzanne Jordan. She is a new arrival to the Jordan household and joins her adopted brother, Adrian. A few months ago a young woman had an option: Should she abort the child she carried or bear it and give it up for adoption? If she had chosen an abortion, my daughter would have joined 1.5 million other unborn children destroyed in America this year. But because of the ministry of Oklahoma Baptists and a young woman who chose life rather than death, I hold the most precious of gifts in my arms.

I appeal to you. Get involved. Please join me in the fight to stop the killing.

Abortion: Myths And Realities

D. James Kennedy

TEXT: Jeremiah 1:5, KJV

SUPPLEMENTAL VERSES: Proverbs 6:16-17, Isaiah 1:18; 44:2, Job 10:11, Psalm 51:5, Luke 2:12

SUMMARY OF MESSAGE: D. James Kennedy's "Abortion Myths and Realities" answers many of the arguments abortion advocates use to win society's support. Kennedy shows how contradictory some of their beliefs are.

Dr. Kennedy also answers questions your audience may have concerning aspects of abortion today, such as "Are legal abortions safer?" "Shouldn't a woman be able to choose?" and "What's the difference between a fetus and a baby?"

PREACHING TRACKS:

➤TRACK ONE: Preach the entire sermon.

➤TRACK TWO: Preach the points on the outline that best apply to your congregation. II looks at who's involved in the issue from a broad viewpoint. You'll want to include information from III. This section answers popular questions and arguments about abortion. Add your own illustrations and Scriptures.

➤TRACK THREE: Preach a combination of points in this sermon and other sermons in this book.

ABORTION: MYTHS AND REALITIES

"Before I formed thee in the belly I knew thee; and before thou camest forth out of the womb I sanctified thee, and I ordained thee a prophet unto the nation."
Jeremiah 1:5

D. James Kennedy

A bortion—the myths and the realities. I would like very much to discuss with you what is probably the most important single moral issue of our time: the matter of abortion. It has been called by numerous writers "The American Holocaust." This topic deals with a matter of vast importance; it deals with the matter of life and death.

The Declaration of Independence says: "We hold these truths to be self-evident, that all men are created equal, that they are endowed by their Creator with certain unalienable Rights, that among these are Life, Liberty and the pursuit of Happiness." More important than liberty, more important than the pursuit of happiness, more important than economics, and more important even than religious freedom, is the question of life itself. If we are deprived of life, then obviously all of our other rights are gone as well.

Since the infamous Roe vs. Wade decision in 1973, more than 30 million unborn babies have been killed. That number is greater than those lost in all of the wars that have been fought in the history of America.

This is a problem of tremendous dimensions. What kind of problem is it? Is it a political problem? It obviously has a political aspect to it. But it is basically a moral problem; an ethical problem; a spiritual problem; a biblical problem. There are over a hundred texts in the Bible dealing with the unborn. It is a subject about which the Bible has much to say, but all too often we have been silent, even as many were silent in Germany when the great atrocities were taking place.

I. WHO ARE THOSE INVOLVED?

Who are the people involved in this issue? There are some who say it is merely a woman's concern. I have great sympathy and empathy for a woman, especially a woman who, out of wedlock, finds herself carrying an illegitimate child. Like others, I feel empathy toward her and am concerned for her plight, so much so that our church has started a home where such women can be cared for, and where we are able to provide a positive, viable alternative to the matter of abortion.

However, this is not merely a woman's issue; there are others concerned as well, including, for example, the father. That newly created life is as much the father's as it is the mother's. Historically, it is interesting to note that when the Roman Empire did away with laws which allowed abortion, it was done, not because of the woman or the harm that abortions were doing to women (and indeed they do vastly more harm than most people are aware), but because the husband was being defrauded of his progeny.

There are others that are involved as well. For example, grandparents. As the father of a marriage-age daughter I want you to know that I would have an interest in her children, as does every grandfather and grandmother who love their grandchildren. It is also true of siblings. How many people have complained because they never had brother or sisters with whom to grow up?

Even society has an interest in the death of millions of its future citizens. I remember reading the story about the birth of a baby where the circumstances were so tragic, the poverty so great, the handicaps so numerous, that by a half dozen different measuring tools used today this baby would, no doubt, have been aborted. But it wasn't. The baby's name: Ludwig van Beethoven.

But, most of all, there is the matter of the child itself. The Bible speaks very strongly about "hands that shed innocent blood" and God's great displeasure with the shedding of innocent blood.

There is also God Himself. These unborn creatures are made in His image and He is greatly concerned about them. So we see there are many people that are involved in this issue.

II. ARE LEGAL ABORTIONS SAFER?

We are told that legalized abortions are much safer than illegal abortions. That, I might say, is contested by people who know the facts. Before the legalization of abortion, the so-called ten-thousand-deaths figure was thrown around before numerous committees in Congress and elsewhere. Where did that figure come from? Dr. Bernard Nathanson, who headed up the movement to legalize abortion, who had performed thousands of abortions, and who then came to recant and repent and now grieves over the thousands of deaths that he created, was asked that question. He said, "We made it up. We thought it would impress the committees." So, if those who favor abortion don't care enough and if they don't have the morals to keep them from destroying thousands of innocent children, then telling a convenient lie is not going to be such a problem, is it?

In 1967 there were 275 deaths in this country as a result of abortion. That was when only a few states had legalized abortions. Interestingly, 164 of those deaths were from legal abortions; that was more than the deaths from illegal abortions at that time.

So, it is a complex problem. The Bible says, "Come now and

let us reason together." Doing away with emotion and hysterics, let us reason together. Let us consider some of the various reasons that are given for abortion and consider them rationally.

III. IS A HUMAN LIFE DESTROYED?

First of all, we are told that abortion is not killing children; that these are not living human beings; that these are simply fetal material; that they are genetic garbage (another term that has been used).

Recently I read where 60 prominent physicians had met in Cambridge, Massachusetts and presented a declaration which said that the biological facts are absolutely conclusive that the fetus is a living human being. These doctors included Drs. Hofmeister and Schmidt, past presidents of the American College of Obstetrics and Gynecology. Also included were Dr. Joseph Faley, past president of the American Academy of Neurology; Dr. Nathanson, the largest committer of abortions in America, and many other prominent physicians. They said this: "The developing fetus is not a sub-human species with a different genetic composition. As clearly demonstrated by 'in vitro' (dish) fertilization, so also in 'in vivo' (womb), the embryo is alive, human, and unique in the special environmental support required for that stage of human development." That is, the fetus is a genetically unique human being. It is medically incontrovertible. Every doctor knows this. Every scientist knows, too, that from the moment of conception this is a specially unique, genetically different human being.

I remember listening to a doctor point out that he had talked to dozens of doctors around the country who had performed abortions, and he asked them if they knew that what they were destroying was a human life. Their responses were very interesting: every one of them became angry. Why were they angry? Because they were destroying human life? No. Because his question implied the possibility they may have been so ignorant they didn't know they were destroying human life? No, of course, they knew. They said they were doing it for a "good reason"!

Every doctor knows what is in the womb. They have known it for centuries. But many women have been deceived by the linguistic gymnastics used to hide what they are doing. The Hippocratic oath, which has been used in Western civilization by doctors for well over 2,000 years, makes it very clear that the doctor will give no abortive remedy. It is interesting that now we are returning to a pre-Hippocratic period. In fact, there are some medical schools that no longer use the Hippocratic oath for that reason.

IV. DOES A WOMEN REALLY HAVE THE RIGHT TO CHOOSE?

We are told that women have the right to choose. That is a very interesting concept. It is an aborted sentence: the *right to choose.* It ends rational discussion, it is an emotional declaration; it is a sentence without a predicate. Obviously, a moment's reflection would indicate that a person does not have an unlimited right to choose anything that he wants to do. The very essence of civilization is based upon the limitation of the people's right to choose.

Do I have a right to choose? I am sure that if I went to a meeting of NOW and asked that question there would be a resounding response: "Yes! We all have the right to choose." Wonderful! I choose to kill you! Do I still have the right to choose? That puts a little different coloring to the question, doesn't it? The ironic thing is that there really is no informed choice given to these people who insist on the "right to choose."

A young man who heads up an organization that had been picketing various abortion chambers, talked to the owner of one of these places. He said to him, "If you will just give me a little desk in the corner of your establishment where I can have a few minutes with each of these ladies to explain what the alternative is to abortion and exactly what is taking place in abortion, and what is within her womb, we will immediately stop picketing." The owner's response: "Never! Forget it." The only choice that the women are given is whether they want the abortion on Tuesday or Saturday. After all, it is only the product of conception!

V. IS IT A "FETUS" OR A "BABY"?

In talking to numerous women who have had abortions, they have told me that never once were they told what was inside of them was a baby. It is called everything but that. The abortionists use the term, "fetus." Why do they use that term? Do you know what a fetus is? Do you know what fetus means? Fetus is a perfectly good Latin word which simply means "an unborn baby."

Martin Luther knew how important it was for the Latin Scriptures to be translated into the vernacular so that people would know what was going on. And the abortionists know how important it is to translate the English words into Latin so that young women won't know what is going on!

We are told that the fetus is not a person. As they back away semantically, they say that it may be a living human being but it does not have personhood. That certainly dredges up some very interesting historical reminiscences. For example: It reminds me of 1857 and the Dred Scott Case where the decision by the Supreme Court indicated that the black man, the slave, was not a person.

It reminds me of Nazi Germany where the Nazis maintained that the Jew was not a person. These people knew that before they could enslave or exterminate human beings, the first thing they had to do was to depersonalize them, dehumanize them. They had to be semantically destroyed before they could be physically destroyed. They had to be made into something less than human. That is exactly what the Nazis did then and that is what is being done today.

It is interesting that the same depersonalizing arguments that were used to support abortion were used to support infanticide in the Baby Doe case: "not a person." They are the same arguments used to support the destruction of the mentally deficient, or defective babies: "not fully persons."

We should never forget that before Adolf Hitler ever killed a single Jew he murdered 275,000 handicapped people. First, abortion had been prevalent in Germany for over twenty years; then there was infanticide, the killing of babies; then there was the destruction of the 275,000 adult handicapped people.

Abortion has been prevalent in Japan for decades. Consider what has happened there. There was a strong push for euthanasia; a strong push to get rid of the elderly and the defective. Why? Through abortion the younger generation was destroyed and now there are so many older people to support that it is becoming economically infeasible; the economic pressures are rising to get rid of the old people. There is a certain poetic justice there: the parents have been killing the children and now the children are rising and killing the parents! God will not be mocked!

"Not a person," indeed! There are over 100 biblical texts that make it very clear who they are. Listen to the personal pronouns: "Thou didst clothe me with skin and flesh." Clothed what? It? "Me, with skin and flesh. And knit me together with bonds and sinews." (Job 10:11)

"Thus says the Lord who made you, who formed you from the womb and will help you." "Behold, I was brought forth in iniquity, and in sin did my mother conceive me." In Jeremiah we read: "Before I formed you in the womb I knew you and before you were born I consecrated you." Consecrated you! We don't consecrate an appendix or a tumor – but a person. (Isaiah 44:2, Psalm 51:5, Jeremiah 1:5)

"When Elisabeth heard the salutation of Mary, the babe leaped in her womb" (Luke 1:41). Elisabeth said that the babe in her womb leaped for joy. It is interesting that you never hear a woman say that the "fetus" inside her leaped for joy. It is always the "babe." The Greek word is *brephos;* the babe in the womb is the *brephos.* It is the same term that was used to describe Jesus: the babe lying in a manger, clothed in swaddling clothes. That is a baby, not a tumor.

VI. ARE THERE REALLY ANY "UNWANTED BABIES"?

Then we are told that babies should be aborted because they are not wanted. This, indeed, brings up a very new and interesting perspective on the unalienable right to life. It now depends upon some popularity contest! If one is not wanted then one surely should not be allowed to be born! It is an interesting philosophical and logical twist of things. Of course, we would all agree that it is nice to be wanted; that everybody should be wanted. Certainly every wife has the right to be wanted by her husband. We would all agree with that.

If some young lady should come into my office and tell me that she is not wanted by her husband and her heart is broken, I would say to her. "My dear, I think that is the saddest thing I have ever heard. It breaks my heart to hear that your husband, that mean old wretch, doesn't want a lovely thing like you. There is only one thing to do." I open my desk drawer, pull out a gun, and BANG, she is dead! That solves the problem! "Bring in the next counselee..." That is so ludicrous, so absurd, so illogical as to be virtually irrational, except that there are millions of people going around saying "not wanted."

In the case of a baby it is not only irrational; it is also a lie. There are one and a half million abortions performed every year in this country. There are two million couples looking unsuccessfully for babies to adopt. Many adoption agencies have had to close because of a lack of babies. They are all in the incinerator! Couples have had to wait five to ten years to adopt a baby. On the black market today babies are selling for as much as $35,000! I want to tell you that nobody spends $35,000 for something that they don't want very, very much. Babies are wanted!

We are also told that because children are not wanted they will be abused. They won't be abused if they are adopted by people who do want them. But, of course, again a lie is involved for we are told that the basic reason for child abuse is that children are not wanted. Yet studies have shown the vast majority of abused children were wanted. Since so many millions of "unwanted children" have been destroyed, child abuse should have virtually disappeared from America! Yet it is epidemic in our time. No, it does not follow that because children are not wanted they will be abused.

Why do we have so much child abuse today? It is because we have devalued human beings, and children in particular. We have destroyed them by the millions in the womb; we are now moving toward destroying them after they are born.

A young college-age girl came to a counselor and told the story of years of child abuse in her home. She said that the thing that hurt her most of all was when her mother said to her after beating her, "And you just remember that we didn't need to have you at all." Have we sunk so low that the day has come when children will have to get up in the morning and thank their parents for not having killed them? What a distortion of everything decent and moral that is!

VII. IS THE MOTHER AND BABY ONE OR TWO?

We are told that a woman has a right over her own body. That is supposed to be so self-evident as to immediately end the discussion. My friends, what shall we say about that? My response would be: Of course a woman has a right over her own body; who would dispute such a fact? But, we should also point out that that right is limited by law. A woman does not have the right to commit suicide. That happens to be against the law. But within reason, she has a right over her own body. The statement is true but it is totally irrelevant because that baby within her does not happen to be a part of her body!

The same 60 prominent physicians referred to previously, including two past presidents of the American College of Obstetrics and Gynecology, said this also: "A human ovum fertilized by human sperm produces a biologically identifiable human embryo." It has separate and unique genetic information and biological material. Every cell in a woman's body has exactly the same 46 chromosomes and exactly identical thousands of genes in those chromosomes. Every single cell is identical in that way except for the cells in that baby. They all have different sets of chromosomes and different sets of genes.

The baby even provides its own nest. Many people do not realize that the baby is the one that creates the placenta. It is the baby that produces the umbilical cord. The baby has its own blood stream. It has a different blood type. It produces its own blood. In half the cases the baby has a different sex. If it is part of the woman's body, then the woman is part male – in some cases!

It is also interesting to see that developments in fetology – the science of the study of the baby (which coincidentally began in the same year of 1973) – are producing some amazing revelations. For example: "In vitro" is the development of the egg and sperm in a dish outside the mother. This has been going on now for some time and scientists are finding that they can keep that newly created life alive longer and longer before implanting it in a womb. At the same time they are able to cause the baby who is born prematurely to survive at an ever-younger age. The fact that they can keep the embryo alive longer "in vitro" and at the same time cause the premature to survive at an earlier and earlier age, causes scientists to speculate that before the end of this century those two figures are going to meet. Which is to say that scientifically a baby could be conceived, fertilized and grow to maturity without ever having been inside of the womb of a woman! I personally don't know that that is so desirable, but nevertheless, it is scientifically true.

VIII. IS VIABILITY A PROPER TEST?

The argument is made that an embryo is part of the body of the mother because it is not viable outside of the womb. But suppose it comes to pass in a few years that there are babies that have been fertilized, conceived and grow up, never to have seen the inside of the mother's womb. Is a woman going to say, "Oh, that is just a part of my body?" It will be self-evident that this is a separate, unique, genetic individual, totally apart from her body. Let me point out to you that when that baby is six weeks old it is still totally dependent upon the woman for nutrition and protection. Because it is not viable apart from the care of the mother and totally dependent on her, then obviously at six weeks of age, after birth, the mother has the right to kill it then, too, because it can't survive without her! What about six months of age? How about a year old baby? Can it take care of itself? Kill them also!

How about a sailor in a submarine submerged for six months. All of the air that he breathes is dependent upon that submarine. The food that he eats; the protection from the pressures and the water of the sea; all are dependent upon the submarine. Obviously, any intelligent person should be able to see that that sailor is simply a part of the submarine! Well, logic is logic, isn't it.?

IX. SHOULD ABORTION BE ALLOWED IN RAPE OR INCEST?

What about the matter of rape or incest? Again, less than two percent of all abortions are done because of rape and incest. Rape is a very violent and evil crime, but do we solve it by committing another violent act? Do we solve it by killing the innocent child who is as much a victim of the rape as was the mother and who had, in fact, nothing to do with it at all? Do two wrongs make a right? In the Bible the child of rape was allowed to live and the rapist was put to death. Today, we find that the penalties against rape have become more and more lenient, whereas the child is the subject of capital punishment. Justice has been totally destroyed and perverted in that the guilty are practically allowed to go free and the innocent are killed. The very antithesis of justice!

X. DO THE UNBORN HAVE RIGHTS TOO?

Rosemary Bottcher, an analytical chemist whose major work deals with protecting the environment, says she doesn't like the very unflattering picture of women that the radical feminist abortionists are setting forth. She doesn't think women are that way at all. She says if that is true and if women cannot handle the stress and pressures of a pregnancy, how are they going to handle the stress and pressures of the presidency! She adds that she does not like the picture the feminists paint of women who deplore the idea that the value of a woman is determined by whether or not some man wants her. But, says the abortionist, the value of a child is determined by whether or not the mother wants it! They become irate at the idea that sexual freedom should allow men the right to rape women, and rightly so. But they insist that their sexual freedom allows them the right to kill unborn children. They lament, she says, men's reluctance to recognize their personhood, but they steadfastly refuse to recognize the personhood of the unborn. And, indeed, I might add they get most furious at pornographers and *Playboy* advocates who see women as nothing but meat—flesh on display, at the same time insisting upon saying that the baby is nothing but flesh, tissue, a product of conception.

XI. WHAT SHOULD CHRISTIANS DO?

My friends, the time has come for Christians to stand up; to become active; to fight this gross moral evil of our time. We have seen that there is not a rational argument that can be presented for this flood of abortions which have launched this nation out in a sea of blood. God warns, by implication in a number of Scriptures, "Woe unto the hand that sheddeth innocent blood." We are, perhaps, going to bring down upon us the very wrath of God. I am certain that this hideous blot on the escutcheon of mankind will be wiped away, just as slavery went the way of other evils; just as the Inquisition passed away. Just as Nazism passed away, so, also, will this butchery of the innocent pass away. However, it will leave a scar on the historical character of our nation.

May God grant because of our prayers, because of our concern, because of our actions, that this evil will pass away soon before many other innocent children are given over to the butchers who have no feeling about taking the life of the silent innocent. One of the signs of character and morality is the concern for the weak, the sick, and the helpless. Even as the chivalrous knights were concerned about women, so should we be concerned about these members of our society who are the most helpless, the most silent sufferers in our time. God grant that soon this evil will pass from our land. May it be!

SPEAKING FOR THE SILENT

*"The only thing necessary for evil to triumph
is for good men to do nothing."*

Beverly LaHaye

Edmund Burke spoke those words over 200 years ago, but the truth of the message has been illustrated in civilization since the beginning of time.

From the slaughter of newborn infant boys in Egypt during Moses' day to the ravages of Genghis Khan throughout Asia in the 13th century, the world has seen the barbarism that results when evil is allowed to triumph.

Even as recent as this century – after mankind had supposedly become civilized – we saw one of Europe's most educated societies embrace a leader and a philosophy that systematically murdered 10 million people in little more than a decade. Today we look back on the Nazi atrocities and ask, "How could a nation allow this to happen? How could a modern, educated society allow itself to be deceived?"

The answer is a simple one: evil triumphed because many good men and women did nothing.

It's easy to turn up our noses in disgust as we consider the barbarism of ages past and criticize those who passively allowed the massacres to occur. It's far more difficult to stand up and rebuke a holocaust in our midst. And what we have in America today is nothing short of a holocaust – perhaps one of the worst the world has ever known. Our society has turned a blind eye as 31 million preborn babies have been systematically slaughtered in just 22 years.

Where are the good men and women of our nation? Evil will continue to flourish until we. As Christian Americans, overcome our political apathy with a righteous passion to fight for what is right and good in the sight of the Lord throughout our land.

I'm not just talking about protests and political rallies. I'm talking about a well-balanced, Bible-based approach: one that begins with prayer, is seasoned with education, and grows into effective action. It's a principle borne out again and again in Scripture and is capsulized in Jesus' Sermon on the Mount when He admonished: "Ask and it shall be given to you. Seek and you shall find. Knock and it shall be opened." (Matt. 7:7 NASB) Asking is prayer. By seeking we learn and educate ourselves on the issue. And finally, the knocking is the action. Activism must be preceded by education and education must be preceded by prayer.

I. Prayer: the Firm Foundation

When Christians' eyes begin to open to the horrors of abortion, many times indignaion overcomes spiritual discretion leading some to jump into the political fray before a firm foundation has been laid.

From its inception, Converned Women for America's motto has been: "Protecting the rights of the family through prayer and action." Prayer must always come before action, if we are to succeed.

What should we pray? The Bible gives us direction. In 1 Timothy 2:1-3 (NASB), Paul wrote: "First of all, then, I urge that entreaties and prayers, petitions and thanksgivings be made on behalf of all men, for kings and all who are inauthority, in order that we may lead a tranquil and quiet life in all godliness and dignity."

We must pray for our President. We must pray for our legislators on both federal and state levels. We must keep all elected and appointed officials in our prayers, asking that the Lord would touch and transform their hearts and grant them wisdom as they make the decisions that affect our lives and the lives of the preborn.

We, as concerned Christians, must also practice wisdom and discernment as we fight this good fight. In James 1:5, Scripture urges: "If any of you lacks wisdom, let him ask of God, who gives to all men generously and without reproach, and it will be given to him." Having the wisdom to know when and how to speak and take action is a crucial element in the battle for the preborn.

We must also pray that God will raise up godly people to run for public office – people who will bring Christian, pro-life values into the political arena, and install those values into public policy.

We must not take lightly this first and most crucial step to influencing legislation and legislators. For as James writes, "The effective prayer of the righteous can accomplish much." (James 5:16 NASB)

II. Education: Learning What to Say and How to Say it

The stakes are too high in the abortion battle for us to plow into the debate hot-headed and half-cocked. After our foundation of prayer has been laid, Christians must take time to educate themselves on the issue. In the abortion debate, we not only have the moral high ground, we also have the logical arguments to win over the uncommitted as well as the opposition through rational discourse.

But no one can articulate what they haven't studied. The Lord urges us in Scripture to study to show ourselves approved. There are innumerable resources available to educate you on the abortion issue and to keep you up-to-date on the abortion debate. Almost all pro-life organizations publish regular newsletters and educational pamphlets that can help you learn the facts. Concerned Women of America publishes a monthly news magazine, called *Family Voice* for the fundamental purpose of educating concerned Americans and keeping them on the cutting edge of the issues that threaten the family. These resources as well as books on the subject, will give you the facts and statistics you need to construct an effective defense.

For example, abortion proponents often argue that the fetus is "just a blob of tissue" not a baby. If pro-life advocates have done their homework, they can point out the medical fallacies in that statement. Only 21 days after conception – before the woman even knows she's pregnant – the child's heart is beating and pumping blood through the body. At 30 days, the child's arms and legs are clearly forming and he has a brain. By the 35th day, facial features become visible – a mouth, ears, a nose. At 40 days, the child's brainwaves can be detected.

Those are all scientific facts – indisputable. Pro-life Americans must be well-versed in such facts if we are going to be successful in saving the preborn.

Beyond the scientific facts, pro-life Americans also need to know how to point out the flaws of logic in abortion proponents' arguments. One popular argument is: Every woman should have the right to choose.

The phrase "right to choose" has a flavor of freedom and liberty. It's as American as apple pie, which is why it has become such an effective battle cry of pro-abortion forces. Certainly the "right to choose" is an appealing concept until we ask: the right to choose what?

Does a man have the right to choose to rape a woman? Does one person have the right to choose to assault another? Of course not. The right to choose ends when another person is harmed by the choice. Abortion stops a beating heart; it snuffs out a human life; and it robs another person of a lifetime of choices.

Many injustices have been promoted throught history under the guise of choice. In early America, slave owners argued that abolitionists were trying to restrict their freedom, by not allowing them the choice to own slaves.

Educating yourself on the issue is something that never ends. Also, pro-life Americans should know the status of abortion-related legislation both on the state and national levels. You can't know when to take action if you don't know where the threat lies.

III. Action: Making a Difference

The American government was constructed to be a government of the people, by the people and for the people. That means we as Americans have been given great opportunity and responsibility to effect change in the political arena when necessary. There are many ways individuals, groups and even churches can go about effecting that change.

The simplest thing someone can do is register to vote and then go to the polls on election day—both in the primary and the general elections. It is easy to sit back and think one vote can't make a difference. However, our nation's history is speckled with examples where a few votes were able to make or break an election.

If Christians would make it a priority to be at the polls and to know the candidates, we could reform abortion laws from the inside out.

Churches can take an active part in the process as well. While churches are prohibited from endorsing or contributing money to candidates, they are free to conduct voter registrations and get-out-the-vote drives.

In 1992, CWA Prayer/Action Chapters in Lancaster County, PA, conducted a "Voter Registration Sunday" in seven different local churches. CWA members manned the tables in ech church providing all the necessary forms needed to register to vote. They also provided candidate surveys and scorecards, which revealed how each candidate stands on the issues.

Church voter registrations reach college students with absentee ballots and missionaries home on furlough as well as new people in the area and those who simply haven't bothered to register in the past.

Churches can also provide transportation to and from the polls. It is perfectly legal for a church to organize cars, buses or vans to help people make it to the ballot box.

Pro-life rallies – many of which include prominent speakers – create a good atmosphere for both educating and encouraging Christians in the fight for the preborn. However, any group planning such an activity should be prepared to meet with opposition. Anytime a pro-life group holds a large public function, abortion proponents naturally see it as a threat and want to counter it.

Many abortion battles today are won or lost in the state legislatures, so an organized group of lobbyists can have substantial influence in this arena. However, legislation can be complicated and the wording is often purposefully misleading, causing many to become intimidated. By being linked to national pro-life groups who have legal and legislative experts to evaluate bills, local pro-life groups can avoid the pitfalls of obscure legislation.

Persistence is the key in this battle. It sometimes seems that for every three steps we take forward, we are pushed two steps back. But we are making progress, and we will continue to make progress if, and only if, the good people of this nation ban together to fight.

Those who don't feel called to lead lobbyists to the state capitol, can send letters to congressmen and senators in Washington and legistlators in the state capitols. Or write a well-researched letter to the editor of your local paper.

Another way to help end abortion is by supporting the local crisis pregnancy centers that are popping up all over the country. These are privately-funded, volunteer-run organizations that provide an alternative to abortion by meeting the financial and emotional needs of women facing unwanted pregnancies. All pro-life pregnancy centers can use volunteers and financial contributions.

You can make a difference.

IV. A Christian's Calling

I believe the abortion issue is a spiritual issue as well as political. Whatever grieves the heart of God is clearly a spiritual issue. Certainly the slaughter of 30 million preborn infants grieves the heart of God. This should spur us to action — both on our knees and in our legislatures.

We've endured more than two decades of Roe v. Wade. We sit passively as 1.5 million preborn babies are thrown into surgical trash cans each year. Again the evil is looming in our land because too many Christians are still doing nothing. We must hear the silent cries of the preborn and take action.

Who Will Stop The Killing?

Richard Land

TEXT: Psalm 139:13-16, KJV

SUPPLEMENTAL VERSES: Jeremiah 1:54, Psalm 51:5, Numbers 35:33, Proverbs 24:10-12

SUMMARY OF MESSAGE: Richard Land's "Who Will Stop the Killing?" looks at aabortion from biblical, historical, societal and personal points of view. Land uses current real life stories of abortion and infanticide and writings of medical experts to reinforce his thesis that in every abortion, a baby is killed.

Land instructs Christians to pray for sensitivity to the horror of abortion, to intervene in society's blindness on behalf of babies and to proclaim the truth about life in the womb. He urges his congregation to take immediate action to stop the killing and further devaluing of life.

PREACHING TRACKS:

➤ TRACK ONE: Preach the entire sermon.

➤ TRACK TWO: Preach the points on the outline that best apply to your congregation. V details the current thinking on abortion in society and exposes Satan's efforts to desensitize us and cause us to compromise. VI and VIII offer ways Christians can help stop the killing. VII includes horror stories about what the mind-set of legalized abortion has allowed to take place in the United States.

➤ TRACK THREE: Preach a combination of points in this and in other sermons in this book.

WHO WILL STOP THE KILLING?

Richard Land

A bortion is a controversial subject. It stirs the emotions. I am thankful that at least it is still objectionable enough to be controversial, although my heart is hearing that our nation is not godly enough to condemn the horrendous practice of the killing of babies with more certainty than is currently the situation.

I. BIBLICAL TEACHINGS REGARDING ABORTION

The Bible is very clear in its teaching on the matter of the nature and value of prenatal life. My presuppositions are biblical and in the present context I do not need to spend much time talking about the biblical teaching on abortion. There are some very definite passages in the Scripture that speak to the abortion issue and the history of Israel clearly indicates that fact. In Psalm 139:13-16, we read:

"Thou hast possessed my reins: thou hast covered me in my mother's womb. I will praise thee; for I am fearfully and wonderfully made: marvelous are thy works; and that my soul knoweth right well. My substance was not hid from thee, when I was made in secret, and curiously wrought in the lowest parts of the earth. Thine eyes did see my substance, yet being imperfect; and in thy books all my members were written, which in continuance were fashioned, when as yet there were none of them" (cf. note in Criswell Study Bible).

The phrase, "possessed my reins," literally "kidneys," means God formed all of the internal organs of David. "Covered me" in verse 13 literally means "knitted me together." "My substance," literally "bones," refers to the skeletal frame. "Made in secret" is equivalent to "made in the womb." "Curiously wrought" is literally "embroidered." "In the lowest parts of the earth" is simply Hebraic poetic language for the formation in the darkness of the womb. "My substance yet being imperfect" in verse 16 refers to the embryo. Verse 16 affirms God's prior knowledge of David's life all the way from the pre-embryonic state to the end of his life and into eternity.

When Jeremiah was being called he was told, *"Before I formed thee in the belly I knew thee; and before thou comest forth out of the womb I sanctified thee"* (Jer. 1:5). God was working, preparing, and embroidering in such a way that the exact, precise genetic pool was available so that the unique genetic combination constituting the great, weeping prophet Jeremiah was created at precisely the time that God intended for Jeremiah to be brought to fruition.

Psalm 51:5 says, *"Behold I was shapen in iniquity and in sin did my mother conceive me."* David was not led by God to say here, as is presupposed in some major non-Protestant traditions, that the marital act is in some sense less than holy. Rather, he is emphasizing his own sinful nature. This is particularly clear in the Hebrew text. David is making reference to the proclivity or bent toward evil which is present in all human beings from conception. The passage indicates that this sin nature is present from conception onwards. Only human beings possess a sin nature.

We have statements in the Scripture which make it very clear that we are dealing in abortion with human life. As far as the Bible is concerned, there is no qualitative difference between the fetus and a human being. The only difference is quantitative. There is nothing about that child that is not determined at conception and does not reveal itself as a process of time.

The World Book Encyclopedia tells us that within four weeks the unborn child has developed a heart, limb buds and muscle tissue. Within five weeks, it develops ears, eyes and minute hands. At eight weeks, its features are recognizably human.

II. HISTORIC CHRISTIAN VIEW REGARDING ABORTION

The nonbiblical evidence for the biblical attitude toward abortion consists of this: every culture in the Mediterranean Basin practiced infanticide, the killing of infants, as a matter of course, and practiced abortion whenever they had the medical expertise to do so. Will Durant estimated that 99 out of 100 families made it a regular practice to abandon all daughters after the first one to die. The only culture which condemned abortion and infanticide universally was the Hebrew culture. Why? Because the Bible had a clear and unmistakable witness in the Old Testament against abortion and against infanticide.

The Protestant Reformation recaptured the correct and accurate biblical tradition which was taught, espoused and legislated by the Jews. That tradition is this: when you are dealing with a human being, you are dealing with a human being from conception onwards. The only legitimate reason for taking that human being's life is in the active defense of the mother's physical life. Not the mother's psychological well-being, but the mother's physical life. That was the position of the Old Testament; it was the position of the Jewish Rabbis up to the introduction of Christianity, and it was the position of the early church.

By the middle of the Fourth Century A.D., when Christianity had won a victory, albeit not a complete victory, over the paganism and humanism of Greco-Roman culture, abortion and infanticide ceased to be legal and acceptable socially. It did not become legal or socially acceptable again in the West until the collapse of the Christian consensus, which unfortunately has occurred in our lifetime.

For example, the National Council of Churches as late as 1961 in its "Statement on Responsible Parenthood" declared that Protestant Christians were agreed in condemning abortion and that "The destruction of life already begun cannot be condoned as a method of family limitations."

I think that we need to understand that anybody who takes the Bible seriously is going to have to come to the conclusion that we are dealing with human life and that the only justification for taking human life is the defense of physical human existence.

I have been concerned about the abortion issue for many years before the 1973 Supreme Court decision. There are several reasons why I feel that it would be helpful for me to share them with you. First of all, I discovered as a teenager that my mother had had two previous pregnancies, both of which had ended in miscarriage, and that when she became pregnant with me in 1946, she was told by her doctor that she must have a legal abortion. He said that it was, in his medical opinion, a threat to her life and a certainty that I would not survive the pregnancy. Then, after she changed doctors, she was exposed to German measles during the maximum danger period. Once again, her doctor encouraged her to have a legal abortion, which she refused to do. And then, in the final trimester of her pregnancy with me, she experienced a serious medical problem that should have caused my death or hers.

Thus, I feel like one who was scheduled for abortion who escaped. I have a burden to speak for those who cannot speak for themselves, who are telling us that they want to live and that they have the right to live. We, as Christians, must speak up for the helpless; we must speak up for those who cannot speak for themselves. We must speak up, because we have not been aborted but allowed to live.

III. THE PENDING JUDGEMENT OF GOD BECAUSE OF ABORTION

We as a society are under the judgment of God for allowing abortion to assume the proportions that it has in our society. God is going to judge those who make their living from abortion. God is going to judge those mothers who kill their children. God is going to judge those of us who know that it is wrong and do not take a stronger stand against it. And God is going to judge us as a nation. I believe that judgment has already commenced.

We have been told by Planned Parenthood and by others that if we allowed abortion to take place, that we would no longer need to worry about child abuse because every child would be a wanted child. Exactly the opposite has taken place. There has been between a 500 and 600 percent increase in child abuse since the Supreme Court decision in 1973, because the logic of child abusers, even if unconscious, is irrefutable: "If I have the right to kill my child before it is born, what is the difference in a calendar date? If I have the right of life and death over my child before it is born, I have the right of life and death over my child after it is born."

We are under the judgment of God because we have allowed the greatest shedding of human life in a shorter span of time than any nation in the history of the world! And we are a supposedly Christian nation. We are a nation where the Gospel is more freely preached than any other nation. We must speak up because it concerns us and it concerns our children and our children's children.

Pastor Martin Neimoller, a Lutheran pastor in Germany at the time of the rise of Adolf Hitler, said,

"In Germany they first came for the Communists and I didn't speak up because I wasn't a Communist. Then they came for the Jews and I didn't speak up because I wasn't a Jew. Then they came for the trade unionist and I didn't speak up because I wasn't a trade unionist. Then they came for the Catholics and I didn't speak up because I was Protestant. Then they came for me...and by that time there was no one left to speak up."

We need to understand that if we allow this wholesale murder of the unborn to continue in the womb and in the nursery, it is going to cause our nation to submerge itself into a chaos of disrespect for human life. We are going to have the old, the aged and infirm being declared unfit to live.

Already in the United Kingdom, if you are over 59 years of age, you are not eligible for a dialysis machine under socialized medicine if you have kidney problems.

Already in this country I am told that there are at least two insurance companies that have on the drawing boards and are seeking legal opinions about whether or not they can, when there is a problem with a pregnancy, demand an amniocentesis to take place and, if the child is perceived to be retarded mentally or to have severe birth defects, then the medical insurance will pay for the abortion. If the mother refuses to have an abortion, then the medical insurance would be terminated. That is not a choice, unless you happen to be able to support a $3,000 or $4,000-a-day medical bill.

We must stand up and do something before it is too late about this terrible stain – the stain of the blood of our innocent brothers and sisters that stains the land and curses the land. We must stand now

If the Christian church will not stand on this issue, on what issue will we stand? If we will not stand now, when will we stand? If we will not stand here, where will we stand? And, if we will not stand, who will stand? God exhorts us: "So ye shall not pollute the land in which you are; for blood pollutes the land and no expiation can be made for the land for the blood that is shed on it, except by the blood of him who sheds it" (Numbers 35:33).

We are bringing condemnation and judgment upon ourselves and upon our children when we do not do that which is necessary to stop this horrible massacre of our unborn. That position is reiterated for us in Proverbs 24:10-12: *"If thou faint in the day of adversity, thy strength is small. If thou forbear to deliver them that are drawn unto death, and those that are ready to be slain; If thou sayest, Behold, we knew it not; doth not he that pondereth the heart consider it? And he that keepeth thy soul, doth not he know it? And shall not he render to every man according to his works?"*

IV. THE CHRISTIAN ATTITUDE REGARDING ABORTION

We are to defend the helpless; we are to defend those that are being drawn to death, and if we do not do so, then we are held as culpable by God.

Let me share with you out of my own conviction about this issue. I have argued it. I argued it at seminary. I must confess to you that in 1973 I was in the minority on a baptist seminary campus, even among those that were inerrantists and conservatives on this issue. They looked upon it as a way to cull the welfare rolls, pagan as that view is. I can understand the National Broadcasting Company having that view – but I have a difficult time when seminary students have that view. I have had to argue this with relatives and others who just won't accept the biblical testimony on this issue.

That kind of callous and heinous disregard of human life is the kind of thing that is bred in the Soviet system. It is not a flaw in the Soviet people – it's a flaw in the Soviet system. They have been taught that people exist to serve the state and that this life is all there is.

I wonder if our society is not, to some degree, crippling and desensitizing us. Do you realize that every hour and 45 minutes as many babies are being aborted in the United States as were killed on a jumbo jet that was shot down by the Soviet Union? I wonder if in living in the society in which we live we have somehow become part of the problem and we have become desensitized.

I am afraid that I see signs in evangelical life at times that we have been more concerned with righteous indignation over the merchants of death that operate our abortion centers than we are in grief and weeping over the children that are being slaughtered. After all, we are part of that generation that has grown up with television, that has seen 18,000 violent deaths on the television screen by the time we turn 18. We can't watch that kind of thing and be subjected to that level of violence without desensitization taking place in our own lives. We need to pray that God will restore unto us the ability to be horrified, grieved and shocked over the death, poisoning, dismemberment and strangling of human beings. God help us!

George Will wrote an article in which he talked about the neglected issue of pain of the aborted. Our babies, who are being killed in the womb, our babies, who are having serrated knives injected into their mother's womb and being sawed apart and cut to pieces, feel the pain—they react against it! We know that fetal

111

pain is felt at 8 to 12 weeks; we can measure it. Doctors believe that it can be felt earlier, but we can measure their reaction to stimulants, negative and positive, at 12 weeks of age.

World-famous pediatrician Dr. H. M. I. Liley has said that "when doctors first began invading the sanctuary of the womb, they did not know that the unborn baby would react to pain" just as "violently as would a baby lying in a crib" as indicated by "flailing his tiny arms, wriggling his entire body, and crying."

Do you realize that we live in a society where your 9th and 10th grade daughter cannot be given a prescription drug without parental permission, but she can obtain birth control pills or have an abortion without parental knowledge or consent? What can we do? If not this, what? If not now, when? If not here, where? If not you, who?

We need, first of all, to evacuate. We need to do all that we can to save individual babies from this holocaust. We must do what the abolitionists did; we must help the unborn to escape. We must have an abortion underground railroad where we do all we can to snatch these babies from the jaws of death and put them into homes where they are wanted and loved. Just as the underground railroad helped blacks to escape before slavery was ended, we must do what we can to save the victims. We must do what the godly in Germany did when they hid the Jews from the Nazi holocaust.

If not this, what? If not now, when? If not here, where? If not you, who? The time has come or else we are going to have to go back and apologize to the Nazis and other Germans we tried at Nuremburg. After all, they were just following orders.

Dr. A. W. Lilley, Professor of Fetal Physiology at the National Women's Hospital in Auckland, New Zealand, known as the Father of fetology, writes of the unborn child:

"Biologically at no stage can we subscribe to the view that the fetus is a mere appendage of the mother. Genetically, the mother and the baby are separate individuals from conception. On reaching the uterus, the young individual implants in the spongy lining and with a display of physiological power, suppresses his mother's menstrual period. This is his home for the next 270 days, and to make it habitable, the embryo develops a placenta and a protective capsule of fluid for himself. By 25 days, the developing heart starts beating. Twenty-five days before the mother ever knows that she might be pregnant, another human heart is beating within her body. The first strokes of a pump that will make three million beats in a lifetime. By 30 days and just two weeks past the mother's first missed period, the baby, now one-quarter inch long, has a brain of unmistakable human proportions, eyes, ears, mouth, kidneys, liver, an umbilical cord and a heart pumping blood he has made himself, blood by the way that is often a different blood type than that of the mother."

There is no medical record ever of one human being having two blood types. That's not the mother's body. That baby is plugged into the mother's body. The baby is a human being.

"By 45 days, when brainwaves can first be measured on an EEG, about the time of the mother's second missed period, the baby's skeleton is complete, in cartilage, not bone. The buds of the milk teeth appear and he makes the first movement of his body and new-grown limbs, although it will be another 12 weeks before his mother notices movement. At two months and three days, he will grasp an object placed in his hand and make a fist. We know that he moves with a delightful grace in his buoyant world and that fetal comfort determines fetal position. He is responsive to pain and touch and cold and sound and light! He drinks his amniotic fluid, more of it if it is artificially sweetened, less if it is given an unpleasant taste."

What do you think his reaction is when the saline poison is injected into the amniotic sac?

"He gets hiccups and he sucks his thumb, he wakes and he sleeps. He gets bored with repetitive signals, but can be taught to be alerted by a first signal for a second one. Finally, he determines his birthday! Of the 45 generations of cell divisions needed to get from the fertilized ovum to the adult, 41 have occurred by the time we were born and the final tedious four occupy childhood and adolescence. This, then, is the fetus we know and, indeed, we each were. This is the fetus we look after in modern obstetrics, the same baby we are caring for before and after birth, who before birth can be ill and need diagnosis and treatment just like any other patient!"

We are dealing with human life! The picture that we find before us is an awesome one in our country.

V. TRAGIC RESULTS OF ABORTION

We hear of children being delivered alive and being strangled by the doctor. I have in my files a **Philadelphia Inquirer** newspaper special edition in which a live birth subsequent to an abortion procedure is called "The Dreaded Complication," with a picture of the height of heinousness being the Nazi holocaust in Europe. I remember reading for the first time about how General Patton forced the citizens of German towns to march through the camps and to see the bodies stacked like cords of wood, to see the crimes against humanity, crimes for which the Allies brought the German nation to trial.

We have an American holocaust now. Most of you know the story about the pathology lab in Los Angels County which collected aborted infants from abortion mills and returned pathology reports. The bodies were stored in a 20-foot-long metal shipping container that was parked in the backyard of the posh Woodland Hills home of the man who ran the lab. When the last manager failed to pay for the container, it was repossessed. After the winch of an industrial crane broke under the 3 1/2-ton-weight of the filled container, workers parked it in the shipping yard. When it was needed for further uses the workers began to unpack the 20-foot container, full from ceiling to floor and front to back. When one of the boxes broke and spilled its contents on the ground, workers were shocked to see the headless body of a small infant. Police were called. The Los Angeles County Health Department came to remove the contents and transfer both human bodies and piles of computer sheets to another truck for delivery to the coroner's office. The stench of decaying flesh and formaldehyde was overwhelming. An investigation was demanded and burial was requested.

State Senator Alex Garcia, who represented part of Los Angeles, filed an official request to claim the bodies for burial. Senator Garcia referred to the situation as mass murder. On March 16, 1982, autopsies were ordered by the Los Angeles County Board of Supervisors. Doctors weighed and measured the infant bodies. Autopsies were performed on those infants whose bodies were fairly intact. They took 43 of the larger bodies for autopsy. The putrid smell, the constant buzz of flies and the pitiful sight of the mangled bodies made the procedure difficult for the doctors. Each body was in its original plastic container labeled with the name of the abortionist. The body count was 17,000 to 22,000 babies. Autopsy reports disclosed bodies as old as 30 weeks!

God help us! Thirty weeks! President Reagan responded by sending a personal letter to Philip Dreisback of the California Pro-Life Medical Association decrying the killing and supporting a memorial service. Public officials held a major press conference to urge release of the bodies. The A.C.L.U. filed suit to block the release of the bodies for burial and giving a decent grave to these unborn children. At the request of the Feminist Women's Health Center (an abortion facility which encourages women to abort themselves, receives one million dollars in public tax funds), the A.C.L.U. filed a restraining order to prevent release of the bodies. Los Angeles Superior Court Judge Dickran Tevrizian issued the order. The A.C.L.U. argued that religious service and burial for the aborted bodies was a violation of separation of church and state. Six months after the discovery, the 43 bodies which were autopsied were still jammed in the plastic containers in the morgue and the remaining 17,000 to 22,000 babies were still in the boxes in an unrefrigerated truck in a maintenance yard in Los Angeles. And we talk about Dachau, Auschwitz, Buchenwald!

In Wichita, Kansas, a sanitary worker complained to the news media that he was being asked to burn the bodies of babies up to 32 weeks of age in the same incinerator where he was being asked to burn dead dogs and cats. We, who were horrified when the Germans burned dead people, are burning the bodies of dead babies.

If not this, what? It not now, when? If not here, where? If not you, who?

There is no end to human ingenuity, or should we call it human degeneracy? French cosmetic firms have taken the lead in the latest revolutionary breakthrough in the creation of the most expensive and exotic beauty treatment ever. Beauty experts have found a magical rejuvenator for old and tired skin that has lost its luster and resiliency. It has long been recognized that living cells if frozen and then applied to old and wrinkled flesh could cause amazing rejuvenation. The was discovered in the 1940s by Dr. Alexis Carrel.

The only problem was it was hard to get anybody to donate living tissue. That problem has now been solved. The cells are being taken from the placenta, the fetus, the spleen, the liver, and the thymus of aborted babies. The results are visible and important. Epidermal circulation is activated, coloring is pinker and fresher, texture is finer, and blotches disappear.

European customs officials have intercepted trucks coming through Central Europe loaded with the bodies of human babies destined for the laboratories of French cosmetics firms to be used as a youth rejuvenator in cosmetics. Do you remember how horrified we were that some of the more perverse guards in concentration camps had made lampshades out of human skin? Where is our horror now? We have done everything but eat our young.

It was always said by those of us who have been fighting against abortion that it would not take long for murder to escape the womb and to get its cold, clammy hands on the nursery. It is happening.

Let me remind you of what type of child we are dealing with in abortions. Dr. Paul Rockwell described his experience:

"Years ago, while doing an anesthetic for a ruptured tubal pregnancy (at two months), I was handed what I believed to be the smallest human being ever seen. The embryo sac was intact and transparent. Within the sac was a tiny (one-third-inch) human male swimming extremely vigorously in the amniotic fluid, while attached to the wall by the umbilical cord. This tiny human was perfectly developed with long tapering fingers, feet, and toes. It was almost transparent as regarding the skin and the delicate arteries and veins were prominent to the end of the fingers. The baby was extremely alive and did not look at all like photos and the drawings of embryos which I have seen. When the sac was opened the tiny human immediately lost its life and took on the appearance of what is accepted as the appearance of an embryo at this stage with blunt extremities, etc."

Then there is the case of Baby Doe. Baby Doe was born on April 9, 1982, in Bloomington, Indiana. For many religious Americans that day was Good Friday. What a perverse sense of humor Satan has. For Baby Doe, it was the beginning of six days of torture he would never understand the side of Heaven. He was one of the those special children, the kind some say that God sends to test our nation's love and care for the least among us. If so, we failed. He had Down's Syndrome, an affliction that usually but not always results in some degree of mental retardation. Some Down's Syndrome citizens have normal intelligence and when retardation does result, it is usually mild to moderate. Over 90 percent of them learn to talk and many are able to hold jobs and lead productive lives. All of them are human beings.

This special child had one other problem. He was born with a small hole between his esophagus and his trachea. This meant that food and water would go into his lungs rather than into his stomach and like every little boy, he needed to eat. Fortunately, he was only a short distance from a children's hospital in Indianapolis. The parents consulted with a three-doctor delivery team and called in Dr. James Locklin, a specialist. Dr. Locklin told them there was no evidence of any other defect and that the esophageal-tracheal problem could be corrected at Riley's Hospital by a serious but routine operation to close the small hole. He said there was a ninety percent chance the operation would be totally successful. In the meantime the 6 lb. baby boy just needed to be fed intravenously and moved the short distance to the children's hospital, but the doctors who had delivered the baby told the parents there was another "treatment." After all, there was no way of telling at birth what degree of mental handicap the child might have. The other treatment was to do nothing—just order that the baby be given no food or water until he starved to death in a hospital dedicated to preserving life in the United States of America. God help us!

As Francis Schaefer has said, if the Christian church won't take a stand on this, what will it take a stand on? The decision was made and the order was given because, you see, the parents had the right to choose.

The child who had now been 24 hours without nourishment was not represented when the hospital's attorney called in a judge to make sure the hospital was in no legal jeopardy. A private secret hearing was convened at the hospital. Everyone was represented but the baby. The judge asserted that the only legal question was whether or not the parents had the right to choose to let the baby die by withholding food and water. The judge agreed that they did. Guilty of only being an unwanted and a helpless child that could not speak for himself, he had been condemned to death without due process and without counsel.

For four days Baby Doe cried. On Tuesday, he stopped crying. With no water, with no food since birth, with his body now racked by the infection that was sure to follow such treatment, he was too weak to make a sound. I wonder if the silence made it easier for the doctors and the nurses who were watching him die?

Monroe County Prosecutor Barry Brown found out what was being done. He was shocked and horrified, and so, after four days the child finally had a civilized human being for a friend. Barry Brown filed an immediate appeal that afternoon. He appeared before the juvenile judge arguing that the treatment being given the baby constituted legal neglect and sought to have the baby put under the care of the County. But Judge Spencer ruled that there was no probably cause to suspect neglect, and the parents were just exercising their right to freedom of choice. What about Baby Doe's choice?

That evening another appeal was filed with the judge on behalf of Infant Doe. A temporary order was sought to nullify the earlier order that the child be starved, but to no avail. Wednesday morning Barry Brown, joined by two Pro-Life attorneys, took the case to the Indiana Supreme Court. By a three-to-one margin the Indiana Supreme Court decided against Infant Doe. The five-day-old baby was now the top news story in Indiana.

Six couples stepped forward and offered to adopt Infant Doe. One of these couples, Shirley and Bob Wright, had a three-year-old Down's Syndrome child of their own. At a press conference, Shirley Wright tearfully showed reporters her three-year-old daughter, Bobbi. Bending down to kiss her own daughter, Shirley Wright told the reporters, "I would like people to see this baby and see if they would still let the Bloomington baby die."

A Pro-Life attorney James Bot joined the case and with Brown and others filed an appeal to the U.S. Supreme Court; a hearing was set before Justice John Paul Stevens at 9:00 a.m. on Friday. Brown again went to Juvenile Judge Thomas Spencer seeking a temporary injunction to preserve the life of Infant Doe until the case could be heard before the U.S. Supreme Court. He pointed out the baby was not being given antibiotics to combat the toxins in his blood and in his system and that even a convicted murderer was routinely given a stay of execution pending an appeal before the U.S. Supreme Court. Judge Spencer denied the motion and stood by the decision condemning Infant Doe to starve to death.

That evening as the Pro-Life attorneys arrived at the airport to fly to Washington, D.C. they were informed that Infant Doe had stopped breathing.

Infant Doe's trial had ended. But the trial of our nation continues. If not this, what? If not now, when? If not here, where? If not you, who?

I am not ashamed of being emotional on this issue. We hear talk about back alley and coat hanger abortions. We are told about women who are pregnant because of rape, though it almost never happens and medically, it is extremely rare. I want to say that if you want to talk about emotion, let's talk about babies that are allowed to starve to death.

We must evacuate, we must save the babies. We must educate, we must proclaim the truth, we must speak for those babies that lie in the garbage cans of abortion clinics. As one shocked and horrified reporter put it, babies whose facial expressions bear the agonized tautness of one that is forced to die too soon. And we must legislate. We must speak for those who cannot speak for themselves, for those that cry to us, their blood cries to us from the ground. We must stop the slaughter of our unborn.

Bible Answers to Abortion Questions

Larry L. Lewis

TEXT: Psalm 100:3, KJV

SUPPLEMENTAL VERSES: Job 33:4; 1:21, Proverbs 6:16-19, Genesis 2:7; 9:5-6, Psalm 139:13-16; 127:3, Isaiah 49:1; 58:1, Jeremiah 1:5, Luke 1:15, 41; 2:6, Numbers 35:16-21, 30, 33, Acts 10:34, Matthew 5:14, Exodus 20:13; 22:18-19; 221:16; 23:7, Deuteronomy 17:6; 22:24-25; 24:7,16, Leviticus 20:2-5, 10-16; 18:22; 21:9

SUMMARY OF MESSAGE: Larry Lewis' "Bible Answers to Abortion Questions" discusses some of the most commonly asked questions concerning the abortion issue, such as "Is an unborn child really a human being?" and "Are we sometimes justified in taking life?" Lewis gives clear scriptural support for his answers to these questions and offers several suggestions for ways Christians can get involved.
Dr. Lewis outlines what the United States Constitution says about the right to life and liberty and tells why, according to the Supreme Court, it doesn't apply to unborn children.

PREACHING TRACKS:

➤ TRACK ONE: Preach the entire sermon

➤ TRACK TWO: Preach the points on the outline that best apply to your congregation. III, IV and V detail the viability and personhood of unborn life. VI-IX explain why abortion is an injustice to the child and to God in any circumstance. X gives suggestions for Christian involvement. Combine information and Scriptures from these points with your own illustrations and facts.

➤ TRACK THREE: Preach a combination of points for this and other sermons in this book.

BIBLE ANSWERS TO ABORTION QUESTIONS

"It is He that hath made us and not we ourselves."
Psalms 100:3

Larry L. Lewis

Some have suggested the Bible does not specifically address the matter of sanctity of life or the abortion issue. Nothing could be further from the truth. The Bible is replete in its teaching regarding the sanctity of life and its obvious inference that the wanton destruction of life at any stage, either born or unborn, is a grave ill. "Thou shalt not kill" surely applies to the unborn baby as well as to the developing child or mature adult.

The serious questions relating to the abortion issue: Is the unborn baby a human being? Is the unborn a person? Is the unborn a soul? Is it wrong to terminate the life of the unborn child? These and other pertinent questions relating to abortion are explicitly addressed and clearly answered in the Word of God.

I. When does Life Begin?

Job 33:4; "The Spirit of God hath made us, and the breath of the Almighty hath given me life."

Genesis 2:7; "And the Lord God formed man of the dust of the ground, and breathed into his nostrils the breath of life, and man became a living soul."

When does life begin?

The fact is that human life began with Adam when God shaped man in His own image and breathed into him the breath of life. This life is transmitted from generation to generation in an unbroken chain that links Adam and Eve with every child that has ever been conceived in its mother's womb. Through the living sperm of the father and the living ovum of the mother, human life is relayed from parent to child. When sperm and ovum unite, another human being is generated and yet another person is formed. How ridiculous to assert or believe that somehow or in some way that marvelous product of conception is not really human life at all! The developing fetus is a human life just as surely as a fully-developed adult.

II. Is The Unborn Child A Human Being?

Isaiah 49:1 NASV; "The Lord called me from the womb; from the body of my mother, he named me."

"Human: having human form or attribute; be'ing: substance, nature, or essence of anything existent, one that exists." (**Webster's Collegiate Dictionary**)

Is the unborn fetus really a human being? Many Bible scholars, even some Southern Baptist theologians, have attempted to suggest that the unborn child cannot really be considered human. Dr. Paul Simmons, ethics professor at Southern Baptist Theological Seminary, cited the following as a reason some give in supporting abortion: "The fetus is not to be equated with the mother as a human being. At best, the fetus is potentially a human being but not in fact a human being, especially in the early stages of pregnancy." (Simmons, Paul. "Abortion in Moral, Legal, Social, and Political Perspective")

How contrary such ideas as these are to the Scripture! The psalmist beautifully declares in Psalms 139:14, "I will praise thee, for I am fearfully and wonderfully made."

How can anyone rationally conclude the unborn child is not a human being? To suggest it is not a "being" is to suggest it doesn't exist. Certainly, whatever it is, it does exist and it is, therefore, a "being." Further, to suggest it is not a human being is to imply it must be some other kind of being. If it is some other kind of being, what kind is it? Is it a pig, a cow, or a duck? Is it a vegetable, or perhaps some inorganic thing? How ridiculous! Surely, a right-thinking person must conclude that the developing child within the mother's womb, from the moment of conception, is a human being with all the potential of an Einstein or a Billy Graham.

Any time we terminate the life of an unborn child, we are, in fact, taking the life of a human being.

III. Is The Unborn Child A Person?

"For Thou didst form my inward parts; Thou didst weave me in my mother's womb. I will give thanks to Thee, for I am fearfully and wonderfully made; Wonderful are Thy works, And my soul knows it very well. My frame was not hidden from Thee, When I was made in secret, and skillfully wrought in the depths of the earth. Thine eyes have seen my unformed substance; And in Thy book they were all written, The days that were ordained for me, when as yet there was not one of them." (Psalms 139:13-16 NASV)

Is the unborn child really a person? Should he enjoy the right to life guaranteed persons by the United States Constitution?

Notice how often the psalmist referred to himself in his unborn condition with the personal pronoun "me" or "I." In this short passage, the psalmist refers to himself with a personal pronoun ten times. Under the inspiration of the Holy Spirit, the psalmist openly declared his personhood even while yet in his mother's womb and affirmed beyond question the sanctity of life of the unborn.

Jeremiah also affirmed his personhood even before he was born by the use of a personal pronoun. Note carefully what he said: *"Before I formed you in the womb, I knew you, and before you were born I consecrated you; I have appointed you a prophet to the nations."* (Jer. 1:5)

Consider that marvelous occasion when Mary visited her cousin Elizabeth, several months pregnant, with the unborn child. When the good news of the Messiah's coming was declared, the Bible says: *"The babe leaped in her womb... "* (Luke 1:41;44) Luke further declares that John was "filled with the Holy Ghost, even from his mother's womb." (Luke 1:15) The Holy Ghost fills people, not tissue or cells.

The Greek word for baby is *"brephos."* It is the same word used here in this passage for the unborn baby in Elizabeth's womb. ***Thayer's Greek Lexicon*** defines *"brephos"* as "embryo, fetus, newborn child, young child or nursing child."

This same word is used to describe Jesus in the manger in Luke 2:16.

Scriptures make no distinction between the humanity and personhood of the born and the unborn.

In the infamous Roe vs. Wade decision of 1973, the United States Supreme Court concluded that the unborn child was not really human nor a person, therefore, was not protected by the right to life assured "persons" by the United State Constitution. The Supreme Court concluded that the unborn fetus was merely a part of the mother's body, not a separate human individual.

Obviously, this reasoning flies in the face of the plain biblical teaching of the humanity and personhood of the unborn child.

It is interesting to note that most often, when one is planning to terminate the life of the unborn, and destroy this miracle of God's creation, they refer to the unborn as the "fetus" or the "embryo." By contrast, when they plan to keep the child and cherish it, it is always known as "my baby" or "my child." Did you ever hear anyone say to an expectant mother, "Oh, I'm so happy to see you're going to have a little fetus"? Did you ever hear an abortionist say, "We're going to kill the little baby?" Our respect for the unborn seems to be strangely affected by the circumstances.

Surely, in God's sight, the unborn baby is the crowning miracle of His creation. I hold in my hand a plastic model—a replica of a 12-week old unborn baby. He is only two inches tall, hardly as large as a human thumb. Yet, even at 12 weeks, every organ of the human body and every attribute of a human being is already developing in place. One can see the tiny fingers and toes, the beautifully formed ears and nose, the arms and legs firmly in place. There is no question but that this 12-week old fetus is a human being and very much a person in his own right. How tragic that every 20 seconds one such as he is utterly destroyed and ripped from the mother's womb, discarded as so much trash. How can the Christian conscience tolerate such carnage without deep concern?

121

IV. Does The Unborn Child Have A Soul?

Genesis 2:7; "And the Lord God formed man of the dust of the ground, and breathed into his nostrils the breath of life; and man became a living soul."

Is the unborn child a living soul from the moment of conception? Or does one possess a soul sometime during gestation? Or does the soul enter the body at the moment when one is born, perhaps when one takes his first breath?

Many evangelicals believe that one gets his soul at the moment he is born and breath enters his body. Of course, there is no Scripture for this idea. It is simply another example of speculative theology without any biblical basis.

The Bible does not teach that man has a soul as a separate part of his anatomy, as one has a liver or a lung, but rather that man "is a living soul." When God created man in His own image from the dust of the earth—that is, from the elements of material substance, He distinguished him from the rest of the animal kingdom by breathing into him the breath of life and he became a living soul. Thus, from that point on, man was both a spiritual and a physical human being, possessing both body and soul from conception.

Admittedly, it is difficult to find Scripture and verses to definitely instruct us as to the moment a soul is established and immortality assured. However, we can most likely conclude that the unborn is also an immortal soul. Surely this is sufficient reason to prohibit abortion, except for the most serious cause.

V. Are We Ever Justified In Taking Human Life?

"Whoso sheddeth man's blood, by man shall his blood be shed; for in the image of God made he man." (Genesis 9:6)

Is taking human life, either born or unborn, ever justified?

Even though the Bible clearly commands, "Thou shalt not kill," and even though the Bible continually affirms the sanctity of all human life, the Bible also justifies the taking of human life in a number of instances.

Capital offenses were sometimes punished by death of the offender. In a number of instances, God Himself ordered the execution:

> *Murder (Genesis 9:5-6; Numbers 35:16-21, 30,33; Deuteronomy 17:6)*
> *Adultery (Leviticus 20:10, Deuteronomy 22:24)*
> *Incest (Leviticus 20:11, 12,14)*
> *Bestiality (Exodus 22:19; Leviticus 20:15,16)*
> *Sodomy (Leviticus 18:22; 20:13)*
> *Rape (Deuteronomy 22:25)*
> *Kidnapping (Exodus 21:16; Deuteronomy 24:7)*
> *Fornication (Leviticus 21:9)*

Witchcraft (Exodus 22:18)
Child Sacrifice (Leviticus 20:2-5)

However, carefully note that in every instance where God allowed or even commanded the death of a human being, it was in response to that person's flagrant and serious crime. God does not command or condone the death of an innocent human being. In contrast, God's Word clearly commands "the innocent and righteous slay thou not." (Exodus 23:7) There is no instance in the Scripture where the Bible teaches or God condones the death of the unborn child.

VI. Should Abortion Be Allowed To Save The Life Of The Mother?

Most Christians have concluded that in those very few instances where the life of the mother is at stake, an abortion is justified. For the past several years, the Southern Baptist Convention has passed or reaffirmed resolutions abhorring abortion "except to save the life of the mother."

Perhaps common sense and Christian conscience would conclude that if the life of the mother is seriously threatened, terminating the life of the baby is justified.

However, many medical authorities feel that seldom, if ever, is a doctor compelled to make this terrible choice. In nearly every case where the mother's life is jeopardized, the baby can be taken by Caesarean Section and the doctor can do all that is humanly possible to keep the baby alive. Thus, the doctor has not destroyed life but has done everything in his power to preserve it.

VII. Is Rape And/Or Incest A Justification For Aborting?

Evidence indicates that less than five percent of the abortions in America today are the result of incest and/or rape. (Willke, J.D., *Handbook on Abortion,* Hiltz, Cincinnati, Ohio, pp 35-36).

Certainly if abortion could be prohibited, except in those rare cases of proven rape or incest, a great victory for the pro-life movement would be achieved. However, many Christians feel even this exception should not be allowed.

Does destroying the unborn baby in any way eradicate the tragedy of the rape? Does an act of violence against the mother justify an act of violence against the unborn child? The tragedy of the woman being raped is not eliminated but compounded by killing the unborn baby. It would seem more logical to kill the rapist, not the innocent baby. (Deu. 22:25; 24:16)

Proverbs 6:16-19; "There are six things which the Lord hates, Yea, seven which are an abomination to Him: Haughty eyes, a lying tongue, and hands that shed innocent blood."

A basic principle of jurisprudence is "hard cases make poor laws." This simply means that when laws are made to accommodate extreme exceptions, bad law results. The law becomes vague and unenforceable.

Nevertheless, hard political realities may determine that no proposed constitutional amendment prohibiting abortion will be passed by the Congress or ratified by the states unless it contains a rape/incest clause. Therefore, for the sake of political expediency, some Christians are supporting a rape/incest exception even though it is contrary to their own particular convictions.

VIII. Should Abortion Be Allowed If An Unborn Child Is Deformed?

Is the possible deformity of the unborn child justification for an abortion? Any time we determine to abort a baby because it may possibly be deformed, we are forced to make serious value judgments which are really beyond human prerogative. It is very difficult for the doctor to determine deformity with certainly. Tests are often inconclusive and sometimes totally erroneous.

Even if it were possible to determine that the fetus is seriously deformed, ordering its death is not a prerogative given to man. "The Lord giveth and the Lord taketh away," Job proclaimed. Spontaneous abortion, which is an act of God, not man, often does eliminate a deformed embryo. Let this be God's election, not the father's or the mother's or the doctor's. Only God can give life and only God can rightfully take it away. "Behold, children are a gift of the Lord; the fruit of the womb is a reward." (Psalm 127:3)

Issues such as "value of life" and "quality of life" are not germane. Possibly the life of a truck driver is not as valuable to society as the life of a trained surgeon, who can say? Maybe the life of a one-year old or one-week old baby is not as valuable to the world as the life of a fully grown adult, who knows? Perhaps an unborn baby is not as valuable as a born baby, who can tell? Possibly a retarded person's life is not as valuable as a college professor, who knows? Regardless, any attempt to justify taking one life while leaving another, on the basis that one is more valuable, is arbitrary and utilitarian! Surely no right-thinking Christian would ever conclude such a thing. Such muddled thinking can easily be twisted to justify infanticide and euthanasia. *"Even everyone that is called by my name, for I have created him for my glory, I have formed him; yea, I have made him. Bring forth the blind people that have eyes; and the deaf that have ears."* (Isaiah 43:7-8) "Who maketh the dumb, or deaf, or the seeing, or the blind? Have not I, the Lord?" (Ex. 4:11) Truly "God is no respecter of persons." (Acts 10:32)

IX. What Can Christians Do?

Isaiah 58:1; "Cry aloud, spare not, lift up thy voice like a trumpet, and show my people their transgressions and the house of Jacob their sins."

The Bible demands that the Christian be a militant and prophetic influence for good in our society. Jesus said, "Ye are the light of the world." (Matthew 5:14) Even many Christians still remain in darkness concerning the terrible tragedy of the blatant destruction of the unborn. Approximately 1.5 million unborn babies are aborted every year. Over 30 million have been aborted since the infamous Roe vs. Wade decision in 1973.

What can and what should the Christian do to curb this wholesale slaughter of the innocent unborn?

1. The Christian should preach, teach and proclaim the sacredness and sanctity of all human life, both born and unborn. The man of God should not hesitate to preach those many Scriptures throughout the Bible that affirm the humanity and the personhood of the unborn.

2. Lead your church to participate in Sanctity of Life Sunday. What a great opportunity to share the clear, plain teachings of the Bible on the sacredness of human life. Perhaps a special Sunday school lesson could be planned for Sanctity of Life Sunday. Perhaps the pastor could preach, either Sunday morning or Sunday evening, an appropriate message. A film or slide presentation might be appropriate during the Discipleship Training hour. It behooves every church to plan for a meaningful observance of Sanctity of Life Sunday.

3. Support the efforts of those seeking a constitutional amendment to prohibit abortion.

Most of us tend to be reticent in our support of any effort amending the United States Constitution. We like to think of the constitution as a bedrock of American jurisprudence, not easily altered or changed.

However, the constitution has needed constant amending from our nation's inception. President Madison wisely observed, "In framing a system which we wish to last for ages, we should not lose sight of the changes which ages will produce."

To date the constitution has been amended 26 times. Without the process of constitutional amendment, African-Americans would still be slaves, and women would not have the right to vote. Our cherished Right To Worship, along with the Freedom of Speech and Freedom of the Press, were all assured by constitutional amendments. Don't forget, even our Bill of Rights is nothing more than the first ten amendments to the United States Constitution. As late as 1964, there was an amendment to abolish the poll tax and in 1971 we amended the constitution to allow 18-year olds the right to vote. In the 200-year history of our nation has there ever been a need more serious or a cause more grievous than the right to life of the unborn?

Some feel an amendment to the constitution is redundant. After all, doesn't the constitution already assure the right to life? Doesn't the constitution state that all men are "endowed by their Creator with certain inalienable rights, among these are the right to life, liberty and the pursuit of happiness."

That beautiful rhetoric concerning "inalienable rights" is found in the Declaration of Independence, not in the United States Constitution! The Fifth Amendment and the Fourteenth Amendment do assure that no "person be deprived of life, liberty, or property, without due process of law." However, since the Supreme Court has concluded that the unborn baby is not a "person," the present constitutional provisions do not assure the right to life of the unborn. Also, we must remember that the provisions of the constitution are for those who are "citizens" of the United States and further defines a "citizen" as one who has been born in the United States or her territories or has been "naturalized." Since the unborn child has not been "born in the United States or its territories" or "naturalized," again the courts conclude the unborn is not eligible for constitutional protection.

True, in the past it was generally assumed that the rights preserved for the mother were also attributable to her unborn offspring. However, that was before 1973!

Many conclude that the only permanent remedy for the abortion fiasco is a duly authorized constitutional amendment prohibiting abortion.

4. Support candidates for office who will work for legislation and/or a human life amendment.

Certainly a candidate's position on abortion and his interest in a human life amendment is not the only concern one should consider when supporting a candidate for office. There are many important issues facing our nation and each of them should be seriously pondered as we make our political choice.

However, the seriousness of the abortion issue merits our deep concern. Many feel that curbing this wholesale destruction of innocent life is surely one of the most, if not the most important issue pending in America today. No matter how a candidate may stand on other issues, if he is not solid in his support for life and anxious to influence some type of legislative remedy, many Christians feel that candidate is not worthy of their support.

5. Preach, teach and proclaim biblical instruction regarding proper sexual relationships. By the thousands and by the millions innocent unborn children have been the helpless victims of promiscuous sex. A playboy philosophy running rampant in our society is the major contributor to this abortion holocaust.

Our people need to realize that the laws of God have never been revised, repealed, or revoked! Premarital sex is just as wrong today as it has ever been. Our young people must be challenged to chastity and decency in their conduct.

Sex is a beautiful gift God has given those created in His image. It must be exercised· responsibly within the bounds of marriage as God ordained. A wanton defiance of God's clear guidelines concerning proper sexual relationship results not only in heartache for the mother but far too often the murder of the innocent unborn baby.

6. Minister and counsel with godly compassion. In our zeal to teach the evil of promiscuous sex, let us clearly denounce the greater ill of destroying the unborn child. "Adoption, not abortion" is more than a cliche. Literally thousands of deserving parents fervently desire to adopt a baby but find all their efforts frustrated because the supply of adoptable children is so very small.

Most adoption agencies have a waiting list of two to five years for adoptive parents. What a blessing a baby would be to these deserving parents!

What a blessing these good and godly parents would be to a child! How terrible for one to take the life of their baby simply to avoid some degree of humility or shame rather than willingly place that baby in a good and godly home.

Let us be quick to accept with love and forgiveness the unwed mother and encourage her to bring that baby to full term so it can be placed in a deserving home and fulfill the prayers of an anxious parent. Or, if the single mother elects to keep the baby, let's encourage her in every way we can to strengthen her in her choice.

How absurd that some should suggest the fact the mother doesn't want the child as ample justification for abortion. The truth is, there are very few "unwanted children." Even though the biological mother may not want the child, there are literally thousands of empty homes waiting to extend loving care to that unborn baby.

Let us pray earnestly and anxiously for God's direction as we seek to affect the serious issue of abortion and preserve the sanctity of life for all persons, both born and unborn.

Abortion: The Slaughter Of The Innocents

John MacArthur, Jr.

TEXT: Psalm 1139:13-16, NASB

SUPPLEMENTAL VERSES: Genesis 20:18; 16:2; 17:6; 21:2, 25:21, Isaiah 43:7; 44:1; 45:9-10; 49:5, Job 10:8-12; 31:15; 33:4, Psalms 22:9-10; 100:3; 104:30; 127:3, 1 Samuel 1:5-20, Ruth 4:13, Judges 13:3, Jeremiah 1:5, Galations 1:15, Luke 1:41, Matthew 1:20-21, Exodus 4:11, Ecclesiastes 11:5

SUMMARY OF MESSAGE: John MacArthur's "Abortion: The Slaughter of the Innocents" is a comprehensive look at the abortion issue from the viewpoint that abortion is a blow against God's sovereignty.

MacArthur begins by giving statistics and explaining procedures of today's abortion industry, showing how confusing and contradictory the abortion advocates' arguments and current abortion laws are. He then traces the history of abortion from the beginning of time until now, showing that Satan has always been the instigator of murder. Finally, he uses Scripture from Genesis to Galatians to teach what God's Word says about abortion, showing that abortion destroys God's creative work and perfect plan.

PREACHING TRACKS:

➤TRACK ONE: Preach the entire sermon.

➤TRACK TWO: Preach the points on the outline that best apply to your congregation. I contains information about today's abortion industry that is not publicized in the media. It is important for people to know what is happening, but because I.C and D are somewhat graphic, you may want to adapt them to your audience. II.A and C and III.B,C and D look at abortion from historical and biblical perspectives.

➤TRACK THREE: Preach a combination of points in this sermon and in other sermons in this book.

ABORTION: THE SLAUGHTER OF THE INNOCENTS

John MacArthur, Jr.

The problem of abortion is primarily defined as a blow struck against the sovereignty of God. It is a direct and overt attack on God. We will see how and why as we look together to this subject and to Scripture.

I. THE HORROR OF ABORTION

If you have read newspapers, magazines, or been alerted to the media in any way over the last few years, you have become increasingly aware that America presently is highly committed by law and by practice to mass murder. We have made that formal commitment, and we are carrying out the execution of that commitment on a wholesale fashion. It's really a very stark transition from the America of history, a nation known for freedom and liberty and privilege and rights. A nation where justice was the protector of the people and which always seemed to pride itself on its humanitarianism, its concern for the poor and the needy, the weak and the defenseless. And yet, it is in this very nation that has stood in the world as the symbol of freedom and right and privilege that mass murder has been taking place for many years.

In some metropolitan hospitals in our nation, abortions outnumber live births. And though I'm always amazed, America has an ability to justify what it's doing and condemn everybody else. Often the same liberal element piously condemning activities in Africa are eagerly leading the parade to massacre babies in our own nation. There are tremendous inconsistencies in such thinking.

The Upjohn Pharmaceutical Company is in the process now of developing a pill that will enable women to abort babies at home so they won't need clinics or hospitals. Planned Parenthood, the originator of the population-control mentality in our country, had a meeting of what they called "The Planned Parenthood Physicians Association." One of their seminar leaders was a Dr. Willard Cates. He presented a paper entitled, "Abortion As Treatment For Unwanted pregnancy—The Number Two Sexually-Transmitted Disease."

What Dr. Cates is saying is that pregnancy is a disease, the number two sexually-transmitted disease next to venereal disease. By his definition, children conceived are simply symptoms of a disease that needs to be eliminated. Planned Parenthood, by the way, has over 700 abortion clinics doing about 60,000 recorded murders a year. They receive millions of dollars a year from the United States government as well as support from the United Way and a lot of other public agencies that funnel funds to them.

One abortionist suggested that abortionists charge according to the length of the foot of the aborted baby.

In Mount Sinai Hospital in New York City, there was a situation where a woman was carrying twins. It was determined through medical examination that one of them was likely afflicted by Down's syndrome and the parents did not want a Down's syndrome baby. So a process known as "cardiac puncture" was used to kill one baby while keeping the other one alive. The heart of that baby was punctured with a needle and all of its blood extracted and in its place some poison added.

When babies do live, there are all kinds of unimaginable consequences. One that never ceases to amaze me is Revenue Rule Number 73-156 of the IRS. That rule says that should you be having an abortion but the baby comes out alive, you can count it as a tax deduction as a dependent. It's a non-person if it's dead; it's a person if it's alive. That is the stupidity of humanism.

I was amazed to read about a woman in Van Nuys, California, who didn't want her family to know that she was illegitimately pregnant. She went into a bathroom to give birth to her child. She was unsuccessful drowning it, so she cut it up with a razor blade. It was determined she should spend a minimum – if convicted – of 11 years in prison, which is an interesting sort of conundrum. If she had gone to an abortionist, she wouldn't have had any penalty at all. Because she tried to kill the baby herself, she's going to be sentenced to 11 years. It won't be considered murder, but rather a sort of "semi-murder" because nobody knows what to do in the hopeless chaos of this dilemma.

The best term I can think of as a parallel term for abortion is "convenience killing." That is basically what it is. It is killing because it is convenient. In fact, 15-year-olds can get abortions without parental knowledge or parental consent. The assumption of the abortion advocate is that parents are enemies of their own children and might try to stop them from having an abortion. Spousal consent, that is the consent of a husband to a wife's abortion, is also unconstitutional. The confusion is unbelievable.

When you talk about what happens to the aborted child, that opens a whole area of unbelievable situations. For example, dead fetuses are used in all manner of experiments and so are live ones. I've been reading over the last couple of months about this and it's a horrifying thing. I cannot imagine anything in human history worse than what is being done both to the living and the dead as a result of the abortive process.

In 1981, according to the *Journal of Clinical Pathology,* fetal organs were being grafted into mice and rats to see how long they could be kept alive. Squibb Company was involved in paying tens of thousands of dollars to Ob/Gyn doctors (Obstetrics and Gynecology), to experiment with fetuses for use in research on high-blood pressure drugs. The U.S. government has funded experiments on live aborted babies purchased from certain hospitals. The *New England Journal of Medicine,* (probably one of the most prestigious medical journals in the world) reports that tissue cultures are obtained by dropping babies who have been aborted into sort of a meat grinder to culture their tissues.

I want you to understand where we are! Dr. J. Dominguez of New York City writes, "On any Monday, you can see 70 garbage bags with fetal material in them along the sidewalks of abortion clinics in New York City." The *New England Journal of Medicine* carried an article by Dr. Raymond Duff and professor A.G.M. Campbell of Yale University. They acknowledged that over a 21-year period, at least 14 percent of all the babies who died at the Yale Hospital did so through the discretionary choice of the physicians.

It is now possible to do to a baby what you couldn't get away with doing to a dog or a cat. It's a strange and bizarre situation. The same people who seem to be screaming "save the whales" are also in the parade yelling "kill the babies."

I was amazed to read about a case in California called "Curlander vs. Bio-science Labs." It is now possible because of that case for children to sue their parents for wrongful life, for letting them live rather than aborting them. In other words, if you are handicapped or deformed or if life isn't all that you think it ought to be for you, there is at least a precedent for you to sue your parents for wrongful life. That was in the newsletter of the American College of Obstetrics and Gynecology.

The stupidity of all of this is demonstrated further by something that happened in Maryland. A wounded American eagle was found and rushed to emergency treatment. The treatment was too late and the eagle died. A $5,000 reward was offered for the arrest of the eagle killer.

In New England, it's illegal to ship pregnant lobsters regardless of which trimester of pregnancy they are in. There's a $1,000 fine for shipping a pregnant lobster because it might do damage to the unborn lobster.

Massachusetts has a law called "The Anti-Cruelty Law." It is illegal to award goldfish as prizes in games of chance. Why? "To protect the tendency to dull humanitarian feelings and corrupt the morals of those who abuse them." Save the goldfish because if we don't, we might be corrupting morals and dulling humanitarian feelings.

You say, "Why is all of this going on?" For one thing, abortion is a one-billion-dollar-a-year business. Abortion is a money maker! Big business! Not only do they get income from the person whose baby is aborted, but also for the sale of the fetal material—the placenta and all that's left, including the baby itself. We became aware here at Grace Church of a particular organization known as "BypMed" having to do with medical by-products. They collect and resell fetal material for about $1.40 a pound. There is evidence that babies have been sold by the bag, $25 a bag. The sale of late-term elected abortions at Washington D.C.'s General Hospital over a ten-year period brought in more than $68,000 which was used to decorate a lounge for visiting professors.

Collagen is the gelatinous substance found in connective tissues, bones and cartilage. Unless your beauty product specifies animal collagen, it could be human, obtained from aborted fetuses. There is triple profit to be had. The first is from the abortion, estimated at half billion dollars a year by *Fortune* magazine. The second comes from the sale of the aborted babies' bodies. And the third profit is from the unsuspecting customer buying cosmetics that contain collagen from babies.

In Japan, since about 1955, there has been an excess of 50 million recorded abortions. The fallout is frightening. There are now in Japan certain Buddhist temples that have been built for the express purpose of memorializing what they call "water babies." (Water babies are unborn infants that are aborted.)

Because of the trauma to the mother and the mother's need to get some resolution as to what happens to that infant that's been aborted, these Buddhist temples have arisen in which a mother – for a price of somewhere between $340 and $640 – can purchase a small stone Buddha as a memorial to her water baby. In just one of those temples in Japan, there are at least 10,000 such little stone Buddhas. Grieving mothers traumatized by the haunting reality they have killed a baby may go back to the temple where the Buddhist priest will, for a fee, offer prayers for the water babies. Religion in Japan is trying to come to the aid of traumatized women.

Psychologists tells us that the suicide rate of women who have had abortions is between 400 and 800 percent higher than the normal female population. There is evidence that hypochondria, depression, withdrawal, guilt, shame, diminished self-esteem, drug and alcohol dependency, and serious psychosis result from abortions.

II. THE HISTORY OF ABORTION

The question comes, "How did this get started? Where did it all begin?" In John 8:44, Jesus said, "You are of your father, the devil. And the lusts of your father you will do. He was a murderer from the beginning."

Where does all of this murder of infants come from? It comes from the devil, Satan. It is a supernatural Satanic conspiracy. It is a reflection of the prince of this world, the god of this age, the spirit that now rules in the hearts of fallen men. It is Satanic. And

Satan has always been a murderer.

Satan has ever been a mass murderer. You can read the history of Canaanitish civilization and find horrific accounts of the Canaanites massacring their babies, burying live babies in walls of new buildings, and offering their born children as sacrifices over the fire to the god Molech.

Satan has always been a murderer and he has always been a murderer of children. He tried in the time of Moses to destroy the Messianic line in the massacre of all of the babies that Pharoah ordered killed. He tried again in the massacre that was carried out by Herod at the birth of Christ. It is God who gives life and Satan is the one who desires to take life. Satan was a murderer from the very beginning and he fosters murderous intent among men in order that he might kill what God has made.

The Jewish Talmud has statements by rabbis throughout ancient history that abortion is murder and has no place in the society of the people of God. Here is one example: "Thou shalt not abort a child." Abortion is nothing new.

Aristotle and Plato both advocated abortion as a way to control large families and stop population development. The Greco-Roman pagan world was busily engaged in abortions even at the time of Christ. I was interested to read the reasons pagans gave for abortion. One was to conceal illicit sex. (Nothing new about that.) Number two, rich women who were illegitimately impregnated in their love affairs with low-class common men did not want to give birth to low-class common children and then have to waste their fortune on them.

The Greco-Roman pagans also said that abortion was convenient because "it allowed a woman to preserve her sex appeal so that she would not be troubling her womb with bouncing babies" (a quote from an ancient source). Abortion was a contraception to conceal illicit sex, to prevent unwanted children, and to preserve one's figure, just as it is today. Nothing new, it's still convenience killing.

I was also fascinated and horrified to read how abortions were done in those days. We sometimes think that ancient peoples were unsophisticated, but that's not the case. They had developed some very effective techniques in aborting babies.

There is a medical journal on gynecology written by a Greek named Soranus at the time of the early church. In it he gives all the procedures for how to go through the birth canal, how to mix the poisons, and how to use them.

They also had a process by which they would tie the woman's stomach tight with ropes so the fetus couldn't develop and eventually would be dead by strangulation. Once the child was large enough, they would try to locate its head and kill it that way.

The pagan world accepted this. The Jews, because of their view of God and His sovereignty and His creative power, upheld the sanctity of human life. They knew abortion was a sin, a horrendous crime of violent murder, and spoke out against it. There is no indication in any Jewish community of ancient times that they advocated abortion.

The church, along with the Jews, stood against abortion for basically the same reasons: that life is a creation of God, a child being cared for and preserved in the most protected place on earth—the womb. To violate that God-given protection and kill the child was considered the ultimate violent act. The early church believed it was an act of lovelessness and an act of murder.

The Didache, which is a codification of early church law, reads, "Thou shalt not murder a child by abortion." In the Epistle of Barnabas (written years after the New Testament), abortion was rejected by the church because it was the opposite of loving your neighbor, for that little one was seen as a neighbor, someone to care for.

The Didache defined the way of life and the way of death very clearly. In defining the way of death, or damnation, the *Didache* said it is full of cursing, murders, adulteries, and the murders of children. Abortionists are called corruptors of God's creatures.

Satan has always wanted to destroy what God has made. The early church taught that abortion brought down the wrath and the judgment of God. "To follow Jesus," said the early church, "was to shed any thought of murder or violence to anyone, including the unborn."

I'm saying the problem isn't new and the church's position isn't new. It is frightening to me the vast number of churches that are pro-abortion or pro-choice. How in the world did abortion ever come to be so pervasive in our country?

It all started with a promotion of abortion as a matter of freedom. "This is a free country," they said. "Women ought to have their freedom." It came out of the new sex ethic "free fornication for everybody with whoever you want with no consequences." Free sex, free love, no consequence.

"So if we're going to have real sexual freedom," the argument goes, "we've got to get rid of the consequences," which are babies. It is the mentality of our society that free sex, free love, free lifestyle shouldn't have any consequences. However, God keeps saying, "But there are consequences."

Many of you will remember the thalidomide babies. As a result of this, English physicians began to advocate what is commonly called "eugenic abortion." That is, abortion because this child to be born is deformed and will cost society a lot of money and be a lot of trouble to everybody. So wipe out all of those deformed children, and you have a sort of post-genetic engineering. So the elimination of defective children became another pressure moving this nation toward wholesale legality of abortion.

Then came the rise of feminism and the cry was a little phrase, "total reproductive freedom." In other words, vile sex life with no consequence. The feminists said, "Women must have abortion as a backup to contraceptive failure."

Then came the ERA and feminists said, "We want on-demand abortion at taxpayers' expense. Women are not equal to men unless they are rid of childbearing responsibilities." Then along came population-control advocates, such as Planned Parenthood, saying, "If we keep having babies, we are all going to be sitting on top of each other. There won't be any food." Nobody ever bothered to say that the entire population of the world right now can squeeze into the state of Rhode Island.

But the final blow was struck by the Supreme Court of the United States, supposedly the most esteemed men and women in our nation. On January 22, 1973 in the Roe Vs. Wade decision they legalized abortion and the wholesale killing of babies. They violated the 14th amendment, which says no person shall be deprived of life without due process of law. They legalized murder.

The court ignored the issue of life. It ignored the issue of personhood, when life begins, when personhood begins. Criminals have been successfully prosecuted for killing an unborn child in an attack on a pregnant woman, but the child is considered a non-person if his or her own mother decides to kill it!

In other words, only the mother can choose to kill her baby. Only China has a more permissive abortion policy than the United States. It is a materialistic, selfish, atheistic ethic that is absolutely hostile to the sovereignty of God.

Now somebody will ask, "Are we sure that at conception a real life begins?" There's no question about it. Dr. Jerome Lejeune, professor of fundamental genetics at the University of Rene Deseartes in Paris, writes, "Life has a very long history, but each individual has a very neat beginning—the moment of its conception. The material link is the molecular thread of DNA. In each reproductive cell, this ribbon of DNA, roughly one meter long, is cut into 23 pieces, or chromosomes. As soon as the 23 paternally derived chromosomes are united through fertilization to the 23 maternal ones, the full genetic meeting necessary to express all the inborn qualities of the new individual is gathered and personal constitution takes place." That's at conception.

Further, he says, "At two months of age, the human being is less than one thumb length from the head to the rump. He would fit at ease in a nutshell, but everything is there—hands, feet, head, organs, brain. His heart has been beating for a month already. His fingerprints can be detected. His little heart is beating 150 to 170 beats a minute. To accept the fact that after fertilization has taken place a new human being has come into being is no longer a matter of taste or opinion."

III. WHAT THE BIBLE TEACHES ABOUT ABORTION

What does the Bible say? The first biblical principle you must understand relating to abortion is this: conception is an act of God.

135

God personally and individually creates every human life. Don't for one moment be under the delusion of the deist who saw God as a great power starting a process and then backing out of it. No, God sustains that process and is aggressive and active and sovereign in that process. It isn't that God made Adam and Eve, then Adam and Eve made everybody else. It is that God starts a procreative process and is active in that process, bringing into existence all those people whom He has foreordained to life. That is His sovereignty.

In Genesis 20:28, we read this statement, "The Lord had completely closed all the wombs of the house of Abimelech." In other words, the women were not having babies because the Lord had closed their wombs. God is in charge of who has babies.

In the 16th chapter of Genesis, Sarah says to her husband, "The Lord has restrained me from bearing," (v.2). They had confidence that life was a gift from God and everyone who was bearing children, was bearing because God energized it and anyone who was not, was not because God restrained it.

In I Samuel 1, Hannah is described in this way: "The Lord had shut up her womb. ...The Lord had shut up her womb" (vv. 5-6). (It's mentioned twice.)

Looking at it from the positive side, the Lord also opens the womb. In Genesis 17:16, God says to Abraham, "I will bless her," referring to Sarah, "and give thee a son also of her and she shall be the mother of nations." God says, "Not only am I going to open Sarah's womb, but as a result a large number of people constituting a nation will come alive."

In Genesis 21:2, the Bible says Sarah conceived and bore Abraham a son in his old age, at the set time of which the Lord had spoken to him. God is sovereign. God has foreordained who will live and when they will live. Life is in His hands.

In Genesis 25, Isaac prayed to God because his wife was barren. And the Lord heard his prayer and Rebecca conceived. Why? Because God answered prayer and gave her a child.

I mentioned a moment ago I Samuel 1, "The Lord had shut the womb of Hannah." After she pours out her heart, the Lord hears her prayer and in I Samuel 1:19-20 it says the Lord remembered her: "Therefore it came to pass after she had conceived that she bore a son and called his name Samuel (El being the name of God), saying, 'Because I have asked him of the Lord.' " She knew that her ability to conceive and bring forth a child was because of God's creative act.

And in that beautiful story of Ruth and Boaz, Ruth 4:13 says, "Boaz took Ruth and she was his wife. And when he went in unto her, the Lord gave her conception and she had a son."

And then there was Manoah and his wife in Judges 13, "And the angel of the Lord appeared to the wife of Manoah and said to her, Behold, now thou art barren and bearest not, but thou shalt conceive and bear a son." And God gave to Manoah's wife a son.

His name was Samson, a judge in Israel.

In Isaiah 43:7 the Lord looks at the whole of the nation of Israel and He says, "I have created him for My glory, I have formed him, yes, I have made him." God takes responsibility as the Creator for every Jew constituting the nation of Israel.

These passages tell us that God is the power behind conception. Every life begins because God has foreordained that life. I believe once life begins in the plan of God, that life is eternal. I also believe that by God's grace, when an infant is aborted, that infant lives forever in the presence of God in the fullness of what God intended in its original creation.

In Job 10:8, Job declares to God, "Thine hands have made me and fashioned me together round about, yet Thou dost destroy me." In other words, his paradox is, "How can You be letting all this evil come into my life when You're the one who made me? Did You make me to destroy me?"

Job discusses God as his maker in verse 9: "Remember, I beseech Thee that Thou hast made me as the clay and wilt Thou bring me into the dust again? Hast Thou not poured me out as milk and curdled me like cheese?" He is saying, "You've produced me: I'm the product of Your efforts." Verses 11-12: "You have clothed me with skin and flesh and have fenced me with bones and sinews, You have granted me life in favor and Your care has preserved my spirit."

In other words, "You made me body and spirit. You formed me. You made me." That's the testimony of Job, perhaps the most ancient book of all the Old Testament. That is a very early and accurate perception, that God is the Creator of all.

In Job 31, verse 15, Job again says, "Did not He who made me in the womb make him? And did not one fashion us in the womb?" In other words, God is the one who creates every person.

This is the key to answering all these questions like: What about a rape? What about the potential death of the mother? What about incest? What about deformity? The point is any creature created in a womb is created by God and therefore it is not up to the discretion of any human being as to its worthiness to live.

In Job 33 and verse 4, the book of Job approaches it from another view in the testimony of Elihu: "The Spirit of God hath made me and the breath of the Almighty hath given me life." He gives testimony to the fact that God is the Creator.

In Psalm 22, verse 9 David writes, "Thou art He who took me out of the womb. You made me hope upon my mother's breasts. I was cast upon Thee from the womb. Thou art my God from my mother's body." In other words, "God, You've been involved in my life since I was in my mother's womb, You are the One who planted me in her womb, You are the one who preserved me in her womb, You brought me out of her womb, and You placed me on her breasts."

How about Psalm 100:3? "Know ye that the Lord He is God,

it is He who hath made us and not we ourselves." Men don't make men, God makes men. He uses the human procreative process, but it is He who ordains life.

Psalm 104, verse 30 says, "Thou sendest forth Thy Spirit, they are created." Creation is a work of the Spirit of God.

There is an absolutely beautiful statement made in Psalm 127, verse 3: "Children are an heritage from the Lord and the fruit of the womb is His reward." Children come from the Lord. Children are not an accident. They are not an inconvenience. They are not symptoms of a venereal disease. Children are not a disruption. Children are a gift from God. He gives them life for His own holy purposes. Ecclesiastes 11, verse 5, "As thou knowest not what is the way of the wind," (You don't know how it works), "nor how the bones grow in the womb of her who is with child, so thou knowest not the works of God who makes all."

Isaiah 44, verse 1, says, "Yet now hear, O Jacob, My servant, in Israel whom I have chosen." He identifies the fact that He had chosen them to be His people. Then in verse 2 He says, "Thus saith the Lord that made thee and formed thee from the womb." Again God identifies Himself as the One who forms from the womb. Verse 24 says the same thing again: "Thus saith the Lord, Thy redeemer and He who formed thee from the womb, I am the Lord who makes all things."

Chapter 45, beginning in verse 9, "Woe to him that fights with his maker." When you abort a baby, you are fighting with God the Creator. And He says in verse 9, "Shall the clay say to him that fashioned it, What are you making?" In other words, "What right do you have to make that?" Do you have a right to question the Maker? Verse 10: "Woe to him that says to his father, 'Why did you beget?' Or the mother, 'What have you brought forth?' " In other words, "Who would ever think to question the One who gives birth? Who would strive with God?"

Isaiah 49:5 states, "And now saith the Lord who formed me from the womb to be His servant." Here Isaiah has the sense that he himself was formed in the womb by God. Jeremiah 1:5 is a good parallel to that: "Before I formed thee in the womb, I knew thee." Before he was conceived in the womb of his mother, God knew that Jeremiah was a person who would exist. The verse continues, "Before you came out of the womb, I set you apart and ordained you a prophet to the nations."

Now when you strike a blow against something that God has created, someone that God has created, you're striking a blow against the sovereign intended purpose of God.

The testimony of the Apostle Paul is similar. In Galatians 1:15 he says, "When it pleased God who separated me from my mother's womb and called me by His grace." Paul had the sense of being the work of God even from his mother's womb.

How about John the Baptist? An angel essentially said to his father, Zechariah, "Your wife is going to have a baby, and the child that is in her will be filled with the Holy Spirit even from the womb."

This was not some nameless non-personal blob in the womb of Elizabeth; it was John the Baptist, a prophet of God. Similarly there was no nameless blob in the womb of the mother of Jeremiah; it was a prophet of God. There was not a nameless appendage to the body of the mother of Isaiah; it was a prophet of God.

In fact, in Luke chapter 1 when Mary came to Elizabeth, John "leaped for joy" while still in his mother's womb. Elizabeth even said to Mary that she would be the mother of the Lord. When Mary conceived through the Holy Spirit, she had in her not some appendage, but the incarnate Son of God. The incarnation did not begin in Bethlehem. It began at conception, for Jesus was fully human even as an unborn infant, from conception to death. When an angel came and announced to Joseph that his wife was pregnant, he went on to explain that "that which is in her is of the Holy Spirit and she shall bring forth a son and you shall call His name Jesus, for He shall save His people from their sins" (Matthew 1:20). He wasn't describing some non-descript blob, some non-personal appendage, some potential life, but the very Son of God, as yet unborn, but a person.

Does this mean that even if a baby is deformed, even if it's crippled or even if it's defective, it's still the work of God? Listen to Exodus 4:11, "Who maketh the dumb, or deaf, or the seeing, or the blind? Have not I, the Lord?" Yes, the Lord made all! Some of the most handicapped people in the world are not handicapped physically, but are handicapped mentally and emotionally. I can't think of any more handicapped people than abortionists! To say that because a person has a physical disability he or she is less than a creature of God is ludicrous. That's not God's purpose.

Dear people, I ask you to stand with me in this fight for life. We simply cannot let this holocaust called abortion go on and not lift our voices in protest. We must speak for those who cannot speak for themselves. We must stand up for these little ones who cannot stand up for themselves!

God bless you as take your stand.

Jesus Christ: The Alternative to Abortion

J. Greg Martin

TEXT: Ephesians 2:1-10, KJV

SUPPLEMENTAL VERSES: Genesis 1:17, Psalm 139:13-16, 1 John 1:5, Revelation 22:15

SUMMARY OF MESSAGE: Greg Martin's "Jesus Christ: The Alternative to Abortion" shows how Jesus Christ brings light, life and liberty to the darkness, death and damnation of abortion. Martin boldly confronts pro-choice advocates, calling abortion what it is: murder of God-ordained, God-created life. At the same time, he calls those who have experienced abortion and have supported it to now experience the grace of God and the forgiveness of Jesus Christ.

Martin also explains what Roe vs. Wade and later Supreme Court decisions allow concerning abortion.

PREACHING TRACKS:

➤ TRACK ONE: Preach the entire sermon.

➤ TRACK TWO: Preach the points on the outline that best apply to your congregation. II.A contains interesting facts about the developing fetus. III is a comprehensive general overview of the current national abortion laws. Martin's theme of light, life and liberty through Jesus Christ can be used to present a compassionate answer to abortion.

➤ TRACK THREE: Preach a combination of points from this and other sermons in this book.

JESUS CHRIST: THE ALTERNATIVE TO ABORTION

Ephesians 2:1-10

J. Greg Martin

W e will have to search long and hard to find a more controversial, emotional and divisive issue than abortion. It seems as though everyone has an opinion on the subject. Our nation is divided. Family members have varying views. It is as though the consensus is there is no consensus.

This dilemma is even realized in the Christian Church. Not all who name the name of Christ value every human life as sacred. In a 1987 survey of 10,000 women by the Alan Guttmacher Institute, it was discovered that one of every six women having an abortion that year identified herself as "born again" or "evangelical."

This raises the question: What does the Bible say about human life? What about abortion in the context of the Church? Does God have any word on the subject? Notice three Biblical statements concerning the sanctity of human life.

I. Advocates of Abortion Are In Darkness, But Jesus Is the Light

People who protest for the right to terminate a fetus are in darkness. They are blinded to truth.

A. Blinded To Truth In the Womb

Many who are pro-choice or pro-death focus on the legal right to abort. They point to the issue of privacy, but fail to grant the same right to privacy for the developing fetus. They do not focus on the divine development going on inside the womb.

Did you know that immediately upon fertilization, cellular development begins and the sex of the baby is determined? By 17 days, the fetus has developed his or her own blood cells. On the 18th day the heart muscle begins to pulsate. At 19 days the eyes start to develop. By six weeks the skeletal system is completed. At eight weeks the brain patterns are discernable. Some fetuses have lived outside the womb at twenty weeks.

Many who advocate abortion turn a deaf ear and a blind eye to the facts about the development of the fetus in the womb. They are in darkness.

141

B. Blinded To The Truth In the Word.

God's Word affirms from Genesis 1 through Revelation 22 that all human life is sacred. Listen to Genesis 1:27: *"So God created man in his own image, in the image of God created he him; male and female created he them."*

Psalm 139:13-16; "For thou hast possessed my reins: thou hast covered me in my mother's womb. I will praise thee; for I am fearfully and wonderfully made; marvelous are thy works, and that my soul knoweth right well. My substance was not hid from thee, when I was made in secret, and curiously wrought in the lowest parts of the earth. Thine eyes did see my substance, yet being unperfect; and in thy book all my members were written, which in continuance were fashioned, when as yet there was none of them."

People who advocate abortions are in darkness. They are blinded to the truth in God's Word.

We are not to cast stones at them or any other blinded individual. We are to have pity on them. We, as God's people, are to lift up a standard of righteousness. We, as the body of Christ, are to show our world of darkness that Jesus, the Light of the world, values every human life. We are to demonstrate that Jesus is the Creator and Sustainer of every human life.

If you want to know what God thinks about abortion, look to Jesus. I John reminds us that in Him there is no darkness. Not on the issue of abortion, eternal life or any other subject is there any darkness in Him. A relationship with Him will lead the blind into the light.

II. Abortion Is Death But Jesus Is Life

Those who advocate abortion tell us that an abortion is little more than having your wisdom teeth removed or your gall bladder extracted. However, the truth is that abortion is death for a developing human being.

A medical professor in an esteemed university asked his students for their suggestions for a lady who found herself pregnant. Her husband was an alcoholic with syphilis. She had one child born dead, another born blind, and a third born quite ill. She was past her prime child-bearing years in life. With those facts in mind the professor asked his medical students for their suggestions. Without fail each recommended an abortion. The professor remarked, "Congratulations class, you just killed Ludwig Von Beethoven."

Although many do not understand abortion in terms of life and death, the Bible makes clear that life begins in the womb. To take that life is nothing short of murder.

It is a sad day when our nation puts more value on the fetuses of animals than humans. If you don't believe that is true just ask Richard Cox of Illinois. In 1985 he was fined $250 for killing a whitetailed doe out of season. He was fined an additional $125 for each of the two fetuses found within the slain animal's womb. Something is wrong when we acknowledge that a deer's fetus is more valuable than a human's. Something is wrong when the termination of a deer's fetus is seen as death and the termination of a human fetus is permissible.

As of January 22, 1990, abortion had taken the lives of at least 28 million American babies since it was legalized in 1973. Worldwide over 60 million abortions are performed every year. Except for biopsies, abortion is now the most common surgery performed in America. Today one third of all American pregnancies are terminated in death. As I look at young people who are 19 years old or less, I realize that for every two who are alive, one is in a mysterious grave forgotten by humanity. Death is a terrible reality for the victims of the abortion industry.

What is most alarming is that many people do not realize abortions can be performed up until the moment of birth. In 1973 the Supreme Court ruled:

➤ that human offspring are not persons "in the whole sense" at *any time* before birth.

➤ that during the first three months of pregnancy, a state may make no laws regulating abortion, except perhaps, if they wish to provide that abortions must be done by licensed physicians.

➤ that after three months and until "viability" (which is not precisely defined but was referred to as being approximately six to six-and-one-half months), states could make only abortion laws aimed at safe-guarding the health of the mother (for example, that abortions be performed in hospitals, etc.).

➤ that from viability until the end of pregnancy, states cannot prevent an abortion if it is performed "to preserve the life or health of the mother."

The Court defined "health" to include "all factors – physical, emotional, psychological, familial and the woman's age – relevant to the well-being of the patient." THUS, ABORTION IS AVAILABLE FOR ANY EMOTIONAL OR CONVENIENT REASON, EVEN DURING THE LAST STAGE OF PREGNANCY.

On July 1, 1976, the Supreme Court extended its original decision and ruled that:

➤ abortions may be performed on minor daughters without the knowledge of their parents.

➤ women (whether married or unmarried) may obtain abortions without the knowledge or consent of the baby's father.

THE SUPREME COURT HAS GIVEN AMERICA ABORTION ON DEMAND UNTIL BIRTH.

Abortion is death, but our dear Savior is the giver and sustainer of life. He gives physical life. He gives eternal abundant life. For this reason you ought to choose Jesus. Choose Him to have light and life over darkness and death.

III. Abortion Is Damnation, But Jesus Is Liberty

Abortionists, promoters of abortions, and people who pay for abortion have an awful future before them. Revelation 22:14-15, discussing those who will forfeit heaven, says that among those who will go to hell are murderers. That is what abortion is. It is murder. I would be less than honest with you if I told you anything different.

However, I want to say that there is forgiveness from all sin through Jesus Christ, even the sin of abortion. Our text in Ephesians says that outside Christ we were all once under judgment and in darkness. Ephesians 2 teaches that God's grace is sufficient to forgive any sin.

If you don't believe that then I challenge you to go to Michigan and introduce yourself to Lorijo Nerad. She has served as the president of WEBA (Women Exploited by Abortion). She is now a born again Christian.

Before she became a Christian and found God's grace, she found herself pregnant soon after delivering her second child. She was eighteen years old. Her husband talked her into it and Planned Parenthood set up the abortion. Two weeks after the abortion, to her surprise, she found a baby's head in her toilet. Lorijo Nerad felt guilt and depression and regret for what she had done. Her doctor passed it off as normal. But Nerad couldn't escape her guilt, depression, and nightmares.

Then, three years later she found God's grace to forgive her of her sin. God's grace was sufficient to set her at liberty from the nightmares, pain, and guilt that followed her abortion.

IV. Conclusion

God's grace is just as sufficient today. We are not here to condemn anyone who has had an abortion, or who has encouraged someone to kill their child. We are here to rebuke you but not to shame you. We are here to tell you that in Jesus there is grace to cover all sins. We are here to tell you He is Light... Life... Liberty.

Come, welcome His grace.

Abortion: The American Holocaust

David Miller

TEXT: Jeremiah 9:1, 17-19, 21, KJV

SUPPLEMENTAL VERSES: Jeremiah 1:5

SUMMARY OF MESSAGE: David Miller's "Abortion: The American Holocaust" focuses on the magnitude of the abortion problem, on the illogical arguments of the pro-abortionists, and on the cowardliness and ungodliness of those who refuse to speak out against abortion.

Miller uses his own life experience of being disabled to defend the rights of all fetuses, including those with impairments, to live.

PREACHING TRACKS:

➤ TRACK ONE: Preach the entire sermon.

➤ TRACK TWO: Preach the points on the outline that best apply to your congregation. III refutes the arguments of pro-abortionists. IV explains that a person's compromise and complacency concerning abortion indirectly make them partially guilty for the blood that's being shed.

➤ TRACK THREE: Preach a combination of points in this and in other sermons in the book.

ABORTION: THE AMERICAN HOLOCAUST

*1Oh that my head were waters, and mine eyes a fountain of
tears, that I might weep day and night for the slain of the
daughter of my people! 17-19aThus saith the Lord of hosts,
Consider ye, and call for the mourning women, that they may
come; and send for cunning women, that they may come: And let
them make haste, and take up a wailing for us, that our eyes
may run down with tears, and our eyelids gush out with waters.
For a voice of wailing is heard out of Zion, How are we spoiled!
21For death is come up into our windows, and is entered into
our palaces, to cut off the children from without...*
Jeremiah 9:1, 17-19a, 21

David Miller

The saddest, darkest day in the history of American civilization
was January 22, 1973 when nine Supreme Court Justices,
appropriately dressed in black robes, instead of interpreting the
Constitution, decreed that it was now legal for a woman to have
her unborn baby put to death. Only three requirements were
made: (1) The baby must still be alive in the mother's womb; (2)
The mother must want to have the baby killed; (3) There must be
a doctor who is willing to kill the baby.

I. THE MAGNITUDE OF THE PROBLEM

As a result of that infamous Roe vs Wade decision in 1973,
one and one-half million babies are aborted annually in this
democracy. Yet, they die without benefit of counsel or trials! Four
thousand babies die every day at the hands of godless doctors in
this nation.

A woman in America may have her unborn child put to death
at any time during the entire nine months of pregnancy – even
while she is in labor! In New York City alone, over 4,000 last
trimester babies are aborted annually. Most of these babies could
have survived outside the womb!

In Arkansas, in 1986, 6,236 babies were killed in abortion
chambers. Today, in the Land of Opportunity, a teenage girl can
receive contraceptives and be educated regarding "safe sex" at a
school based health clinic. If she becomes pregnant, she can
receive an abortion at a Planned Parenthood Clinic. Furthermore,
she can do all of this without her parents consent! Yet, school
administrators will not allow that same teenage girl to be given
an aspirin without her parents knowledge and consent!

147

In my opinion, this is awful, atrocious, and an abomination. It is bad, brutal, and barbaric! Abortion is cruel, carnal, and crazy. It is depraved, demoralizing, and demonic! It is meanness, madness, and murder. Abortion is sick, sorry, and satanic!

In my opinion, abortion is the greatest problem facing America. It is worse than Aids, adultery, and alcoholism! It is worse than cancer, cigarettes, and cocaine. Abortion is worse than iniquity, incest and insanity! It is worse than pot, pornography and prostitution! Abortion is the worst kind of vice, violence and vandalism! It is the worst kind of wretchedness, wickedness and war!

One cannot be excessive in articulating the horrows of abortion. The English language is inadequate to properly describe the magnitude of the problem. It is America's holocaust!

II. THE MENTALITY OF THE PRO-ABORTIONIST

Illogical, ill-conceived, lacking basic intelligence and bordering on insanity – such are the arguments of the pro-abortionists. Let me share with you four of their common arguments in favor of abortion.

A. The woman should have the right to decide what happens with her own body

This sounds very noble on the surface, but I have some news for the pro-abortionist – we are not dealing with just the woman's body. We are dealing with another human life who just happens to be a guest in her womb. A woman has no more right to kill a baby who is a guest in her womb than she would to kill a baby who is a guest in her home. Isn't it frightening that the most dangerous place in the world for a baby to be is inside its mother's womb!

B. We don't know when human life and personhood begins. We are not aborting a baby, it's only a fetus - a glob of protoplasm

I will begin my response by affirming that human life begins at conception. In the Bible no distinction is made between pre-natal and post-natal life. (Jeremiah 1:5) For the sake of the argument, let's *suppose* for a moment that we really do not know for certain when human life begins. Wouldn't common sense tell us to wait until we were positive about the beginning of human life before we abort millions of fetuses that just might in fact be living human beings?

I am a deer hunter. Because of my physical handicap. I have engineered a portable, freestanding, automated, elevator deer stand that lifts me up ten feet in the air. I flip a switch and my seat turns completely around right or left. I wonder what the pro-abortionists would think of me if I were to go to my stand before daylight and just as it begins to dawn, I see some movement in the bushes and, not being able to tell for sure what it was, I open fire only to discover that I had killed another hunter who was slipping through the woods? A deer hunter is required by law to exercise certain precautions – not the least of which is knowing for certain what he is shooting at! Should not the pro-abortionist doctor do the same regarding a human life?

C. What about rape and incest?

Shouldn't a woman have the right to an abortion in such cases?

I want to say up front that rape is an unspeakably terrible crime against women. It invokes our deepest compassion for its victims and arouses our greatest indignation against the perpetrators. The pro-abortionists are very much aware that abortion for rape victims is a highly emotionally charged issue for all of us. Consequently, they use abortion for rape victims as their big gun for keeping abortion legal in this country.

I believe Christians should know the bare bones facts about abortion and rape victims. In the first place, only 3-5 percent of all rape victims conceive a child. Hardly any would conceive if they sought medical treatment immediately after the rape. The Minneapolis-St. Paul hospital did a ten year survey of 3,500 rape victims who sought treatment immediately and not one of them conceived! Today only one-tenth of one percent of all abortions are performed on babies conceived from rape or incest. This translates into only one in one thousand! This means that for every one thousand abortions performed in America, nine hundred ninety-nine of them are for convenience sake!

D. What if the fetus is severely physically deformed and mentally deficient? Wouldn't it be better to abort them?

Forgive my sarcasm at this point, but I get unusually nervous around these kind of folks. You see, I was a deformed fetus! I'm glad my mother did not go to a Planned Parenthood clinic for pre-natal counseling when I was a guest in her womb. I have not been able to run the Boston marathon, but I have enjoyed abundant life for 42 years! I am also excited about my next 42 years. I have not enjoyed being physically handicapped, but the pro-abortionists' alternative does not excite me at all! (David Miller suffers from muscular atrophy and is confined to a wheel chair. Ed.)

III. THE MADNESS OF THE PARTICIPANTS

The women who have abortions and the men who fathered the children and encourage the abortions are guilty of the worst kind of madness. Obviously, the doctors who perform the abortions are also guilty. For many of these doctors, abortion is a very lucrative business.

Moving beyond the obvious, I want to mention three groups of participants in abortion.

A. Conspiring Politicians

Abortion is the greatest moral issue of our day, but it is a political "hot-potato." Few politicians have the character, convictions, and courage required to speak out against abortion. To do so could mean the demise of their political careers. Therefore, the most politically wise thing to do is to avoid making any strong stand either way. Engaging in political double talk seems the easiest way out for many political leaders. For example, in October of 1988, then Governor Bill Clinton visited in Heber Springs during the parade. A young girl approached him on the sidewalk and asked, "Governor Clinton, do you believe in abortion?" Clinton's asinine reply was, "Honey, no one believes in abortion." The wise retort of the girl was this, "Governor Clinton, if no one believes in abortion, then why do we have so many of them!" Even this child could see through the hypocritical rhetoric of conspiring politicians! I personally would rather my voting hand be cut off up to my elbow than to vote for a politician on any level who did not have strong anti-abortion and pro-life positions.

B. Compromising Preachers

Those of you who know the history of this democracy know that there was a time when in every city, village and crossroads pulpits were aflame with God-anointed preaching which shaped the moral and ethical standards of our nation. Alas, those days are gone. While America is killing 4,000 babies per day, most of the pulpits are silent! It is not true in every case. Thank God there are still some preachers who call sin by its name and call sinners to repentance. However, preachers today lack either the conviction or the courage to speak out against abortion and consequently they compromise their calling. By their compromise, they become indirect participants in the meanness of abortion!

C. Complacent People

It is not my problem. It does not affect me. There's nothing I can" do – it's out of my control." These are the statements of uninformed and complacent people – folks who don't want to know and don't want to be bothered. These people are as much to blame for this holocaust as the pro-abortionists. All that is required for evil to triumph is for good men to do nothing! This has happened regarding abortion. What can be done? We can pray until our "eyes run down with tears and our eyelids gush out with waters." We can call for the "mourning women" and the "cunning women." These are people who have the heart and the head to address the problem. We can contact our elected officials and urge them to pass pro-life legislation. We can picket abortion clinics. We can start crisis pregnancy clinics and homes for unwed mothers. There is much that we can do. God help us to do it!

Innocent Blood

Adrian Rogers

TEXT: Proverbs 6:16-19, KJV

SUPPLEMENTAL VERSES:Proverbs 24:11-12, Psalm 139:13-17, Jeremiah 1:5, Luke 1:41, Matthew 7:12, Romans 1:31, Isaiah 58:1; 5:20, 2 Chronicles 7:14

SUMMARY OF MESSAGE: Adrian Rogers' "Innocent Blood" used both Old and New Testament Scriptures to explain that abortion destroys God's creation, Violates God-given principles and instincts and causes society to become callous to other kinds of murder such as euthanasia. He explains why the argument that the mother has the right to choose is unbiblical, illogical and unfounded.
He brings up other questions and exccuses pro-choice advocates use in their arguments for abortion and answers them with Scripture, illustrations and common sense. Rogers then tells what Christians should do to help stop the killing

PREACHING TRACKS:

➤TRACK ONE: Preach the entire sermon.

➤TRACK TWO: Preach the points on the outline that best apply to your congregation. IV explains why abortion is wrong from a biblical perspective. V answers arguments from proabortion advocates. VI offers some ways Christians can get involved. Add your own illustrations and Scriptures

➤TRACK THREE: Preach a combination of points in this sermon and in other sermons in this book.

INNOCENT BLOOD

Proverbs 6:16 & 24:11-12

Adrian Rogers

I speak to you today on the tragic, horrendous, pathetic, grisly abortion business. Hands that shed innocent blood. Here's the diary of a little girl.

October 5: Dear diary, today my life began. My parents do not know it yet. I am so small, I'm as small as the pollen of a flower, but it is I already. I will be a girl. I will have blonde hair and blue eyes. Nearly everything is settled already even that I shall love flowers.

October 19: I've grown a little, but I'm still too small to do anything by myself. My mother does almost everything for me. Though she still does not know she is carrying me under her heart. She does not know that she is already helping me and that she is even feeding me with her own blood. She is so good, but is it true that I am not yet a real person? That only my mother exists? I am a real person just as a small crumb of bread is still real bread, my mother is and I am.

October 23: My mouth is just now beginning to open. Just think, in a year or two I'll be laughing and I will start to talk. My first word will be "mama."

October 25: Today my heart began to beat! It will beat softly for the rest of my life, never stopping. After many years it will tire, then it will stop and I shall die.

November 2: I'm growing continually. My arms and legs are taking shape, but I must wait a long time before those tiny legs will raise me to my mother's arms, and before those little arms will be able to conquer the earth, and befriend people.

November 12: My fingers are beginning to form on my hand. How small they are. One day I will stroke my mother's hair with them. I shall take her hair in my mouth and she'll say, "Oh nasty!"

November 20: Only today that doctor told my mother that I am living here under her heart. How happy she must be. "Are you happy, mother?"

November 25: My mother and father are probably thinking about a name for me. They don't even know that I am a little girl, so they're probably calling me Andy. But I want to be called Barbara. I am growing so big.

December 10: My hair is growing. It is as bright and shiny as the sun. I wonder what kind of hair my mother has.

December 12: I'm almost able to see though it's night all around me. When mother brings me into the world it will be full of sunshine and overflowing with flowers. I've never seen a flower, you know. But more than anything, I want to see my mother! How do you look, mom?

December 24: I wonder if my mother hears the delicate beat of my heart. Some children are born with sickly hearts, and then the gentle finger of the doctor performs miracles to make them healthy. But my heart is healthy. It beats so evenly, tap, tap, tap. "You shall have a healthy little daughter, mom!"

December 28: Today my mother killed me.

A diary of a preborn child.

Today and every day in the United States of America, four thousand innocent babies will be slain. Today and every day in so-called "God Blessed America" these little babies will not have a chance to have a trial to see whether they should have capital punishment performed upon them. There will be no jury. They will not have a counselor or lawyer to argue their case. They will be executed in a cruel and inhumane way. You may watch your watch and every twenty seconds one will be killed; a precious little baby.

I. Who Is Responsible for Abortions?

Who are the conspirators in this atrocity? How did this thing come to pass? Who do we look to; to whom do we point a finger? First of all, to the Supreme Court, the judges. Secondly, governmental social planners, intellectuals, eggheads. Thirdly, physicians, doctors. Fourthly, owners of abortion clinics. Fifthly, willing mothers and willing fathers.

About one and one-half million precious babies will have their lives snuffed out in America this year. Herod, go to the back row. Pharoah, you've been outdone. One and one-half million lives in so-called "God Blessed America." How did it come to pass?

January 22, 1973. Nine men robed in black issued a decree that it is now legal to kill a baby. Only three requirements: (1) the baby still lives inside its mother's body, (2) the mother wants the baby killed, and (3) a doctor is willing to do the killing. Those are the three requirements to legally kill a baby. The baby lives inside the mother, the mother wants the baby killed, and a doctor is willing to do the killing.

Did you know that in the United States of America it is now legal to take the life of a baby even while the mother is in labor? In these so-called "God blessed" states of ours.

Here's what the Supreme Court said in Roe vs. Wade, January

22, 1973: "A state is forbidden to proscribe." The word proscribe means to forbid abortion at any time prior to birth. At any time prior to birth, if in the opinion of one licensed physician an abortion is necessary to preserve the life or health of the mother.

Very few people would argue with saving the life of the mother. But what do they mean by the health of the mother? Here's the court's own definition of health. It means "the medical judgment may be exercised in the light of all factors, physical, emotional, psychological, familial, and the woman's age relevant to the wellbeing of the patient." All these factors may relate to health. And so, it means this, that if having a baby would force a distressful life and future on a woman, she may kill her baby. If it is determined that it would produce psychological harm to her, she may have her baby killed. If it would tax the mental and physical health of the mother by the child care that would be necessary to take care of the baby after the baby is born, she may kill the baby. The baby may be killed if there is distress associated with the unwanted child.

I went to Washington to testify before a Senate committee on abortion. Senator Orin Hatch questioned me along with some others. They had me there because I was the past president of the Southern Baptist Convention. When I went outside in the hallway I was accosted by a young woman. (I shall not call her a lady.) She claimed to be a Baptist and she was also a lawyer and a "pro-choice" advocate. She looked at me and said, "Sir, you just don't understand how traumatic it is for a woman to have an unwanted pregnancy."

I said, "Now let me see if I can get your line of reasoning. What you're saying is that people who traumatize other people ought to be eliminated; exterminated. Is that right? Because right now you're traumatizing me." And I said, "Is it your philosophy that if one person traumatizes another person, then the person who's being traumatized ought to eliminate the other person?" I said, "Suppose I jump on you right now and put my thumbs in your throat and throttle you." She looked at me up and down.

I said, "At least you could run. At least you could cry out for help." I said, "Who can a little baby go to? A little baby can't even run!"

I'm sure she ran off and told everybody "that Baptist preacher threatened to strangle me."

Oh, but you say, "Brother Rogers, abortion just happens to little blobs of protoplasm."

Last year in New York state alone 4,000 third trimester babies were killed. In one state alone, 4,000 who were in the third trimester, that is, they could have lived outside the mother's body.

A while back I preached on "An Old Fool With A New Name," about humanism. I told you about a 19-year-old girl, Marie, who went into her doctor's office to have an abortion, this removal of a little piece of protoplasm, something I suppose she thought was like a tonsillectomy. The girl had been carrying the baby for 28 weeks. When the doctor performed the procedure, he took that little so-called blob of protoplasm and laid it on a table. It was a perfectly formed baby. It was still moving. He wrapped it in a towel and completed his procedure. Then he took that piece of humanity and put it in a sack and gave it to a friend of the girl who was having the abortion. She took it home. It continued to move. It continued to make noises. They got frightened and they took this little baby that weighed one pound and 13 ounces back to the hospital. A team of physicians was called in. They unwrapped that child in an unbridled heat. They began to do all of those things necessary to save its life. They spent $150,000 to preserve the life that a few moments ago was supposedly just a blob of protoplasm. Today that little baby is alive and well.

Now I want to ask you a question. Was that human life or was that not human life? Should that baby have been killed or should that baby not have been killed?

A young man, John DeHaas, today almost five years old, was aborted in Korea. When they took him from his mother's womb, they noticed life. Some in that operating room said, "No, you'll not continue to commit this murder!" And they took little John, his head all bent out of shape because of what they'd done to him, his body mangled, his arms twisted and mutilated. But they went to work. Today John DeHaas is a happy little boy. How glad he is to be alive. Don't let anybody tell you that these little creatures are not human beings!

II. When Does Human Life Begin?

Turn to Psalm 139:13, *"For thou hast possessed my reigns: thou hast covered me in my mother's womb." Me* in my mother's womb. *"I will praise thee; for I am fearfully and wonderfully made: marvelous are thy works; and that my soul knoweth right well. My substance was not hid from thee..."*

Dear friend, God knows the baby in the womb. *"...when I was made in secret, and curiously wrought in the lowest parts of the earth. Thine eyes did see my substance, yet being unperfect..."* God sees the embryo as it develops. *"...and in thy book all my members were written, which in continuance were fashioned, when as yet there were none of them. How precious also are thy thoughts unto me, Oh God! how great is the sum of them!"*

Do you know what that passage tells us, ladies and gentlemen? It tells us that when a woman is pregnant, that God is forming a child within that woman. And it tells us that is a wonderful and a fearful thing. It also tells us that preborn life, that child, is the object of the Father's love and affection. How wonderful are God's thoughts toward that preborn child.

Now when does life begin? Who's going to settle it? God who made us all.

Listen to what God said to Jeremiah, the prophet. *Jeremiah*

1:5: "Before I formed thee in the belly I knew thee; and before thou camest forth out of the womb I sanctified thee, and I ordained thee a prophet unto the nations."

Do you know when Jeremiah was ordained to be a prophet? In his mother's womb. I sanctified you even before you came into your mother's womb. I ordained you. Do you know who Jeremiah's mother was carrying around? A fetus, an embryo? No, a prophet, a prophet of God! Had that baby been aborted, a prophet of God would have been killed. That's what the Bible says.

Jesus was being carried in the womb of Mary. John the Baptist was being carried in the womb of Elizabeth. By today's standards Mary would have had an abortion. After all, the baby was bringing shame. She was very young; she was impoverished; she was a member of a minority race. Today she would have been a good candidate for an abortion. But she had within her womb our Lord.

In the womb of Elizabeth was John the Baptist. Luke 1:41 records it. *"And it came to pass, that, when Elisabeth heard the salutation of Mary, the babe leaped in her womb; and Elisabeth was filled with the Holy Ghost."*

I am telling you that John the Baptist in the presence of his Lord, even in his mother's womb leaped with joy. Are you going to tell me that was not a child, not a human being, not made in the image of God, just a mass of protoplasm, that it's all right to take a little baby that can leap with joy in the presence of the Lord Jesus, and put it to death? No! I tell you no.

III. Why Is Abortion Wrong?

A. Destroys A Human Life

It is the taking of an innocent life. "These six things doth the Lord hate: yea seven are an abomination unto Him..." One of those seven is hands that shed innocent blood.

Dr. Bernard Nathason is an obstetrician and a gynecologist and at one time was assistant professor at Cornell University Medical School. He had been for a long time a pro-choice advocate. What they mean by that is that people ought to be given a choice to kill babies. He worked with the national association for the repeal of abortion laws. He became the director of the first and largest abortion clinic in the western world. He performed 60,000 abortions.

Let me tell you what Dr. Nathason now says, "I am deeply troubled by my own increasing certainty that I had in fact presided over 60,000 deaths." Can you imagine how that man must feel? The certainty, the increasing certainty, that he had presided over 60,000 deaths.

How did he come to this conclusion? In this clinic the doctors and the nurses began to tell him of the nightmares and the depression that they were experiencing and the personality changes that were taking place in the clinic where they were working as they were systematically and clinically snuffing out the lives of these precious little babies. Why is it wrong? It is the taking of innocent life! No one to speak for these children. No one to stand up for them.

B. Violates The Golden Rule

Do you know what the golden rule is? *Matthew 7:12, "What thing you would that men should do to you, do ye also unto them."* Or as we have said, "Do to others as you want others to do to you."

I wonder if there is a mother here who would like for her daughter or her son to kill her.

I wonder if there is a doctor here who would like to be placed into a cell where he couldn't get out, trapped in a cell, and then have someone come into that cell and pour over him a corrosive liquid that would eat his skin and fill his lungs and let him die a painful and excruciating death in convulsions. Is there a doctor here who wants somebody to do that to him? Then, I don't you think you ought to do it to anybody else.

Is there a judge here who would like somebody to take some powerful machine and reach into that judge's house and rip him out of that house and dismember him and tear him and rip him apart with that powerful machine until he's dead. Is there a judge here that wants that done to him? Now if there's not a judge here that wants that done to him, he ought not to do that to somebody else.

C. Violates Natural God-Given Instincts

God gives every mother an instinct to protect her unborn. Every father has that instinct. To destroy that instinct is to go against God. As the Bible says in Romans 1:31, there will be some so vile that they will be "without understanding, covenant breakers, without natural affection..." And that word natural affection literally means without family love.

Don't get the idea that most abortions are caused because the baby is deformed. Or most abortions are caused by rape or incest or these kind of things. Most abortions are are rooted primarily on selfishness. We've been taught to believe that abortion is primarily for the overburdened and the poor. But 76 percent of those who are aborting are unmarried, 53 percent have no other children, most are over 20. They're not teenagers. They are not minorities. Most are white, middle and upper class. Over one third of the women who have had are going back for the second, third, and fourth abortions. They don't want to be bothered with a baby. Just plain selfishness!

Another reason is greed. Did you know that the abortion business is a moneymaking business? If you have an abortion clinic, you've got a little gold mine. It's a way to make a fast buck.

You say, "Brother Rogers, what you say sounds so clear and so plain but how do they rationalize it? Surely they've got some answers."

Well, they say things like this, "The baby is not really a human being until it begins to breathe. God breathed into Adam's nostrils the breath of life and Adam became a living soul." And so they say the baby doesn't become a living soul until it begins to breathe.

Friend, that little baby does breathe inside its mother. Through the umbilical tube it receives oxygen necessary for life. You take that little baby from that mother's womb and bring it into the open air and if it has reached the age of viability, it will immediately breathe the open air of space.

Somebody says, "Sometimes isn't it necessary to abort a baby to save a mother's life?" I think almost all would agree that the mother's life should be saved. But I want you to listen to what a very prominent doctor has to say. Dr. Jerome Lejume, a world famous geneticist says, "I would never attack and kill an unborn child." What he meant by that is that his purpose would never be to kill the child, his purpose would be to save the life of the mother. If the child died in the process then that's tragic, but he would never attack and kill the child. His aim is to save the life of the mother.

We're talking about those who attack and kill that innocent life, "hands that shed innocent blood."

Oh, but what about the danger of deformity? What about these little babies that may be deformed? Are you going to say that defectives ought not to live? If you're going to take the lives of those who are defective before birth, don't you realize that before long we will be taking the lives of those who are defective after birth? I want to tell you something. Ain't nobody perfect here today. Right? Just how defective do you have to be? And what Hitler is going to set himself up as the judge to say who is defective and who is not defective?

Where's it going to end? First, abortion. Secondly, infanticide. Thirdly, euthanasia.

Some of you folks here, 30, 40, 50, are feeling pretty good right now. You let this thing continue and, I tell you, the social engineers have already got it planned. When they get tired of warehousing you in an old folks home, they've got a plan for you. They are going to put you in a beautiful room, they're going to play serene music, they're going to give you some nice food, all your loved ones are going to come, they're going to numb you a little bit, put a little dope in your food and that nurse is going to come in and put a little sharp needle in your arm, and "goodbye!"

We have taught a generation it's all right to kill the babies. That same generation is going to believe it's all right to kill the old folks. You think I'm exaggerating? I'm not a prophet or the son of a prophet, but I stand here before God, absolutely, totally convinced that what I'm prophesying will take place unless there is a turnaround in America. It will and we're snowballing in that direction. Hitler would have loved that plan.

Somebody says, "Well the mother's life and the mother's body, it's her own. I don't want some Baptist preacher telling me what I can do with my body."

Listen, my body is not my own, when you think about it. Suppose I reached under this pulpit and took out a hatchet and started to chop off my fingers one at a time. My thumb, there it goes; this finger, there it goes. By the time I got to the third finger, I hope you'd be up here brother. You'd say, "There's something wrong with a man who is destroying his own body, and whether he wants it done or not, we will stop him!" Would you just let me chop off my fingers and say, "Get away, I know my rights. It's my body."

We don't have an absolute right to our own bodies. They won't even let you ride a motorcycle in this state without a helmet. A little girl has to get permission from her parents to have her ears pierced, but she doesn't have to get permission to kill a baby, to have an abortion.

The woman says, "Well it's my body." We're not talking about your body. That baby is not your body. I don't have a right to kill an unwanted guest in my home. And you don't have a right to kill an unwanted guest in your body. They are living within you.

No woman under heaven has a right to kill a baby. Nobody! I don't care how much rhetoric you put to it. That baby is not her body. That baby now lives within her body.

But somebody says, "It's so unfair. The abortion laws now, they're unfair. If you prohibit abortion, then you're going to have all those illegal abortions. You're going to have those back alley abortions, and the rich people are going to be able to have abortions and the poor people are not going to be able to have abortions. It's going to be more dangerous for them."

Let me tell you what the social engineer would say. "Since the rich can have drugs more easily than the poor, it is our duty to supply heroin for the poor." That's the twisted logic. "Since the rich can have an abortion more easily, now it is our duty to supply an abortion for the poor."

The fact that some can get away with sin doesn't make sin right. The fact that it's easier for some does not mean that it's right and that I as a taxpayer should pay to take the lives of little babies.

Someone says, "Oh, but the population explosion. We have so many babies we're not going to be able to feed them all."

Did you know that in the United States we're under zero population growth? Did you know that our population is shrinking? Did you know just to stay even we have to have a 2.1 birth rate per family? We're at 1.9. Did you know that there are people who are wanting babies, begging for babies, wanting to adopt babies, and can't get them? What should we do?

IV. What Should Christians Do?

Proverbs 24:11: "If thou forbear to deliver them that are drawn to death, and those that are ready to be slain; if thou sayest, Behold, we knew it not; doth not he that pondereth the heart consider it? and he that keepeth thy soul, doth he not know it? and shall not he render to every man according to his works?"

Do you think you can be neutral in this thing? Do you think that it's Congress's problem? Do you think that it's Adrian Rogers' problem; that it's not your problem? You say, "I'm not pro-abortion. It's not my problem."

I tell you it is your problem.

Number one, you better be informed. You cannot afford to be ignorant. Number two, you better work for and pray for a constitutional ammendment to outlaw abortion in America except in those instances where the life of the mother may be at stake. You better be able to see to it that sexual morality is being taught at home and in the church.

The one voice that ought to speak has been primarily silent! The government, Hollywoood, the social engineers, the atheists, and the humanists have all spoken. It's time for God's people to speak. We need to speak out clearly. Isaiah 58:1, *"Cry aloud, spare not, lift up thy voice like a trumpet, and shew my people their transgression, and the house of Israel their sins."* We need to speak with a voice of a trumpet. No stutter, no stammer, no apology, and no fear; no let up, back up or shut up until we're taken up!

Number three, we need to learn to forget our self-righteousness and have more compassion for unwed mothers. Show them love and compassion and understanding. So many times we are driving them right into the arms of the abortionist. We need to give them some understanding and to pray for them.

Do not be swayed by high sounding arguments of the liberals, the humanists, the social planners and the experts. Don't let them sway you. *"Woe unto them that call evil, good, and good, evil; that put darkness for light, and light for darkness; that put bitter for sweet, and sweet for bitter."* (Isaiah 5:20) It's wrong to kill babies. Wrong! I don't care how much rhetoric you drape over it, it is wrong, wrong, wrong before God. *"These six things doth the Lord hate, yea seven are an abomination unto Him. Hands that shed innocent blood."*

The last thing we must do; we must pray to God that He will have mercy upon us and give us space to repent. We'd better get right with God. I thank God that the Bible still teaches in II Chronicles 7:14, "If my people, which are called by my name, shall humble themselves, and pray, and seek my face, and turn from their wicked ways; then will I hear from heaven, and will forgive their sin, and will heal their land."

I'm living for that day when we have a revival of righteousness in America. I want to believe it's coming. That God, not any preacher, not any president, but God will do something in America. Lord, haste that day!

Life Worth Saving

George Sweeting

TEXT: Genesis 1:26; 2:7

SUPPLEMENTAL VERSES: Exodus 20:13, Judges 13:5, Psalms 58:3; 106:38, Luke 1:15, Genesis 4:10; 9:6, Isaiah 14:13-15

SUMMARY OF MESSAGE: George Sweeting's "Life Worth Saving" gets to the root of the abortion issue. Sweeting says abortion is a result of society's unbiblical values, and he outlines some of the wrong attitudes and values we hold. Sweeting explains – using Scripture and information from current popular sources such as TIME magazine – that innocent human beings are undeniable the victims of abortion. He also shows that American adults are, in a way, victims of abortion both spiritually and financially.

PREACHING TRACKS:

➤ TRACK ONE: Preach the entire sermon.

➤ TRACK TWO: Preach the points on the outline that best apply to your congregation. II reveals that a human life is terminated in every abortion. III is a unique look at the underlying causes of abortion.

➤ TRACK THREE: Preach a combination of points in this sermon and in other sermons in this book.

LIFE WORTH SAVING

Abortion: Throwaway Life – Can We Afford It?

George Sweeting

When is human life expendable? The question seems to have an easy answer—-never! There is no life not worth saving. Two persons, or fifty, or even an entire nation will team up to find a child lost on a mountain, rescue a miner trapped by an explosion, or free a terrorist's hostage.

And yet millions of lives are being written off, snuffed out quietly and efficiently with scientific expertise. In fact, in the United States the legal act of abortion is causing more deaths than heart disease or cancer.

I. The Effects Of Abortion

Abortion was legalized by the Supreme Court in 1973, and since then the problem of "throwaway life" has not lessened. In fact, it has multiplied astoundingly. Today it presses on the American conscience as have few issues. And it should. Millions of legal abortions are on record in the United States since the Supreme Court upheld abortion as a right.

A *Moody Monthly* editorial asks, "Have we been sitting, Lot-like, in the seats of the scornful, in the gates of our individual Sodoms, quite at home, quite unruffled, even critical of those who are so easily alarmed about – babies?

"If the blood of Abel – one innocent adult – cried out to God from the ground, how much more the millions of babies since 1973?"

Many who justify this form of extermination do so on the grounds of safeguarding human rights – the rights of mothers to avoid the consequences of conception. Others have vested interests – the fathers who want no further responsibility, or possibly the doctors and medical assistants who make abortions a financially rewarding business.

The effects of this harvest of willful death are far greater than we think. We could well be moving toward a society of middle-aged and older people. The present generation is not replacing itself with younger life. Consequently, fewer and fewer workers will be left to support a growing population dependent on Social Security.

Columnist Joan Beck writes: "Doubts about abortion are growing, not diminishing. A kind of collective uneasiness seems to be increasing in this country, not so much among those who have always opposed abortion as among some who welcome it and still support it."

But most important, abortion is affecting our relationship with Almighty God. Few nations in history have so invited divine judgement while needing God's favor.

II. The Evils Of Abortion

Many argue that abortion does not involve taking a human life. They say there is no proof that life begins until a child is born. In its historic Roe v. Wade decision, the United States Supreme Court concluded that it could not decide when human life begins – that the fetus may be destroyed "for any reason or no reason."

Many believe, however, the Supreme Court overlooked overwhelming evidence. One aspect of that evidence was dramatized and documented in 1979 in a historic feature on CBS television. For the first time in history, television viewers coast to coast saw motion pictures of the human fetus in the womb. The pictures made plain that even at the age of 40 days, a fetus in the womb has a beating heart, a slender spine, and a brain that is already sending out nerve impulses. The feature stressed this was a human life, a "life never seen on earth and never to be repeated."

Time magazine makes a similar point. "Even in the earliest stages of pregnancy," the magazine says, "the embryo is amazingly baby-like. By the ninth week the fetus is kicking and wiggling.... Its sex can be recognized, and at one point it seems to be trying to shield its eyes from the lights of the camera."

Is a fetus only flesh? Dr. C. Everett Koop, well-known for his outstanding work in surgical pediatrics, has this to say in his book *The Right to Live: The Right to Die:* "Once there is the union of sperm and egg, and the 23 chromosomes of each are brought together, that one cell with its 46 chromosones has all of the DNA (deoxyribonucleic acid), the whole genetic code that will, if not interrupted, make a human being just like you with the potential for God-consciousness." He asks a crucial question: "At what point can one consider this life to be worthless and the next minute consider the same life to be precious?"

Dr. Koop, who is a Christian, says, "As recently as 1967, at the first international conference on abortion, a purely secular group of people said, 'We can find no point in time between the union of sperm and egg and the birth of an infant at which point we can say this is not a human life.' "

It is this human life that is the victim of abortion. Some fetuses are removed from the womb by suction, in a mass of blood and tissue. Some are destroyed by scraping from the womb, and some are drowned in an injection of salt solution. Still others are removed by surgery not unlike a Caesarian operation, and the fetus is left to die if it is not already dead. In every case, regardless of the means, a precious life is blotted out.

Some people are quick to point out that the Bible does not specifically speak out against abortion. But the Bible does not specify every sin. It does say, "Thou shalt not kill." And the Bible clearly speaks of human life as beginning in the womb. The mother of Samson was told that her child would be a Nazarite from the womb (Judges 13:5), the implication clearly being that his status as a person began before his birth. Psalm 58:3 says that the wicked are estranged "from the womb." The implication is that even as unborn babies they are living persons. Speaking of John the Baptist, Luke 1:15 declares that this great man of God would be "filled with the Holy Ghost, even from his mother's womb." Only a living person can be filled with the Holy Spirit.

So the nature of the human fetus, medical science and the Word of God all testify that the tiny creature in the womb is a unique and living person. If that is true, no one can commit abortion without destroying human life.

III. The Errors Of Abortion

That brings us to the real heart of the problem – wrong values that have been accepted by our society without regard to God's Word. What are some of these wrong values? First, there is a wrong attitude toward human life.

What is a human life? When God made man, He said, *"Let us make man in our image, after our likeness" (Genesis 1:26).* And the record goes on to say, *"God created man in his own image, in the image of God created he him" (Genesis 1:27).* Every human life, even in its fallen state, reflects to some degree the likeness of Almighty God. When man dares to take another human life, he lifts his hand in rebellion against the image of the Almighty God. When Cain killed Abel, God said, *"Thy brother's blood crieth unto me from the ground" (Genesis 4:10).* The very universe records the violation of a human life.

God spelled out to Noah the seriousness with which He views the taking of human life. In Genesis 9:6, He says, *"Whoso sheddeth man's blood, by man shall his blood be shed."* And then He gives the reason for demanding such a penalty: *"For in the image of God made He man."* Never forget that God condemns the taking of human life and demands the ultimate penalty. Again and again the Bible tells us that judgment came to men because of blood guiltiness.

God judges nations, too. Israel – God's own people – was sent into captivity. Psalm 106:38 reminds us that this judgement came in part because the Hebrew people had dared to take the lives of their own children – a sin only a hair's breadth from the abortion we flaunt so openly today.

A second wrong value that gives rise to abortion is a wrong emphasis on self. Perhaps the most often heard argument for abortion is that the mother has the right to decide what happens to her own body. On the surface the argument seems reasonable. The mother is the one chiefly involved. Her future and well-being are at stake. But wait a minute. What about the child she has helped conceive? What about the obligation to the human life already conceived? What about the future and well-being of the unborn child? Are not his rights to be considered?

God gave the sex relationship to strengthen the marriage bond and to bless the home with children. No privilege is more sacred than that of bringing a new life into the world. No privilege should be exercised more carefully. And it should be viewed as holy responsibility.

The Word of God says plainly that sex is for marriage only. Abortion would virtually disappear tomorrow if it were not for the willful violation of God's great charter of marriage and purity. The abortion problem begins with rebellion that says, "I will do as I please for pleasure. I reject the limits prescribed by God in favor of personal satisfaction."

And that is the essence of the wrong values of which we are speaking. The root of all wrong value systems is a rebellious attitude toward God.

To put one's will above God's will, one's rights above God's rights, is to rebel against the Sovereign of the universe. You cannot seize sovereignty for yourself without challenging Almighty God. That is what Satan did in his fall. Isaiah 14 describes how Satan went from being God's highest angel to become the enemy and deceiver. In verse 13, God, speaking to Lucifer (Satan's name before he fell), says, *"Thou hast said in thine heart, I will ascend into heaven, I will exalt my throne above the stars of God ... I will be like the Most High. Yet thou shalt be brought down to hell."* When we flout the will of God, we are walking in the footsteps of a doomed and defeated Satan. We are not the Creator; we are His creatures. We are not God, but people subject to His will and wishes.

For generations our nation has pushed aside the principles taught in the Bible. We have defied the voice of God. We challenge Him at our peril. Pride and rebellion are deadly sins. Part of their harvest today is the tragic and bloody snuffing out of millions of tiny lives.

Although we have made abortion legal, although we have made it respectable, although we have made it commonplace, the fact – the sin – is unchanged. Like Cain, we are daring to strike down human life, life with potential, life made in the image of Almighty God.

"But," someone will say, "is abortion always wrong?" "Always" is a broad and sweeping word. There are difficult questions we are not able to answer in this brief chapter. For example, what about "defective" babies? What about abortion in the wake of rape?

These are special circumstances that represent only a small fraction of the total number of abortions. There are answers for such problems. We can trust God with the hard situations in our lives if we set ourselves to do His will. We cannot expect His help or blessing if we ignore His Word and set aside His precepts.

And God's will seems clearly to stand in opposition to the wanted destruction of precious lives.

The heart of the abortion issue is stated by R.F. Gardner in a booklet published by the *Christian Medical Society Journal.* He writes, "From the moment of conception the couple concerned have not the option whether a proffered gift be accepted, but rather whether an already bestowed gift should be spurned." That is the issue – what will we do with a human life that has been given to our keeping?

Meanwhile abortion, like all sin, is not standing still. The tide is rising fast. Judicial decisions continue to make abortions easy, even for teenagers and wards of local government.

In this country many believe that only an anti-abortion amendment will change the situation. If so, let's get behind it.

I am well aware that few who read these pages have had or will have responsibility for the abortion crisis. But we are guilty if we fail to raise our voices in opposition. God's judgment is not far from any nation that complacently accepts the slaughter of its unborn babies. Once His judgment falls, it will be too late.

May we stop being neutral on this issue. If abortion is wrong, we cannot be silent. Besides taking a stand, we need to help others realize what is happening – and put our influence as Christians where it will count.

PRO-LIFE RESPONSES TO TOUGH QUESTIONS

Kristen White

Pro-abortionists are everywhere – in the workplace, at rallies, even in churches. As believers in God's Word and as supporters of life, we must be prepared to answer the accusations and questions of those who approve of abortion. Here are some comments and questions you may encounter and possible responses. The sermons in this book give more detailed responses. In giving pro-life information, always be sure your statistics and information are correct. Answer gently and kindly to inform without arguing.

You say you're pro-life because the Bible is pro-life, but not everyone believes the Bible is the final authority.

The pro-life position is not only based on belief in the Bible. It is based on scientific evidence and on sincere concern for babies. From the moment of conception, a person with an individual genetic structure – and possibly different blood type from the mother – is growing and developing. By eight weeks of age. The baby in the womb has every body system and feature he or she will have as a born person.[1] All that is required is growth.

Also, the pro-life position is not only based on concern for babies, but also on concern for the women who are not informed about all their options and about the possible physical and psychological effects of abortion. Women must be given complete information. Abortion clinics do not regularly tell women about the development of the child in the womb or about alternatives. Pro-life supporters care about the women affected by abortion as much as the babies killed by it.

These psychological questions you are concerned about don't happen to all women who abort. And besides, couldn't there be another common reason for these women experiencing such problems?

Not all women who abort experience the signs of postabortion syndrome (which can include physical effects such as sterility or death and psycological effects such as depression, sleeplessness, nightmares and anxiety). But there is no real way to determine how many do. If a woman suffers deep guilt and depression from having an abortion, she may never seek help or reveal the cause of her pain. But isn't just one woman's experiencing death or emotional or physical problems (because she wasn't warned about potential side effects of abortion) a terrible crime against women, an awful form of deceit?

It is doubtful there is another common denominator. Women who have abortions come from all walks of life – all races, age groups, and economic levels. They get abortions for a variety of reasons. We ignore women's pain if we insist that women can get abortions without side effects; physical or psychological. Abortion is the opposite of what our bodies and emotions do by instinct (bear and protect children).

But the world has too many people. Abortion prevents overpopulation.

Many nations – including Western and Eastern nations – currently have too low a birthrate. Even in Third World countries, population growth has slowed significantly.[2] If current trends continue, more people will die each day than are born. This has serious economic and social consequences.[3]

Even if your world's greatest problem were overpopulation, is killing people to prevent such overpopulation a correct response? It certainly isn't a moral one. Nor is it very wise. What will happen when we have prevented the overpopulation problem to such an extent that there aren't enough workers to support elderly people? Would we then "solve" the problems of large numbers of dependent elderly people with the same method?

Every child should be a wanted child; wanted children aren't abused. Abortion prevents child abuse.

Unplanned pregnancies do not necessarily result in unwanted and unloved pregnancies. In fact, one study shows that 90 percent of child abuse cases occur in homes where children were deeply wanted. Parents who abuse were often victims of child abuse themselves.[4] That doesn't mean we should abort babies who are wanted or whose parents grew up in abusive situations. It means that women who keep unexpected babies do not characteristically abuse their babies. Neither do adoptive parents.

Also, the nature of abortion may actually contribute to child abuse. Legal abortion communicates that it is okay to terminate an unexpected pregnancy. Even the statement "Every child a wanted child" implies that it is okay to do away with those babies who aren't wanted and to keep those who are. Consequently, subconsciously society's conviction of the value of life has lessened, and reported cases of abuse are more numerous now than before Roe vs. Wade passed. And since babies in the womb can feel the pain of abortion, whether it be salt poisoning/burning or suction aspiration or another means, isn't abortion the ultimate child abuse?

You say child abuse has increased significantly since abortion was legalized. You imply a relationship that may not be.

But it probably is. Dr. Phillip Ney conducted a study in 1979 that found that parents' resistance to harming and abusing children was lowered because of abortion.[5] Abortion goes against all natural processes and instincts. It is highly controversial. Why? Because people know it is innately wrong, but they continue to insist on their "right to chose." So abortion remains, and the message is communicated that it's okay to go against everything your conscience says is proper. You have a right to get your way. It's okay to physically do away with unborn people. It's okay to destroy people with words, neglect and actions.

Reported cases of child abuse have increased from 167,000 in 1973, the year abortion was legalized, to 2.4 million in 1989.[6]

Many pro-life supporters believe aborted babies go to heaven. Why not be excited when a baby is aborted? He or she has a guaranteed place in heaven and won't have the grief of earth and the potential of going to hell.

God's Word clearly indicates that life in the womb is precious and that shedding innocent blood angers Him (Ps 139; Prov. 6:16-17). God's Word indicates that God recognizes individual personalities and has a plan for them from the beginning of their existence. (Jer. 1:5; Ps. 139). We as Christians must do what God's Word instructs us to do. On the matter of killing innocent people, the Bible says, "Rescue those being led away to death; hold back those staggering toward slaughter." (Prov. 24:11, NIV).

The Bible also says, "Love does not delight in evil but rejoices with the truth" (1 Cor. 13:6, NIV). No matter how exciting it is that people go to heaven, as Christians we cannot rejoice in the evil of abortion or the supposed "good" it brings about. The suggestion to rejoice in aborted babies is totally against God's character. Yes, He does want people to go to heaven, but not by being killed. He wants people to choose Him freely. Taking life out of God's hands into our own to guarantee people a place in heaven is playing God.

Also, this statement ignores the pain and problems the woman who aborts faces. Pro-life in its fullest meaning includes caring for the mother and others abortion touches. Not only is killing babies to get them into heaven appalling; so is doing it at the expense of woman's physical and psychological health.

Is the church prepared to pay for the upbringing of the 1.5 million babies who are now aborted each year?

The Bible instructs Christians to tell others of the good news of salvation through Jesus Christ and to provide and care for the poor, the fatherless and the widow. As Christians, we are responsible for doing what we can to provide for others' needs lovingly and unselfishly. We should also educate people about sex/abstinence, alternatives to abortion (adoption, single parenting, etc.), child development and parenting. Ultimately, however, paying for the upbringing of a child is the responsibility of the parents.

Also, if abortion weren't an option, those getting them might more seriously consider the consequences of the actions that bring about pregnancy, thus reducing the number of unwanted pregnancies.

Since many women can't afford to have a child, shouldn't abortion be an option until people become more responsible sexually? It isn't fair to overpopulate the world with unwanted babies just because people don't use birth control.

Allowing abortion simply because some are sexually irresponsible is illogical. It puts the consequences on the child.

Further, abortion will never encourage responsible sexual behavior. It is an excuse, an escape for others to continue having sex without facing the consequences of their actions (so abortion advocates tell them, but women who abort and those who encourage it often do suffer guilt and other physical and psychological harm as a result of abortion).

It isn't fair to overpopulate the world with unwanted babies: It's not fair to the world or to babies. But the answer is not abortion; the killing of the innocent. It is abstinence – not getting pregnant in the first place.

But isn't abortion a relief to babies who will be disabled. Isn't is a relief to their parents who will have to pay for treatment?

Disabilities are sometimes difficult to cope with, but we should not judge another person's ability or desire to cope with these and choose death for them. In fact, people with disabilities say they want to live despite the handicaps they face.[7] We should not be allowed to kill people because caring for them may be costly. Life is priceless. We should allow natural progression of these pregnancies and after birth, we should support and encourage people with disabilities to become all they can and want to become.

Often this argument is used as the reason we should keep abortion legal. Realistically, however, relatively few abortions are done for this reason, because babies are rarely deformed. The majority of abortions are performed for reasons of convenience, not for the "benefit" of the children.

To be fully pro-life means to be supportive of life no matter the difficulties and sorrows the individual may face.

Pro-life advocates often use the emotional pull, "Think of all the doctors, musicians, etc., the world doesn't have because of abortion." Think about all the Hitlers and mass murderers the world is missing, too.

Again, just because a child has the potential to choose to do things that don't benefit society (or just because he or she is unexpected or possibly disabled) doesn't mean we have the right to take his or her life. Realistically, very few people who are born will commit heinous crimes such as mass murder and rape. If we were to prevent every person's life who might harm another in some way, none of us would be alive.

Also, God allows sinners to be born. If that weren't so, none of us would be alive. Who are we to be God's police officers and try to prevent sinful people from coming into the world? God's perfect will and greatest desire is for all to choose forgiveness and love (see 2 Peter 3:9). To be fully pro-life means to tell others about God's good news so they can experience abundant and eternal life. It means we should teach others ethical and moral behavior. It means we should establish laws that don't allow people to harm and kill others.

But even the Bible doesn't say abortion is wrong.

The Bible never uses the word abortion, but the message that God believes children in the womb are living, valuable human beings and the message that God hates the taking of innocent lives are certainly communicated in God's Word, just as the word missions is never used in the Bible, but the concept is certainly there.

In Psalm 139, David praises God for being intimately involved in his life, even in the womb. In Jeremiah 1:5, the Lord God tells Jeremiah that before he was formed in the womb, God called him to be a prophet. Elisabeth recognized that Mary was carrying her Lord before Jesus was born. She asked Mary, "But why am I so favored, that the mother of my Lord should come to me." (Luke 1:43, NIV)? In His omniscience, God knows when each person is created, or conceived, before anyone else knows. In His grace, He loves people from the moment of conception and places in them a measure of faith to believe in Him (see Romans 12:3) so that they can come to know Him and commune with Him. Unborn babies are alive to God. God hates abortion because it kills lives He created, lives He has ordained.

If God is omniscient, then He knows who will be aborted. That means His plans for those lives is that they be aborted, right?

In His omniscience, God knows how long each person's life will be, how each person will die and what each person's eternal destiny is. That does not mean that what happens in each person's life is God's perfect plan.

God's perfect plan is for each person to accept Christ Jesus as Savior (see 2 Peter 3:9), for each person to turn from sin so they won't have to experience His wrath (see Ezek. 18:23) and for each person to experience abundant life (see John 10:10). Not all people experience God's perfect plan for their lives, not because He's not powerful enough to bring it about, but because not everyone submits to His plan out of his or her free will.

God established a system of free will so people could themselves choose to love God and live for Him. Without free will, humankind would offer God forced, robotic obedience rather than obedience out of love and gratitude. Without free will, humankind could not understand or experience the sacrificial love of God through the sacrifice of Christ Jesus.

God knows all that will happen, but all that happens is not necessarily His plan.

The Bible says that life begins when the first breath is taken, doesn't it? When do you believe life starts?

Genesis 2:7 is sometimes quoted as biblical "proof" that life begins when a child takes the first breath. However, the verse says nothing about the man taking a breath. It says, "[God] breathed into his nostrils the breath of life, and the man became a living being" (Gen. 2:7, NIV).

"The breath of life" does not mean that the child becomes a valid life when he or she takes the first breath. God's breathing into Adam was the starting point of Adam's life since he was not formed in a mother's womb. The starting point for life now is conception. That is, after all, when God begins His handiwork creating a new individual.

It is also the scientific starting point. At conception a new human being with a completely unique, never-to-be-repeated set of genes begins. The new life grows and develops more rapidly in the first two months than it ever will again. By the end of the eighth week, everything that this new life will have as a born person is already in place.[8]

It is okay to abort in the first trimester, but not in the second or third. That's when the baby is more fully developed.

To draw arbitrary, human-defined lines in development (such as trimester) is an insult to our continual development. Development doesn't stop or change in nature after three months and six months in the womb. The baby does what he or she always has since conception – grow and develop. We continue to grow and develop physically, mentally and emotionally throughout our lives.

To draw arbitrary lines is also confusing. At what hour, minute and second does a three-month-old fetus in the womb suddenly become a baby? What if you abort after this dividing line?

To disregard the validity of a fetus' life because he or she doesn't "look like" a baby or isn't as developed as a baby is disrespectful to all human beings. We all went through these stages of development, and all future lives and all current lives in the womb must go through these stages also. And then you must draw another arbitrary line: When does a baby in the womb look enough like a human to be a valid life?

To disregard the validity of life because a fetus is dependent on his or her mother is unreasonable. Even after "viability" and even after birth, we are dependent on others for care and nourishment.

If life in the womb is valid at any stage in development, it is valid at all stages of development. The only difference in a one-day-old embryo and a nine-month-old baby in the womb is time. Everything a baby needs to become a born human – even an adult – is present from conception.

If God values life so much, why did He allow so many people in the Old Testament – including unborn children – to die when He exercised His wrath?

God's allowing unborn children to die this way, or through miscarriage or abortion, does not mean He does not value life. God's perfect will for each life is to experience salvation and abundant living (see question about God's omniscience). Humankind's free choice to do evil has brought destruction and disease into the world. God allows these evils to take place because they are the natural result of disobedience to God. If He didn't allow them, humankind would continue in sin, leading to the even more painful destruction of their souls for eternity.

In the Old Testament, God sometimes destroyed groups of people for their stubborn evil. He never did this without years of patience and warning. Pregnant women were killed in God's punishment of these people. That doesn't mean God didn't love the unborn children within these women or that His plan was for them to die before they were born. The sinful mothers, in these cases, were the ones who led to the destruction of their children. These women's stubborn disobedience was hated by God, not only because it was disobedience and not only because it ruined God's perfect will for the women's lives, but also because it led their children to premature death.

God has a special heart for children. Jesus welcomed children, loved them, instructed people to care for them, and often talked about the punishment people would receive for leading little ones away (see Matt. 10:42; 19:13-15; Mark 9:42). Jesus even answered the disciples' question of who is greatest in the kingdom of heaven by calling a little child to Him (see Matt. 18:1-4).

Why aren't pro-lifers adopting if adoption is the answer?

Many have. Many more want to. The number of couples and single adults wanting to adopt is about 3 million.[9] The problem is, there aren't enough babies to adopt. *Newsweek* reports, "Only 2 percent of unmarried mothers placed their children for adoption in the 1980s."[10] The average number of adoptions of non-related children each year is 50,000, according to the National Committee on Adoption.[11]

There are waiting lists for white babies without disabilities. There are waiting lists for children with disabilities such as spina bifida and Down syndrome.[12] There are many who want to adopt babies of different races, but there are trans-racial barriers that make adopting minority children difficult for nonminority families.[13]

So what's the answer?

The answer is abstinence before marriage; faithfulness and responsible behavior within marriage; adoption in crisis cases; single parenting with encouraging, effective support systems; and a love of life that accepts people just as they are – no matter their disability or gender,

Kristen White

no matter their parents' circumstances or financial status.
    This is what we must teach and live.

1. Lennart Nilsson, *A Child is Born* (New York: Dell Publishing Co., Inc., 1977) p. 71.
2. *U.S. News and World Report*, June 22, 1987, p. 57.
3. Dr. and Mrs. J.C. Willke, *Abortion Questions and Answers* (Cincinnati: Hayes Publishing Co., Inc., 1990), p. 159-167.
4. Willke, *Questions and Answers*, p. 144.
5. Willke, *Questions and Answers*, p. 146.
6. Willke, *Questions and Answers*, p. 216.
8. Lennart Nillson, *Child is Born*, p. 71.
9. Willke, *Questions and Answers*, p. 313-314.
10. "The Politics of Adoption," *Newsweek* (March 21, 1994)p. 65.
11. Willke, *Questions and Answers*, p. 313.
12. Willke, *Questions and Answers*, p. 251 and 314.
13. "The Politics of Adoption," p. 64-65.

IDEAS FOR PROMOTING THE SANCTITY OF HUMAN LIFE

Greg Martin

Biblical preaching is a powerful tool for communicating God's message. For pastors it is the primary instrument for divine instruction. However, a preacher should not limit himself to the pulpit in his effort to communicate God's truth. This chapter is offered to help preachers with some creative methods of communicating the sanctity of human life.

➤ 1. Have children dress up in costumes of professional people (firemen, policemen, doctors, painters, farmers, ballet dancers, business persons, school teachers, and/or judges). Have one leave every 20 seconds to illustrate the loss to society because of abortion.

➤ 2. Before the conclusion of the service have all the children assemble on the stage. Instruct one to leave through the side door every 20 seconds to emphasize the point that one child is aborted every 20 seconds in America. Remind the adults how different church would be without children.

➤ 3. Have a child's voice sing or talk to his/her potential parent over a loud speaker.

➤ 4. Show a series of slides of a baby developing from the fetal stage through toddler age. Play appropriate background music.

➤ 5. Have a gynecologist or obstetrician explain to the congregation various stages of pregnancy. It would be helpful to have a mother at a few weeks, three months, six months, and full term on stage with the doctor. The mothers could testify of their desire for their children.

➤ 6. Invite a speaker from a crisis pregnancy center to share the platform.

➤ 7. Use testimonies from people who have had experiences with the sanctity of human life issue. Potential testimonials could come from:

—*Foster parents who have experienced the joy of helping an unwed mother.*
—*Parents of retarded or disabled children.*
—*A woman who has had an abortion and experienced God's grace.*
—*A man who paid for an abortion and experienced God's grace.*

—Grandparents of an aborted child.
—Siblings of an aborted child.
—Former abortionist who has been saved.
—Former abortion clinic owner who has been saved.
—A medical doctor describing abortion.
—A forgiven and loved unwed mother.
—A single mother who faced her crisis alone.
—A single mother who was unloved by her church.
—Parents who considered abortion but chose life.

➤ 8. Place one cross on the lawn of the church for every million babies that have been lost in abortion chambers since Roe vs. Wade.

➤ 9. In an informal worship service provide paper, pens, and addresses for worshippers to write their legislators about pending legislation.

➤ 10. On Mother's Day give a rose to all pregnant mothers.

➤ 11. Preach a sanctity of human life sermon holding a newborn sleeping baby.

➤ 12. Have a baby dedication day on Sanctity of Human Life Sunday.

➤ 13. Use bulletin inserts from a pro-life agency.

➤ 14. Take a special offering for a crisis pregnancy center.

➤ 15. Conduct a funeral service after church on sanctity of Human Life Sunday for all the babies that died during the year.

➤ 16. If your church sponsors an institution that is involved in saving the lives of children, place a white rose in a special vase every week for each child that was saved during the week.

➤ 17. Give the little baby model "Young One" to each person as he/she arrives for church on sanctity of Human Life Sunday.

➤ 18. Show the film "Your Crisis Pregnancy" from Focus on the Family.

WHAT CAN I DO?

Sylvia Boothe

➤1. Pray.

➤2. Become educated.

➤3. Educate others.

➤4. Ask your pastor to preach on sanctity of life or related topics.

➤5. Organize others of like concern.

➤6. Get involved.

➤7. Ask your doctor's opinion on abortion—tell him or her of your convictions.

➤8. Learn who your senators and representatives are on state and national levels. Learn their voting records on abortion and family issues.

➤9. Write your senators or representatives, asking them to initiate or support legislation on life issues. One letter is worth thousands of opinions.

➤10. Write a letter to the editor of your local newspaper. (Know your facts; be courteous.)

➤11. Become involved in or start a crisis pregnancy center. The director will train you. Needs are:

- *Volunteer counselors (16 hours of training)*
- *Advocates for the mothers*
- *Advisors with expertise in related fields*
- *Professionals: physicians, attorneys*
- *Services: maintenance helpers, printers, advertisers, public relations*
- *Office space, equipment, supplies*
- *Maternity clothes—new and **good** usedapparel*
- *Newborn baby clothes and supplies*
- *Baby furniture*
- *Prenatal vitamins*
- *Childbirth coaches*
- *Breastfeeding information*
- *Financial assistance:*
  — *groceries, insurance, rent*
  — *housing*
  — *job training for clients*
  — *resources such as books, films, and brochures*
- *Information on finishing high school education / GED*
- *Opportunity for further training*

➤ 12. Ask churches to provide:
- *Facilities for meetings, banquets, support groups*
- *A yearly banquet for staff and volunteers*
- *Parenting classes*
- *Child care for counselors' children or single parents' children*
- *Climate of welcome and caring*
- *Bible studies*
- *"Adoption" of an unwed mother; give her a baby shower*
- *Forgiveness*
- *Support groups for unwed parent(s), parents of the unwed, or postabortal women*

➤ 13. Testimonies of people who were adopted. Testimonies of people who adopted.

➤ 14. Ask business leaders to:
- *Talk to key business people about support, equipment, facilities, jobs*
- *Provide civic club exposure and support*
- *Provide speaker's bureau personnel*

➤ 15. Provide public, school, and church libraries with the best books available on related subject.

➤ 16. Expose school administrators to sex education material teaching chastity (Sex Respect).

➤ 17. If Planned Parenthood is in your local school system, ask for equal time to present your viewpoint.

➤ 18. Run for the local school board.

➤ 19. Provide every pastor with good books for his library on abortion and the alternatives.

➤ 20. Provide a billboard.

➤ 21. Put an ad in the local newspaper.

➤ 22. Give away pamphlets.

➤ 23. Keep informed on family issues.

➤ 24. Keep your church informed on family issues.

For more information, contact: Sylvia M. Boothe, Coordinator, Alternatives to Abortion Ministries, Home Mission Board, 4200 North Point Pkkwy, Alpharetta, GA 30202. 1-800-962-0851.

SCRIPTURES REGARDING SANCTITY OF LIFE AND ABORTION

Genesis 2:7; Then the Lord God formed man of dust from the ground, and breathed into his nostrils the breath of life; and man became a living soul.

Genesis 9:6; Whoso sheddeth man's blood, by man shall his blood be shed: for in the image of God made He man.

Exodus 4:11; And the Lord said unto him, Who hath made man's mouth? Or who maketh the dumb, or deaf, or the seeing, or the blind? Have not I the Lord?

Exodus 20:13; Thou shalt not kill.

Exodus 21:22-24; If a man strive, and hurt a woman with child, so that her fruit depart from her, and yet no mischief follow, he shall be surely punished, according as the woman's husband will lay upon him; and he shall pay as the judges determine. And if any mischief follow, then thou shalt give life for life, Eye for eye, tooth for tooth, hand for hand, foot for foot, burning for burning, wound for wound, stripe for stripe.

Exodus 23:7; Keep thee far from a false matter; and the innocent and righteous slay thou not; for I will not justify the wicked.

Deuteronomy 18:10a; There shall not be found among you anyone that maketh his son or his daughter to pass through the fire...

Deuteronomy 24:16; The fathers shall not be put to death for the children, neither shall the children be put to death for the fathers; every man shall be put to death for his own sin.

Deuteronomy 30:19; I call heaven and earth to record this day against you, that I have set before you life and death, blessing and cursing: therefore choose life, that both thou and thy seed may live.

Job 33:4; The Spirit of God hath made me, and the breath of the Almighty hath given me life.

Psalm 100:3; Know ye that the Lord He is God; it is He that hath made us, and not we ourselves; we are His people, and the sheep of His pasture.

Psalm 106:37-38; Yea, they sacrificed their sons and their daughters unto devils and shed innocent blood, even the blood of their sons and of their daughters, whom they sacrificed unto idols of Canaan and the land was polluted with blood.

Psalm 139:13-16; For thou has possessed my reins; thou hast covered me in my mother's womb. I will praise thee for I am fearfully and wonderfully made: marvelous are they works, and that my soul knoweth right well. My substance was not hid from thee when I was made in secret and curiously wrought in the lowest parts of the earth. Thine eyes did see my substance, yet being unperfect; and in thy book all my members were written, which in continuance were fashioned, when as yet there was none of them.

Proverbs 6:16-17; These ... things doth the Lord hate; yea, seven are an abomination unto him: A proud look, a lying tongue, and hands that shed innocent blood.

Isaiah 43:7-8; Even every one that is called by my name; for I have created him for my glory, I have formed him; yea, I have made him. Bring forth the blind people that have eyes, and the deaf that have ears.

Isaiah 49:9 and 49:5a; Listen, isles, unto me, and hearken, ye people, from far; the Lord hath called me from the womb; from the bowels of my mother hath he made mention of my name. And now, saith the Lord that formed me from the womb to be his servant...

Isaiah 58:1; Cry aloud, spare not, lift up the voice like a trumpet and show my people their transgression, and the house of Jacob their sins.

Isaiah 59:3; For your hands are defiled with blood, and your fingers with iniquity, your lips have spoken lies, your tongue hath muttered perverseness.

Jeremiah 1:5; Before I formed thee in the belly I knew thee, and before those camest forth out of the womb I sanctified thee, and I ordained thee a prophet unto the nations.

Ezekial 16:4-6; And as for thy nativity, in the day thou wast born thy navel was not cut, neither wast thou washed in water to supple thee; thou wast not salted at all, nor swaddled at all. None eye pitied thee, to do any of these unto thee, to have compassion upon thee; but thou wast cast out in the open field, to the loathing of thy person, in the day thou wast born. And when I passed by thee, and saw thee polluted in thine own blood, I said unto thee when thou wast in thy blood, Live: yea, I said unto thee when thou wast in thy blood, Live.

Ezekiel 16:20-21; Moreover thou has taken thy sons and daughters, whom thou hast borne unto me, and these hast thou sacrificed unto them to be devoured. Is this of thy whoredoms a small matter? That thou hast slain my children, and delivered them to cause them to pass through the fire for them.

Luke 1:15; For he shall be great in the sight of the Lord, and shall drink neither wine nor strong drink; and he shall be filled with the Holy Ghost even from the mother's womb.

Luke 1:41 and 44; And it came to pass that, when Elizabeth heard the salutation of Mary, the babe leaped in her womb; and Elizabeth was filled with the Holy Ghost. For lo, as soon as the voice of thy salutation sounded in mine ears, the babe leaped in my womb for joy.

Luke 17:2; It were better for him that a millstone were hanged about his neck, and he were cast into the sea, than that he should offend one of these little ones.

Acts 10:34; ...Of a truth I perceive that God is no respecter of persons...

Romans 2:11; For there is no respect of persons with God.

Galatians 1:15; But when it pleased God, who separated me from my mother's womb, and called me by his grace.

Revelation 21:8; But the fearful, and unbelieving, and the abominable, and murderers, and whoremongers, and sorcerers, and idolaters, and all liars, shall have their part in the lake which burneth with fire and brimstone, which is the second death.

SOUTHERN BAPTIST CONVENTION RESOLUTIONS 1980-1991

On June 12, 1980, the Southern Baptist Convention passed for the first time a strong resolution not only opposing abortion (except to save the life of the mother), but also opposing the use of tax funds or tax-supported facilities for the performance of abortions and supporting anti-abortion legislation and a human life constitutional amendment. Although this resolution has been revised and rewritten several times since 1980, the sense of it remains unchanged.

Resolution No. 10—Abortion

WHEREAS, Southern Baptists have historically affirmed the Biblical teaching of the sanctity of all human life, and

WHEREAS, All medical evidence indicates that abortion ends the life of a developing human being, and

WHEREAS, Our national laws permit a policy commonly referred to as "abortion on demand,"

Be it therefore, RESOLVED, That the Southern Baptist Convention reaffirm the view of the Scriptures of the sacredness and dignity of all human life, born and unborn, and

Be it further RESOLVED, That opposition be expressed toward all policies that allow "abortion on demand," and

Be it further RESOLVED, That we abhor the use of tax money or public, tax-supported medical facilities for selfish, non-therapeutic abortion, and

Be it finally RESOLVED, That we favor appropriate legislation and/or a constitutional amendment prohibiting abortion except to save the life of the mother.

June 11, 1981, Southern Baptist Convention, Los Angeles, California:

Resolution No. 18—Family Planning

Therefore be it RESOLVED, That we call upon elected and employed government officials to work toward the return of parental or guardian control of minors in the matter of sexual information and devices, and we oppose any governmental agency withholding or threatening to withhold funds from public-funded agencies that require parental consent or parental knowledge

184

before dispensing medication or devices, and

Be it further RESOLVED, That we oppose the distribution of birth control devices to minors except with parental or guardian consent.

June 17, 1982, Southern Baptist Convention, New Orleans, Louisiana:

Resolution No. 11—Abortion and Infanticide

Therefore, be it RESOLVED, That the messengers to the 1982 Southern Baptist Convention affirm that all human life, both born and pre-born, is sacred, bearing the image of God, and is not subject to personal judgments as to "quality of life" based on such subjective criteria as stage of development, abnormality, intelligence level, degree of dependency, cost of medical treatment, or inconvenience to parents.

Be it further RESOLVED, That we abhor the use of federal, state or local tax money; public, tax-supported medical facilities; or Southern Baptist supported medical facilities for the practice of selfish, medically unnecessary abortions and/or the practice of withholding treatment from unwanted or defective newly born infants.

Be it finally RESOLVED, That we support and will work for appropriate legislation and/or a constitutional amendment which will prohibit abortions except to save the physical life of the mother, and that we also support and will work for legislation which will prohibit the practice of infanticide.

June 14, 1984, Southern Baptist Convention, Kansas City, Missouri:

Resolution No. 8—Abortion

Therefore be it RESOLVED, That the Southern Baptist Convention meeting in Kansas City, Missouri, June 12-14, 1984, encourage all of its institutions, cooperating churches, and members to work diligently to provide counseling, housing and adoption placement services for unwed mothers with the specific intent of bringing them into a relationship with Jesus Christ and /or a sense of Christian responsibility; and

Be it further RESOLVED, That we deplore the practice of performing abortions, as well as dispensing to minors without parental consent or even notification, contraceptive medications which have potentially dangerous side effects, and deplore also the use of tax funds for such activities, and

Be it further RESOLVED, That we call upon all Southern Baptists to renew their commitment to support and work for legislation and/or a constitutional amendment which will prohibit abortion except to save the physical life of the mother; and

Be it further RESOLVED, That we encourage Southern Baptists to inquire whether or not their physicians perform abortions on demand or give referrals for abortions, and that we commend those of the medical profession who abstain from performing abortions or making abortion referrals; and

Be it finally, RESOLVED, That we urge our agencies and institutions to provide leadership for our cooperating churches and members, by preparing literature to take a clear and strong stand against abortion, and to inform and motivate our members to action to eliminate abortion on demand.

June 11, 1986, Southern Baptist Convention, Atlanta, Georgia:

Resolution No. 10—Sex Education and Adolescent Pregnancy

Be it therefore RESOLVED, That we, the messengers to the Southern Baptist Convention, meeting in Atlanta, Georgia, June 10-12, 1986, affirm the urgency for families and churches to educate children about spiritual insights and Christian understanding of sexuality as essential not only for the avoidance of unwanted pregnancies, but also for the development of Christian character. We also affirm that abortion is unscriptural and has harmful effects on the mother as well as the elimination of the unborn child.

June 18, 1987, Southern Baptist Convention, St. Louis, Missouri:

Resolution No. 9—Abortion

Therefore, be it RESOLVED, That we, the messengers of the Southern Baptist Convention, meeting in St. Louis, Missouri, June 16-18, 1987, encourage the Christian Life Commission to continue the expansion of program services related to the sanctity of human life and to actively lobby for legislation to protect the lives of the unborn; and

Be it further RESOLVED, That we encourage the Christian Life Commission to continue to make the abortion issue a priority on its agenda; and

Be it further RESOLVED, That we encourage the Home Mission Board to train churches for ministry in crisis pregnancy centers and residential care homes for pregnant women and children; and

Be it further RESOLVED, That we encourage churches, associations, and state conventions to expand their children's homes ministry to include outpatient and residential care for unwed mothers; and

Be it further RESOLVED, That we encourage all agencies and institutions of the SBC to use their resources and program ministries to promote the sanctity of human life; and

Be it further RESOLVED, That we encourage individuals to minister to those who need physical, emotional and spiritual support in the midst of a crisis pregnancy; and

Be it finally RESOLVED, That we encourage all churches of the SBC to observe Sanctity of Human Life Sunday on the Convention's calendar, January 17, 1988.

June 16, 1988, Southern Baptist Convention, San Antonio, Texas:

Resolution No. 8—Pro-Life Actions of SBC Agencies

Therefore, be it RESOLVED, That we, the messengers of the Southern Baptist Convention, meeting in San Antonio, Texas, June 14-16, 1988, express our appreciation to the trustees of the Home Mission Board, the Christian Life Commission, and the Sunday School Board; and

Be it finally RESOLVED, That we call upon all Southern Baptists to take an active stand in support of the sanctity of human life.

June 15, 1989, Southern Baptist Convention, Las Vegas, Nevada:

Resolution No. 3—Encouraging Laws on Regulating Abortion

Therefore, be it RESOLVED, That we, the messengers of the Southern Baptist Convention, meeting in Las Vegas, June 13-15, 1989, do strongly urge the fifty state legislatures and the Congress to enact legislation to restrict the practice of induced abortion; and

Be it further RESOLVED, That we urge the Christian Life Commission and the various state Baptist conventions, and their Christian Life Committees, affiliated with the Southern Baptist Convention actively to promote the passage of such legislation; and

Be it finally RESOLVED, That we do reaffirm our opposition to legalized abortion and our support of appropriate federal and state legislation and/or a constitutional amendment which will prohibit abortion except to prevent the imminent death of the mother.

June 5, 1991, Southern Baptist Convention, Atlanta, Georgia:

Resolution No. 2—Sanctity of Human Life

Be it RESOLVED, That we the messengers to the Southern Baptist Convention, meeting in Atlanta, Georgia, June 4-6, 1991, affirm the biblical prohibition against the taking of unborn human life except to save the life of the mother; and

Be it further RESOLVED, That we call on all Southern Baptists to work for the adoption of pro-life legislation in their respective states, which would expand protection for unborn babies; and

Be it further RESOLVED, That we call on all Southern Baptists to work with equal fervor to compassionately encourage and assist girls and women with unplanned or unwanted pregnancies to carry their children to term and to prepare for the best life possible for their children; and

Be it further RESOLVED, That we oppose all efforts by the United States Congress to limit the rights of states to restrict abortion-on-demand and call upon Congress to maintain current pro-life policies which prohibit the use of federal funds to encourage, promote, or perform abortions except to save the life of the mother; and

Be it further RESOLVED, That we oppose the testing, approval, distribution, and marketing in America of new drugs and technologies which will make the practice of abortion more convenient and more widespread; and

Be it finally RESOLVED, That we support the current federal government ban on funding any transplantation of tissue from induced abortions for purposes of experimentation and research and call on the federal government to maintain the ban despite pressure from the scientific community and pro-abortion organizations.

BIBLIOGRAPHY

Baker, Don. *Beyond Choice: The Abortion Story No One Is Telling.* Portland, Oregon. Multnomah Press, 1985.

Bendroth, Norman B. **Sanctity of Human Life Sunday: A Worship Manual.** Falls Church, Virginia. The Christian Action Council.

Boothe, Sylvia. **No Easy Choices.** Birmingham, Alabama. New Hope, 1990.

Brown, Harold O. J. **Death Before Birth.** Nashville. Thomas Nelson Publishers, 1977.

Davis, John Jefferson. *Abortion and the Christian: What Every Believer Should Know.* Phillipsburg, New Jersey. Presbyterian and Reformed Publishing Company, 1874.

Exley, Richard. *Pro-life by Conviction; Pro-choice by Default.* Honor Books, 1989.

Falwell, Jerry. *If I Should Die Before I Wake.* Nashville. Thomas Nelson Publishing, 1986.

Fowler, Paul B. *Abortion: Towards an Evangelical Consensus.* Portland, Oregon. Multnomah Press, 1987.

Garton, Jean Staker. *Who Broke the Baby?* Minneapolis, Minnesota. Bethany House Publishers, 1979.

Gorman, Michael J. *Abortion and the Early Church.* Downers Grove, Illinois. InterVarsity Press, 1982.

Hyde, Henry. *For Every Idle Silence.* Ann Arbor, Michigan. Servant Publications, 1985.

Kennedy, Dr. D. James. *A Nation in Shame.* Fort Lauderdale, Florida. Coral Ridge Ministries, 1985.

Klasen, Thomas G. *A Pro-life Manifesto.* Westchester, Illinois. Crossway Books, 1988.

Koerbel, Pam. *Abortion's Second Victim.* Wheaton, Illinois. Victor Books, 1986.

Koop, C. Everett. *The Right to Live, The Right to Die.* Wheaton, Illinois. Tyndale House, 1976.

Lewis, Larry L. *The Bible and Abortion* (booklet). Nashville, Tennessee. Christian Life Commission, 1988.

Montgomery, John Warwick. *Slaughter of the Innocents.* Crossway Books, 1981.

Nathanson, Bernard N. *Aborting America.* Garden City.

Doubleday, 1979.

Shaeffer, Francis and Koop, C. Everett. *Whatever Happened to the Human Race?* Old Tappan, New Jersey, Revell, 1979.

Shelbourne, Lila. *When Evil Strikes*. Hannibal, Missouri, Hannibal Books, 1992.

Shoemaker, Donald P. *Abortion, the Bible, and the Christian.* Grand Rapids, Michigan, Baker Book House, 1976.

Swindoll, Charles R. *Sanctity of Life.* Dallas, Texas. Word Publishing, 1990.

Whitehead, John W. *The Second American Revolution.* Elgin, Illinois. David C. Cook Publishing Company, 1982.

Whitehead, John W. *Arresting Abortion: Practical Ways to Save Unborn Children.* Westchester, Illinois. Crossway Books, 1985.

Wilke, Dr. and Mrs. J. D. *Abortion: Questions and Answers.* Cincinnati, Ohio. Hayse, 1985.

Young, Curt. *The Least of These.* Chicago. Moody Press, 1983.

Please send me:

"Mama, it ain't over 'til the pink marble comes!" by Sandee Williams with Jeanne Todd. The humorous and moving story of Dorothy Williams as she helps her family cope with her diagnosis and death from cancer.

_____ Copies at $9.95 = _____

Escape from America by Wallace Henley. A spine-chilling novel of suspense and intrigue that warns of what America could become.

_____ Copies at $8.95 = _____

When Evil Strikes by Lila Wold Shelburne. Despite seemingly impossible circumstances, Romans 8:28 is validated in this powerful story that reads like fiction.

_____ Copies at $9.95 = _____

In His Steps Today by Marti Hefley. The novel that asks the question "What would Jesus do if he were living today?" A best seller that is fiction with a challenge.

_____ Copies at $7.95 = _____

Just for Jesus by Marti Hefley. The work goes on in this updated version of **God Called: A Family Answered.** This book shows what God can accomplish through "just plain folks" who are willing to rely on His leadership.

_____ Copies at $8.95 = _____

The Secret File on John Birch by James & Marti Hefley. The shocjing true story of missionary and war hero John Birch.

_____ Copies at $12.95 = _____

The Truth in Crisis: The Controversy in the Southern Baptist Convention. Volumes 1-4 available on a limited basis. Call 800-747-0738 fior availability and prices.

Please add $2.00 postage and handling for first book, plus .50 for each additional book.

Shipping & Handling _____

MO residents add sales tax _____

TOTAL ENCLOSED (Check or money order)_____

Name _____

Address _____

City_____State____ Zip _____ Phone_____

MAIL TO HANNIBAL BOOKS, 921 Center, Hannibal, MO 63401.

Satisfaction guaranteed.VISA & MasterCard orders phone 800-747-0738